PRAISE FOR *ROAD FR*

"The issues [Mejía] has raised deserve a close reading by the nation as a whole . . . he has made a contribution to the truth about Iraq."

— Bob Herbert, *New York Times* columnist

"Camilo's most revolutionary action was not refusing to return to Iraq, but recognizing the humanity of those he was told were his enemies.... He inspires not only veterans and soldiers, but all of us by showing that the most revolutionary acts happen in the minds and hearts of individuals."

— Kelly Dougherty, Iraq veteran, cofounder and
executive director of Iraq Veterans Against the War

"Camilo Mejía, one of the Iraq war's earliest critics, has delivered a poignant, illuminating memoir of courage, resistance, and compassion for the innocent Iraqis he left behind. *Road from ar Ramadi* is a must-read in the canon of Iraq war literature."

— Laila Al-Arian, journalist and co-author of
Collateral Damage: America's War Against Iraqi Civilians

"Sergeant Mejía served his country bravely and well in Iraq; but he is serving his country better, and just as bravely, in his publicly announced refusal to participate further in what he correctly identifies as an illegal war using illegal means."

— Daniel Ellsberg

"*Road from ar Ramadi* should be required reading for every Iraq war defender who claims to 'support our troops.' Camilo Mejía, the first U.S. soldier to publicly refuse redeployment to Iraq, documents in heart-wrenching detail how his own experiences as a Staff Sergeant in Iraq convinced him that the U.S. military is guilty of war crimes against the Iraqi people. Mejía is among the bravest of troops—one who has dared to stand up and fight against the atrocities of U.S. Empire."

— Sharon Smith, author of *Subterranean Fire:
A History of Working-Class Radicalism in the United States*

"Camilo Mejía's voice is strong and clear. Although trained to kill, soldiers have consciences, too. Camilo's conscience told him to stop his soldiering in Iraq—for his soul. The path to conscience for a person who has volunteered for the military is difficult; parting with colleagues in the military and sometimes with family over one's participation in a war is particularly gut-wrenching. Camilo's journey to conscience reminds us of what is important in life—being true to one's self."

—Ann Wright, retired U.S. Army reserve colonel and U.S. diplomat who resigned in March 2003 in opposition to the Iraq war

"Sgt. Mejía and his 600 co-deserters could well be the harbingers of a new GI movement."

—Clancy Sigal, the *Guardian*

"The moving memoir of the first U.S. soldier to publicly refuse to fight in Iraq…. We have much to learn from his story."

—*International Socialist Review*

"Camilo Mejía did indeed have his private rebellion during this Iraq War. We are so fortunate to garner from his difficult experience an elegant, honest, and compelling tale in Road from ar Ramadi. His response to this war so early on should inspire all of us to ask ourselves the hard questions we tend to whisper in the dark about ourselves and the war. Just begin with: 'What would I do?' Camilo is a brave soldier, but a much braver human being."

—Patricia Foulkrod, producer and director, *The Ground Truth*

"The courageous journey of Staff Sargeant Camilo Mejía from warrior to military resister. A powerful and important book."

—Ron Kovic, Vietnam veteran and the author of *Born on the Fourth of July*

"Camilo Mejía's memoir of combat, growing doubts, resistance, and redemption is a riveting and compelling tale…. No history of the present conflict is complete without it."

—Christian Parenti, correspondent for the *Nation* and author of *The Freedom: Shadows and Hallucinations in Occupied Iraq*

ROAD FROM AR RAMADI

ROAD FROM
AR RAMADI

The Private Rebellion of
Staff Sergeant Camilo Mejía

An Iraq War Memoir

CAMILO MEJÍA

Haymarket
Books
Chicago, Illinois

A NOTE ABOUT THE TITLE: the name *ar Ramadi* was chosen over the more properly transliterated *al Ramadi* in order to emphasize the proper pronunciation.

© 2007, 2008 by Camilo Mejía
First published in 2007 by the New Press, New York.
This edition published in 2008 by Haymarket Books
P.O. Box 180165
Chicago, IL 60618
773-583-7884
info@haymarketbooks.org
www.haymarketbooks.org

Trade distribution:
In the U.S. through Consortium Book Sales, www.cbsd.com
In the UK, Turnaround Publisher Services, www.turnaround-psl.com
In Australia, Palgrave MacMillan, www.palgravemacmillan.com.au

This book was published with the generous support of the Wallace Global Fund.

Cover design by Josh On.
Author photograph © Jared Rodriguez, www.jaredrodriguez.com.

CIP data available
ISBN 978-1931859-53-0

Printed in Canada by union labor on recycled paper containing 100 percent post-consumer waste in accordance with the principles of the Green Press Initiative, www.greenpressinitiative.org.

10   9   8   7   6   5   4   3   2   1

CONTENTS

To the war resisters,
to those facing the imperial powers of the earth.

With my deepest-felt apologies,
with much respect and admiration,
and with all my heart,
to the people of Iraq.

PREFACE
by Chris Hedges

There are two types of courage—physical courage and moral courage. I witnessed physical courage on the battlefield in my two decades as a war correspondent in Latin America, Africa, the Middle East, and the Balkans but I rarely saw moral courage. Moral courage is harder. It requires the bearer to walk away from the warm embrace of comradeship and denounce the myth of war as a fraud, name it as an enterprise of death and immorality, and condemn himself, and those around him, as killers. It requires the bearer to become an outcast. We do not like our myths, the ones we tell about ourselves, challenged. We like to feel empowered by our strength, and the fiction of our nobility and goodness. We do not want to hear or see what is being done in our name. So those who summon up moral courage—like Camilo Mejía—to condemn the barbarity of war and the futility of the U.S. occupation and refuse to partake in its depravity stand among us like ironic points of light in a sea of darkness.

Military machines and state bureaucracies, who seek to make us obey, seek also to silence those who return from war to speak the truth. So read this book as a cautionary tale, as

a stark reminder that war is industrial slaughter, that its
essence is death, that it deforms all those who engage in it,
and that in war the old always sacrifice the young, the cynics
send idealists to die, and politicians sell out the very soldiers
they lure into battle. War is always, finally, about betrayal.
Those in power, including the ambitious senior officers who
sent Mejía and his squad out looking for combat to advance
their own careers, did not fight for God and country but personal gain and ambition. And those who pay the price in war,
the common soldier or marine, are usually crumpled up and
discarded when they come home, left to struggle with the
nightmare of what they did and what was done to them.

Mejía is the son of Nicaraguan revolutionaries who
helped topple the dictatorship of Anastasio Somoza. His father, one of Nicaragua's most famous musicians and activists,
was in hiding during the dictatorship. Mejía was named after
two Latin American revolutionary heroes: Camilo Torres, a
Colombian Catholic priest who died in combat, and Ernesto
"Che" Guevara, a leader of the Cuban revolution. Mejía's
heritage, along with his intelligence and compassion, were as-
sets when it came time to question authority and defy military
authorities in Iraq. His fortunes and those of his family rose
and fell with the political tides that beset his Central American homeland; but what never wavered was his conscience
and his realization, given to him by his parents, that blind
obedience to any cause or any source of power—even the
leftist Sandinista movement—was a form of slavery.

By the time he was eighteen he and his mother were living in poverty in Miami. His mother's salary as a supermarket
cashier was not enough to cover the rent and feed the family.
As a teenager, Mejía got a job in a fast-food restaurant where
he swept the parking lot, put chairs down from the tables,
and cleaned the bathrooms every morning before working six
hours in the kitchen. He had a two-hour break before starting

night school to get his high school diploma. His days began at 5:30 A.M. and ended at 10:00 P.M. After earning his high school diploma he started attending a community college but ran out of money. Like many young men and women for whom America never offered much more than dead-end jobs, the army was the last hope.

"The recruiter didn't really have to work hard to get me to sign the treacherous contract," he writes. "The army offered financial stability and college tuition, two benefits that seemed tough to find anywhere else." But in that contract was a clause that required all who join to make an eight-year commitment to the military, even if they are only on active duty, as Mejía was, for three years. His eight-year obligation to the military was about to end in May 2003 when George W. Bush, whose privilege and wealth insulated him from the hardships of people like Mejía, declared war. In January of that year Mejía was activated in support of Operation Iraqi Freedom. His commitment to the army was extended until the year 2031. Two-and-a-half months later he was in Iraq.

The ugly side of American racism and chauvinism appeared the moment his unit arrived in the Middle East. Fellow soldiers instantly ridiculed Arab-style toilets because they would be "shitting like dogs." The troops around him treated Iraqis, whose language they did not speak and whose culture was alien, little better than animals. The word "hajji" swiftly became a slur to refer to Iraqis, in much the same way "gook" was used to debase the Vietnamese or "rag head" is used to belittle those in Afghanistan. Soon those around him ridiculed "hajji food," "hajji homes," and "hajji music." Bewildered prisoners, who were rounded up in useless and indiscriminate raids, were stripped naked and left to stand terrified and bewildered for hours in the baking sun. They were subjected to a steady torrent of verbal and physical abuse.

These scenes of abuse, which began immediately after the American invasion, were little more than collective acts of sadism. Mejía watched, not daring to intervene, yet increasingly disgusted at the treatment of Iraqi civilians. He saw how the callous and unchecked abuse of power first led to alienation among Iraqis and then spawned a raw hatred of the occupation forces. When army units raided homes the soldiers burst in on frightened families, forced them to huddle in the corners at gunpoint, and helped themselves to food and items in the houses.

Iraqi families were routinely fired upon for getting too close to checkpoints, including an incident where an unarmed father driving a car was decapitated by a fifty-caliber machine gun in front of his small son—although by then, Mejía notes, "this sort of killing of civilians had long ceased to arouse much interest or even comment." Soldiers shot holes into cans of gasoline being sold alongside the road and then tossed incendiary grenades into the pools to set them ablaze. "It's fun to shoot shit up," a soldier said. Some opened fire on small children throwing rocks. And when improvised explosive devices went off the troops fired wildly into densely populated neighborhoods, leaving behind innocent victims who became, in the callous language of war, "collateral damage."

The absurdity and brutality of the occupation fueled the insurgency until Mejía and his squad found themselves living in a sea of hostility. At one point the unit was surrounded by an angry crowd protesting the occupation. Mejía and his squad opened fire on an Iraqi holding a grenade, riddling the man's body with bullets. Mejía checked his clip afterwards and determined that he had fired eleven rounds into the young man. The elusive enemy, whom the American troops rarely saw and whose bombs began to take a deadly toll, left Mejía and those around him turning every Iraqi into the enemy. Units nonchalantly opened up in crowded neighborhoods with heavy M-240

Bravo machine guns, AT-4 launchers, and Mark 19s, machine guns that spit out grenades. The world spun out of control. The U.S. occupation had become an endless atrocity.

American soldiers swiftly lost their moral compass. They abused the corpses of Iraqi dead. In one incident Mejía related how soldiers laughed as an Iraqi corpse falls from the back of a truck.

"Take a picture of me and this motherfucker," one of the soldiers who had been in Mejía's squad in third platoon says, putting his arm around the corpse.

The shroud falls away from the body revealing a young man wearing only his pants. There is a bullet hole in his chest.

"Damn, they really fucked you up, didn't they!?" the soldier laughs.

The scene, Mejía reports, is witnessed by the dead man's brothers and cousins.

One of the most poignant moments in the book comes when Mejía and fellow soldiers are baptized in the waters of the Euphrates by a military chaplain, but the baptism is not enough to remove the curse of violence and blood. The sickness of war had become Mejía's sickness. Consumed by fury one day at a roadblock Mejía raised his M-16 assault rifle to shoot a wounded Iraqi in an ambulance, afraid that the vehicle had a bomb. He was restrained when another soldier intervened. But the incident was a watershed for Mejía, who became disgusted at what he had become, what war had turned him into, and what was being done in Iraq. He made, at this point, a decision that saved him as a human being. He decided he would no longer shoot at Iraqis. He would become a conscientious objector. And he would endure the ridicule of fellow soldiers rather than be part of the warrior cult and surrender his conscience.

Few senior officers even seemed troubled by the killing. Most stayed as far away from combat as possible, sending troops on futile missions in the quest to be awarded Combat Infantry Badges. This recognition, Mejía writes, "was essential to their further progress up the officer ranks." This pattern meant that "very few high-ranking officers actually got out into the action, and lower-ranking officers were afraid to contradict them when they were wrong." When the badges— bearing an emblem of a musket with the hammer dropped resting on top of an oak wreath—were finally awarded the commanders immediately shipped in Iraqi tailors to sew the badges on the top of the left breast pockets of their desert combat uniforms.

Mejía, on leave in Florida, finally goes AWOL. He turns himself in to military authorities five months later to be court-martialed.

"Sergeant Mejía-Castillo," the colonel in charge said at the hearing, "this court-martial sentences you to be reduced to the grade of E-1, to forfeit pay per month for twelve months, to be confined for twelve months, and to be discharged from the service with a bad conduct discharge."

As Mejía was escorted out of the courtroom in handcuffs to jail he embraced his mother, aware that in his act of defiance he had gained his freedom.

INTRODUCTION TO
THE SECOND EDITION

The idea behind writing *Road from ar Ramadi* first occurred to me while I was living underground in New York City. At the time, I was contemplating the various consequences that could befall me for being critical of the U.S. occupation of Iraq. I knew that if I spoke publicly about why I had refused to return to my unit in Iraq, the U.S. Army would want to silence me. Although I had always wanted to be an author, writing this memoir was separate from that aspiration. Writing *Road from ar Ramadi* was a way to ensure I would not be silenced even if I ended up behind bars.

The reasons I wrote the manuscript have turned out to be more complex than simply wanting to get out my version of the story. The Argentinean writer Ernesto Sábato once wrote in one of his novels that he could not be held responsible for the actions of his characters. I think the same is true for memoirs and for other nonfiction writing. There are driving forces behind everything we do that can be found outside of our intentions. In the case of this memoir, the original purpose was to tell my version of the story because I did not know if I was going to be in jail for a long time. But I did not start working on the manuscript until after I was released from military prison. The need to make my voice heard from behind bars was no longer a consideration when I began the actual work. I now realize that writing the memoir had a different purpose in my life: it was something I had to do in order to begin my healing process.

Shortly after my return from Iraq, my stepsister asked me if I had been in any combat missions and if I had fired my weapon. I began to tell her about the time my squad was ambushed (a story I recount in chapter four). For the first time, my voice broke as I described the event. I had spoken about the incident after it happened with members of my platoon in Iraq, but back then we were too concerned about what would happen next to truly discuss our feelings. Keeping our guard high always meant that the horrible things we experienced in the war were thrown in a trunk of suppressed memories. These emotions and memories only resurfaced after I started working on the manuscript, over a year after my public surrender to the military and almost four months after getting out of jail. Most of the year it took me to write the memoir was actually spent staring at a blank computer screen, remembering, reliving, and coming face to face with painful experiences for the very first time since I left Iraq.

Dealing with the memory blanks I had and still have made writing difficult, but perhaps even harder was understanding why my memory failed me when I tried to revisit very difficult moments. It was never the whole incident but bits of information that were missing from my recollection of events: the age, face, and emotional expression of a child who had just witnessed the brutal killing of his father or the face of a young man who was gunned down for throwing a grenade at our building. It is mostly the faces of people who carry the pain we inflicted in their lives that are hard to remember. Those faces may be missing, but the pain they carried we now carry with us.

Negotiating those memory gaps meant that I had to initiate a sincere dialogue between the part of me that had gone through the experience of war and the part of me that wanted to write about it. That dialogue became problematic when I tried to provide answers to the many haunting questions that, time after time, remained unanswered.

It is clear to me now that there are limits to what we can share, not only with other people, but also with ourselves. Those missing memories are part of an experience far too overwhelming to be fully contained, understood, or explained. Their *missing* is not a form of absence, but rather a statement of how war can profoundly change the human soul, removing memories and banishing them into dark and inaccessible corners of the subconscious, while pain, guilt, and despair occupy center stage in our daily lives.

After I reached an agreement with myself to leave out the missing details, I was able to write, and I found the process less painful and more therapeutic. But the joy of finishing the manuscript was short-lived, to say the least. The product of a year's struggle to reclaim memories buried beneath layers of fear in order to bring them to light was now to be cut down during another agonizing process—editing, which would last six months.

By the time my editor and I finished working on the original manuscript, close to a third of the manuscript was gone. Although I understood the logic behind keeping the book concise, I could not help feeling like a parent at a maternity ward who is told by the doctor that for the baby to survive all its extremities had to be amputated.

The book was officially published six months after we were done with the editing, a year after I finished writing the manuscript. At that time, the writer's vanity took a hold of me. I started to obsessively look for reviews and sales rankings on the Internet. What had begun as the need to express myself in the face of imposed silence, punishment for my rebellion, and

which had later become a process of self-exploration and healing, was now reduced to a selfish need for literary recognition.
Things began to change when I went on a pre-release
book tour in Southern California, sponsored by the San
Francisco chapter of Veterans For Peace (VFP). In two
weeks of speeches and readings, we did not visit a single book-
store. We concentrated on community centers, churches, and
alternative high schools where troubled and disadvantaged
youth went after traditional schools gave up on them. These
students, who lived their lives in the margins of society and
who were the prime target of military recruiters, could not afford to buy the memoir, but my conscience could not afford to
leave them empty-handed. We started donating the book to
the school libraries and letting students buy it at cost, or for
whatever money they had, which many times meant giving it
away for free.

I slowly began to realize that the success of *Road from ar
Ramadi* was not to be found in literary magazines or sales
rankings, but at the community level, where grassroots activists battle against a system that refuses to place human interest above profit and that feeds on poverty and disadvantage
to fill the ranks of its military.

Not too long ago, I received a phone call from a group of
students from a Catholic high school in California. They had
read about me in one of their classes and wanted to interview
me for an assignment. They had been really touched by my
actions and thought I was a prophet. By any stretch of the
imagination I remain sure that I am no prophet, I told them,
but knowing how my actions and words are having a positive
impact on young people is a reward that cannot be matched
materially.

The memoir before you has been transformed yet again —
this time into a tool of activism, a sort of chisel I hope will
contribute to the carving of a new world, beginning by work-

ing on ending the occupation of Iraq through organizing around military resistance. A few words about that resistance would be appropriate.

...

When I first refused to return to Iraq in October of 2003, no combat veterans had taken a public stance against the war. air force captain Steven Potts and marine reservist Stephen Funk had been the only two public resisters, but their resistance occurred prior to the invasion and their cases received little to no attention from the media. At that time, when the nation was rallying behind the president and the antiwar movement was just beginning to gain strength, resisting the war from within the military was a lonely path to walk.

The political climate has significantly changed since October of 2003, when the news was that morale among the troops in Iraq was high, and when only twenty-two service members had failed to report back for duty after their mid-deployment furloughs. Only five months later, the number of GIs who didn't report back to their units had grown to five hundred. When I got out of military jail in February of 2005, after serving nine months on a desertion charge, the same number was five thousand five hundred.

Today's military, developing from blind and unwavering obedience to entire units refusing to go out on combat missions, has come a long way in resisting the war. But those of us organizing in the military cannot take full credit for that change, nor can civilian organizers. It will take a deeper analysis of what is happening inside the military, and outside the antiwar movement, to understand why service members are saying "no" to their superiors.

The military's attempt to repress dissent within the ranks has mostly concentrated on suppressing public criticism of

the war, and it has remained strong since I spoke out. A
month after my court martial, Army Sergeant Abdullah Webster, a U.S. Muslim, was sentenced to fourteen months of in-
carceration for refusing to deploy to Iraq. Webster was
followed by Navy Petty Officer Third Class Pablo Paredes,
who refused to board his amphibious assault ship, *Bonhomme
Richard*, as it sailed off to transport marines to the Middle
East. Paredes was sentenced to three months of restriction
and two months of hard labor. Other high-profile cases include that of Sergeant Kevin Benderman (fifteen months),
Specialist Agustín Aguayo (eight months), and Lieutenant
Ehren Watada, the first commissioned officer to publicly refuse orders. Lieutenant Watada called the war illegitimate
and cited the Geneva Convention and UN Charter as the legal basis of his defense. Though his court martial was dismissed, the military is still pursuing a retrial.

While most of the prominent cases of GI resistance have
revolved around political opposition to the occupation of
Iraq, it would be a mistake to generalize the current military
resistance as purely political, or even as purely antiwar.

As early as July of 2003, a platoon from my infantry unit
engaged in negotiations with our company commander to
modify an ongoing mission after unsound practices cost that
platoon four casualties and a vehicle, and led to the killing of
an innocent Iraqi civilian. In October of the following year,
an army reserve platoon of truck drivers made the news after
seventeen of its members refused to go on a supply mission
that they called "suicidal." And in 2007, as reported by *Democracy Now!* in December, after losing five of its members to an
improvised explosive device (IED) attack, a U.S. Army infantry platoon refused to go back out after the incident, citing
fear of committing a massacre in retaliation for the loss of
their fellow soldiers.

We also have the resistance of Specialist Katherine Jashinski who, in November of 2005, refused deployment orders to Afghanistan, declaring herself a conscientious objector, but avoiding being politically critical of any war. In 2006, Army Specialist Suzanne Swift refused a second deployment to Iraq with the same supervisors who had forced her into a sexual relationship in exchange for not sending her on senseless, suicidal missions, a practice known as "command rape." Army Reserve Colonel Janis Karpinski, during a public tribunal on war crimes committed by the Bush administration, said that female soldiers were dying of dehydration in Iraq. The reason was that, in those extreme heat conditions, they would purposely stop drinking water after noon so they wouldn't have to urinate at night, thus avoiding the risk of being raped by fellow soldiers on their way to the latrine.

In the case of units refusing to go out on missions, as well—as in the cases of Jashinski and Swift—military resistance originated not from a profound political analysis of the invasion and occupation of Iraq but from a more primal, human refusal to participate in one's own detriment, be it physical or spiritual.

The supply and infantry units that refused their missions are not necessarily antiwar. Just as in the case of the two female resisters, these are people who are simply saying, "I refuse to kill or be killed." And, "I refuse to be raped." An effective antiwar movement should recognize the diverse nature of military resistance in order to work with these individuals and involve them.

When people join the U.S. military, in the overwhelming majority of the cases to escape poverty, the understanding is that the possibility of war will *only* come after all other venues to peaceful resolution have been exhausted. There is trust in the government to act within the parameters of national and international law and in the people of the United States to hold its government responsible for any misuse of the armed forces. War, we are told before signing the enlistment document, will only be our last recourse, and will only occur to protect our country—or perhaps to advance freedom and democracy.

It is no wonder then that servicemen and servicewomen have a hard time seeing the bigger picture, understanding that the senseless missions, that the risk of being raped by their peers, that the fear of taking human life without a noble reason, are all directly tied to the policies behind military action.

The propagation of an inhuman, cruel, misogynist, and racist subculture in the military (to a significant degree a reflection of the larger culture) is necessary to create the conditions in which a land and its people can be denied their sovereignty through military force. Military resisters don't necessarily know that—not right away, sometimes never. They may not be ready to tell themselves they were misused by their government to fight for profit or for reasons other than freedom and justice. They just know they don't want to go out there when they know they will commit a massacre, or when they know their lives will be surely wasted, or when they know they will be subject to command rape.

By and large, people resisting in the military, the ten thousand deserters reported last year, the units refusing to commit massacres, the truck drivers refusing suicide missions, the female soldiers who died of dehydration (they too resisted), are not necessarily progressive political thinkers. They just got punched in the face, and fell flat on their backs. The antiwar movement needs to become that hand that helps them get up. They have to be on their feet before they can move forward.

Before there can be a united front to end the occupation of Iraq, the antiwar movement should understand that the many struggles waged by servicemen and servicewomen against their mission and leadership are part of a painful process of realization that something has gone awfully wrong.

In chapter two, I write about my first real act of resistance, which took place in Jordan right before the invasion. It was a matter simple enough to go unnoticed in the United States, but which I conducted with the secrecy of one who is engaged in treason. I asked a soldier in my squad to take a picture of me holding a sign that said: GIVE PEACE A CHANCE. When that picture was taken, I was not a politically aware person. I was informed enough to be against the war on political grounds, but had I gotten out of Iraq shortly after that picture was taken, I would have never considered becoming an activist, nor would I have ever believed that I could be one.

That first act of resistance was followed by a slightly bolder one when I stood up for a soldier who was being abused by our leadership. At the time, I did not know that the same cruelty applied to that soldier would be applied to the people of Iraq once we got there, only with more force and on a much greater scale.

Small acts of resistance that respond to very specific situations in the battlefield or elsewhere in the military are directly tied to the larger injustice of war and occupation, but GI resisters may need help seeing that connection. In order to help them see the broader picture, we must meet them exactly where they are and not where we want them to be. That is why I think the work of Iraq Veterans Against the War (IVAW) is so crucial in ending the occupation of Iraq.

IVAW was founded by seven Iraq war veterans at the VFP convention in Boston, Massachusetts, in July of 2004. Our membership consists of active duty and reserve service members as well as of veterans who have served in the U.S. military since September 11, 2001.

The three stated goals of IVAW are the immediate and unconditional withdrawal of all occupying forces from Iraq, U.S. government reparations to the people of Iraq so they can rebuild their country *on their own terms,* and full benefits to all servicemen and servicewomen, and to all veterans. In order to reach our goals, we are dedicating ourselves to removing military support for the war. We are organizing active duty bases and guard and reserve armories, reaching out to veterans, and going into schools to teach the youth about war and military life so they can make informed decisions about joining the service.

The most ambitious project we have at this time is the organizing of the Winter Soldier Investigation: Iraq and Afghanistan. From March 13 to 16, 2008, we are bringing to Washington, D.C., more than one hundred U.S. veterans and civilians from Iraq and Afghanistan to testify about atrocities committed by our military in those countries. We hope not only to provide an honest picture of the awful reality of those two wars, so that people in the United States can finally see what their government is doing in their name, but also to organize the servicemen and servicewomen who may feel alone in their opposition to the occupation of Iraq.

With the larger peace movement and with the mentorship of our predecessors in Vietnam Veterans Against the War and VFP, we can help young servicemen and servicewomen channel their energy into a path of resistance that leads to justice. Their journey, and ours as we walk with them, is a long and winding one, but one we cannot afford to abandon.

As with the writing of this memoir, the reasons why GIs embark on their different journeys of resistance may vary over time, and may have little to do with what we initially tell ourselves. But when we find our voices as a way to reclaim our love for humanity and our dedication to justice, there can be no punishment severe enough to keep us quiet. Speaking out becomes the moral fabric that keeps our existence together.

Camilo Mejía
February 2008

There will be wailing in all the streets and cries of anguish in every public square.

—Amos 5:16

How did I end up in this place? It was a question that visited me often while serving in Iraq during the summer of 2003. I would find myself riding in the back of a truck through the dusty streets of war-torn ar Ramadi, a Sunni triangle city west of Baghdad. I was supposed to be giving all my attention to watching out for the insurgents, who had made the stretch of road we were on a death trap for the American forces. But then I would catch sight of the children running to the front gates of their homes to watch our vehicles rolling by and they would remind me of the children I had seen back in Nicaragua, my country of birth: barefoot kids with skinny bodies and dirty, weather-beaten faces. They would appear at traffic lights by the dozens, fighting for the opportunity to wipe windshields, or trying to get people to pay them for having watched their cars while they were grocery shopping. My mind would wander off the task of scanning for the countless perils like roadside bombs and snipers as I realized these were the *same* children. I'd go back to reflecting on my own childhood in post–Somoza Nicaragua, where I had been the son of leading Sandinistas, a privileged child of revolution. And again, the question would echo within, *How did I end up in this place?*

ONE

It had been a long time since I left Nicaragua in late 1991. Following the fall in the previous year of the Sandinista government, my mother, single since separating from my father right after my birth in 1975, decided to return with her two sons to her native Costa Rica.

I was sixteen years old at the time, the same age my mother had been in 1971, when she first met my father, a well-known radio personality eleven years her senior. Besides being celebrated for his populist on-air style, which appealed to the common people, my father had risen in popularity after publicizing a hefty fine imposed on him by the Somocista dictatorship for being critical of the regime's unashamed corruption. With street humor, my father's radio show would ridicule government corruption by satirizing the regime's militarized police, known as the National Guard. The radio parodies would depict scenes much too familiar to the people, like guardsmen taking bribes from citizens in order to drop bogus traffic violations, or using international relief funds to line the pockets of the dictator and those closest to him.

One day my mother visited the radio station where my father worked; she was neither political nor very impressed by his radio stardom, having simply gone to place a radio announcement to relay a message to relatives. Since telephonic communication was a luxury many couldn't afford, people listened a lot to the radio, and frequently used its waves to communicate nationwide.

One of my mother's sisters had an in-law who had just undergone cataract surgery, and the message to be broadcast was that everything had gone well, that he would be arriving home on a particular day, and that they needed someone to bring a mule to the entrance of the farm, so that he could be transported to the main house.

My father was attracted by my mother as soon as he set eyes on her and used all his pull at the station to make sure that her announcement went out straight away. In return, my mother sold him a ticket to a party she was attending. On the night of the party he rushed back from a concert he was giving some distance outside Managua to meet my mom. Their relationship started on that evening.

My mother's parents were thrilled that their daughter was going out with someone so closely identified with the political resistance in Nicaragua. Though my mother found him charming and good-looking, her principal reason for dating my father was that it allowed her to get out of the house and meet people with someone she really liked. But she didn't meet just anyone. She was soon being introduced to the top figures in the Sandinista resistance, which at the time was a mixed bag of students and workers, middle-class as well as poor people, priests and atheists, illiterates and poets, theorists and guerrilla fighters. Before long, my mother was both married and an active revolutionary, involved in underground recruiting and grassroots campaigns against the Somoza dictatorship. Already with one child, and pregnant with me, she worked hard to organize poor Nicaraguan neighborhoods for an armed insurgency.

My father had for a long time used his radio show, *Corporito*, to mount criticism of the Somoza dictatorship. Corporito was a radio character, impersonated by my father on air, who satirized the dictatorship and the much feared and very ubiquitous National Guard in "coplas" or songs. At first the government regarded my father as little more than a harmless nuisance and limited its response to fines and the occasional prison threat, which my father in turn publicized, much to the public's delight and his own popularity. But not long after he met my mother his involvement with the clandestine insurgency took a more direct and combative turn. He kept this involvement secret from my mother for a long time, until one day he admitted to her that he had joined the *Frente Sandinista de Liberación Nacional* (FSLN), or Sandinista Front for National Liberation, the main revolutionary organization fighting the Somoza dictatorship.

The organization had taken its name from General Sandino, who had fought against the U.S. Marine occupation of Nicaragua in the 1920s and 1930s and who was assassinated by General Anastasio Somoza, the head of the National Guard in 1936. Somoza himself became president the following year, heading a corrupt regime that ruled Nicaragua with great brutality and the official blessing of the U.S. government for nearly forty years. The FSLN was created as a response to this military dictatorship.

My mother told my father that she, too, had been an active member of the insurgency. My father voiced his opposition to her involvement in the revolution, claiming it was too dangerous for the two of them to take such risks. But my mother didn't care: she was young and full of passion, and she wasn't about to watch from the margins as the revolution unfolded before her.

At around this time a rupture occurred in the Sandinista leadership. In 1974, a group of insurgents stormed a house party given by one of Somoza's closest friends. Armed guerrillas, faces covered by bandanas in the red and black of the Sandinista flag, took the house by force, killing the host and taking everyone inside hostage. Their demands included money, freedom for several guerrillas who were incarcerated by the regime, safe passage out for those holding the party guests hostage, and the publication of a call for the Nicaraguan people to raise up in arms against the dictatorship.

The regime acceded to all demands but then unleashed crude repression throughout the country in an attempt to crush support for the revolution. People were detained on the mere suspicion of having aided the rebels, and torture and disappearances became commonplace. This pressure created internal tensions in the FSLN, with some in the organization pushing for a more combative posture inside the cities and others advocating a more moderate approach. Factions were created, resulting in a deep fracture in the leadership.

During this particular repressive period, and while the Sandinista leadership restructured itself and the various leaders and thinkers figured out the new directions and methods they wanted to adopt, many people were left without guidance and either went into exile or became dormant. My mother, a grassroots organizer, was one of the people left without direction; she dropped out of activity at that time and concentrated more on her personal life and family.

Not so my father. Operating largely outside the direct control of the Sandinista commanders—not directly involved in armed operations and largely unconcerned with the masterminding of the movement—my father continued to perform his subversive songs at clandestine gatherings and sometimes in the open, at community centers, churches, and the Autonomous University of Managua, where students continued to mobilize at full throttle. Among his songs from this period were "La Tumba del Guerrillero," or "The Tomb of the Guerrilla," which tells the story of the disappearance of fallen guer-rilla fighters whose bodies were taken by Somocista guards, never to be seen again. Another song titled "Las Mujeres del Cua," or "The Women of Cua," was an account of peasant women from a mountainous region of Nicaragua who were raped and slaughtered by members of the National Guard af-ter refusing to give away the location of revolutionary fighters.

One rainy night, while my mother was still carrying me inside her, my father pushed his luck to the limit. He and my mother had gone to a concert in a really poor neighborhood of Managua, where the residents had assembled a stage in an open field for my father's performance. The place was packed with people tired of the dictatorship when my father sang a song called "Soldado Hermano," or "Brother Soldier." The lyrics were directed to members of the National Guard and included the line "You have the right to think even though those over there (the government), the inhumane gorillas, place in your hands the machines to kill." A National Guard lieutenant who was in the audience ordered my father's im-mediate arrest. A big commotion started as the guards moved to detain him; they couldn't get through the crowd quickly enough and by the time they reached the stage my father had vanished. Minutes later my mother received his accordion from a stranger who told her that he had been taken to a se-cret location to keep him from being arrested and that she should go home without him.

On the way back to the house my mother was pulled over by a military convoy. She was with a friend of my father's and with my brother Carlos, who was then two years old. National Guardsmen ordered my mother out into the rainy night.

"Get the fuck out of the car," she remembers a guard yelling.

The young man accompanying her tried to persuade the guards to let the pregnant woman and her small child stay in the car. He insisted that my father wasn't with them and that they did not know where he was. But they wouldn't have it, and they dragged her outside, yelling insults and manhandling her, demanding that she tell them of my father's whereabouts. Eventually they let her go. My father returned home three days later.

While my father continued performing his subversive music whenever and wherever he could, my mother largely dropped out of revolutionary activity. It was during this relatively calm period of my mother's life that I was born, in Managua, on August 28, 1975. My parents named me after two Latin American revolutionaries: Camilo, for Camilo Torres, a Colombian Catholic priest who died in combat; and Ernesto, for Ernesto Che Guevara, the Argentine guerrilla commander who was one of the leaders of the Cuban revolution and who died in combat in Bolivia.

Things changed drastically for my family after my birth. Following the post–hostage negotiation oppression, the main ideologues and commanders of the Sandinista insurgency were occupied with restructuring the movement. The problem was that while they decided on new strategies to overthrow the dictatorship, they forgot to pass down information and provide direction to lower-ranking rebels like my mother. Having largely lost contact with the Sandinista leadership, and tired of my father's infidelities, my mother began to feel isolated and without a purpose, until one day she decided to leave my father, Nicaragua, and the revolution; she took my brother and me to New York to live with my grandmother.

This was my mother's first visit to the United States and she soon realized that the Spanish Harlem of the mid-1970s was definitely not what she had in mind when it came to raising her two children. My grandmother had migrated to the United States in search of a higher standard of living and had found work making clothes sold under designer labels in fancy stores. But she saw very little of this money, and her cramped two-bedroom apartment on Lexington Avenue turned out to be far too small for our young family.

Not wanting to return to Nicaragua, where she considered her work with the Sandinistas over, and where she knew my father would try to get her to reconcile with him, my mother decided to move back to her native Costa Rica, a country where she had lived to the age of thirteen and which she knew quite well.

And so, barely a year old, I moved with my mother and brother to San José, Costa Rica's capital city, where my mother intended to live a quiet life raising her two children. Things didn't quite turn out as she'd planned. Almost immediately after our arrival she was contacted by exiled operatives and sympathizers of the Sandinista movement, some of whom were on the run in Costa Rica from the mounting persecution in Nicaragua. Her first such encounters were with people whose engagement with the revolution was largely intellectual and who held political meetings at their comfortable homes to discuss Marxist and Socialist theories. But before long she was meeting with representatives of the so-called tertiary group (the third to appear), which had been created some years earlier by factions within the Sandinista leadership and which pushed for an immediate popular uprising inside the cities. The group was led by, among other people, the Ortega brothers—Daniel, Humberto, and Camilo.

And so, within a month and a half of our arrival in Costa Rica, my mother was again a full-fledged revolutionary. She was given various tasks, including renting homes in upscale neighborhoods, where she would pretend to be a well-to-do married woman. Her supposed husband was another Sandinista insurgent. These wealthier neighborhoods were chosen over poorer ones because they were more private and had fewer eyes watching the constant movement of the Sandinista rebels, who went in and out of these homes under the cover of night for political and military training, and to conduct logistical operations. But the relative privacy provided by these upper-class neighborhoods did not prevent the occasional leak, and the safe houses were raided a couple of times. For this reason, we had to keep on the move, never staying in any particular home for more than two months.

Command meetings, where leaders of the tertiary faction would meet to plan the overthrow of the Somoza regime, took place in these houses. By this time my mother was reporting directly to Humberto Ortega, who would later become the commanding general of the Sandinista army. His brother Daniel, who went on to serve as president of Nicaragua, also frequented the safe houses rented by my mother. The third brother, Camilo, the youngest, was described to me by my mother as ". . . a mystic, tall and scrawny looking, a charming idealist with a sweet expression." He and my mother fell deeply in love during the insurgency, and many who learned of their affair assumed he was my father. But I was a year old when they first met. Even though he died in combat in 1978, my mother still sheds a tear when she talks about him.

In the meantime, my father had left Nicaragua to perform his songs in Europe. He became quite popular in Spain as well as in the communist bloc of nations, where he was seen as a cultural ambassador of the Sandinista revolution. One of his most celebrated works is "The Peasants' Mass," a cycle of songs representing the different musical stages of the Catholic service, composed in the language of the rural townspeople, traditional Nicaraguan musical instruments, popular expressions, daily situations, etc. The aristocracy and the Catholic Church in Nicaragua were both quick to reject the Mass and censure my father for it. But in Europe it was warmly received, particularly by progressive factions of the Catholic Church in Spain.

Toward the end of 1978 the Sandinistas mounted the opening of their final offensive. My mother was now heavily involved in providing logistical support for them and this involved our moving back and forth between San José and the mountainous frontier between Costa Rica and Nicaragua.

On July 19, 1979, the Sandinistas officially declared the overthrow of the Somoza regime and the liberation of the Nicaraguan people. Television footage of the toppling of Somoza's statue in the center of Managua looked a lot like that of the toppling of Saddam Hussein's in Baghdad some twenty-four years later.

I was four years old and have only fragmentary memories of this time, but I do recall when, within a couple of months of the revolution, we moved back to Nicaragua, where my mother worked at a variety of jobs for the new government, including in the military and in covert operations for the state security department. Her irreverent spirit and lifelong habit of questioning everything and everyone got her fired on more than one occasion and certainly did not assist her progress upward in a political system that required blind allegiance to its leaders.

Despite my mother's frequent brushes with the Sandinista elite, we led a privileged life in the years that followed the revolution. Though my family never amassed large amounts of money, influence mattered most in the new Nicaragua, and both of my parents had plenty of that. We lived in one of Managua's most expensive neighborhoods, taking up residence in a large house with five bedrooms, a small library, three living rooms, two terraces, front and back yards, and a small garden outside my mother's room. We employed a maid and a gardener.

My father, who by this time had remarried, lived a few blocks from us in the same neighborhood. Besides a maid, he also had a chauffeur, whom he politely referred to as "the comrade who drives for me." The school my brother and I attended was almost exclusively for the use of government officials' children; the president of Nicaragua, along with several of his top ministers, sent their children there as well. The foreign language we learned there was Russian.

Later we attended a private Jesuit school in Managua. The Jesuits, or at least the ones in Nicaragua, have a reputation of being more progressive and open-minded than the larger Catholic Church. Most of the Jesuit priests who worked at the school saw no contradiction between scientific study and religion, and some even held degrees in science. In their interpretation of the Bible, God was not a tyrannical figure but rather a loving parent and friend. In religion class, we were taught that faith and the teachings of Christ were to be applied to how we lived our lives and not restricted to the chapel.

In spite of this, I considered myself an atheist, although whenever I found myself in a difficult situation I would pray to God for forgiveness. It was only later in life that I realized that to fear God requires some degree of faith.

During this time my father served as a deputy in the Nicaraguan National Assembly, where, he told me, he had an aide who would vote for him when he fell asleep or was writing a song. He also worked as a cultural attaché in the Nicaraguan embassy in Madrid, Spain. My most vivid recollections of his work come from the many performances of his that I attended, often watching from backstage. Looking back, it seems astonishing that I regularly saw thousands of people singing along with my father as he performed, but at the time I wasn't terribly impressed. As far as I was concerned my father had always been famous.

But the memories of my father that I treasure most are not of him as an influential political or artistic figure, but just as a human being who loved his people and his country. I would sometimes travel with him to the poorest and most remote regions of Nicaragua to see him perform. In places like these, people still had to go to the river for water and their houses were made of little more than cardboard, yet my father seemed always to feel at home. The people really loved him and greeted us as part of their family. After a concert my father would eat the traditional foods he was offered with much delight. On our journey back we would often stop in places that at first seemed insignificant, until we noticed the sun setting in the backyard of a little wooden house on a hilltop, or we would stop so my father could take pictures of a sunflower, or a rainbow, or we would go into the middle of a cornfield being irrigated to shower. My father never lost the sense of awe and wonder in simple things that most people seem to leave behind as they grow up.

Despite the great benefits and life improvements the revolution brought to the people, the Sandinista government's popularity among Nicaraguans started to deteriorate a few years after they took power. The revolution had started one of the highest profile social justice movements in the world, and though it was never a full-fledged communist regime, it did have close associations with Cuba, Eastern Europe, and the USSR. Such friendships, coupled with the government's appropriation of private land and resources for the poor, made Nicaragua a prime target for the United States, which soon started channeling significant support to the armed opposition to the revolution, the mercenary army known as the "contras."

This U.S. aggression required the Nicaraguan armed forces to introduce mandatory military service and to take an ever larger chunk of government revenues, money which could otherwise have been spent on social programs, to fight the war. A U.S. economic embargo further choked the economy, undermining the revolution's effort to combat widespread hunger and disease. With the economy stagnating and with no end in sight to a low-intensity war that claimed the lives of more than fifty thousand Nicaraguans, support for the revolution steadily slipped away. Finally in 1990 the Sandinistas lost the presidential elections, and a new oligarchic government that enjoyed friendly relations with the United States took power.

After the fall of the government, it became evident that some of the Sandinista leaders had become multimillionaires. They were well placed to flourish in Nicaragua's new economy, which opened its doors to the U.S. capitalist agenda. My father was not among those who had made substantial fortunes, but he continued to find favor with the Nicaraguan people and was able to live comfortably from his music and art. My mother, on the other hand, was part of a dying, broken-down political aristocracy that was left without resources or influence after the collapse of the revolution. Unable and unwilling to find work in the new government, and ignored by many of her now-rich Sandinista friends, she decided to return to her native home. By January 1992, my brother Carlos and I were living once again in San José, where we would be joined by our mother just a few months later.

At first I thought of our move back to Costa Rica as a return to my second home, a place of sweet childhood memories. But I soon discovered that things in San José were different than before. I had lived in Nicaragua for twelve years and felt as one with its culture and people. But Nicaraguans were looked down on by many Costa Ricans. Often described as the Switzerland of Central America, Costa Rica enjoyed an economy that was light-years ahead of its poorer neighbor to the north. As a result, many Nicaraguans crossed the border looking to improve their living standards, and they would take the worst jobs for the lowest pay. This, in turn, led to sharp discrimination against all Nicaraguans.

My brother and I were enrolled at a private Catholic

school attended by the children of many of Costa Rica's elite families who were not at all welcoming to outsiders like us. One painful recollection from my time there related to a spiritual retreat in the countryside, sponsored by the school priests. I arrived late at the assembly point where the bus was waiting, and as I climbed aboard everyone started yelling at me, mocking my Nicaraguan accent and calling me derogatory names. At first I tried to laugh it off, but the barrage did not stop and I was forced to take my seat and wait for the sea of insults to subside.

Aggressive discrimination of this sort was commonplace throughout Costa Rican society, extending from people on the street to the news media and even politicians. At times I felt like the entire collective sense of humor was hostile to Nicaraguans. Many foreigners from other countries also felt the sting of Costa Rican xenophobia, particularly those from Mexico and Guatemala, who tended to be of darker skin than Costa Ricans; but when it came to being discriminated against and marginalized from society, Nicaraguans always fared the worst.

The general atmosphere in my new home had a profound effect on me and on the way I regarded other people. In Nicaragua I had been a privileged child of the revolution. There was always someone on hand to cook for me whenever I wanted to eat, and if I came home with dirty clothes they would be washed, dried, and neatly folded in my closet before the day was out. I was well liked at school and had many friends. All that came to an end during the two years we spent in Costa Rica, and I became an introverted and lonely teenager.

Lacking a circle of friends to hang out with, I was forced to learn to do things on my own, which, though tough at the time, had its compensations. I started going to concerts and the theater, even taking some acting lessons, and I began to read classical literature and poetry. Inspired by Edgar Allan Poe, I wrote a few horror tales. Toward the end of my stay in Costa Rica I did manage to make some new friends, some of whom were foreigners themselves. My friendship with them further broadened my outlook and interests, and to this day they remain close to my heart.

At the beginning of 1994 we heard from my grandmother—who by then was a naturalized American citizen—that she had been able to obtain permanent resident status in the United States for my mother. Because my brother and I were still minors, we too received permanent residency. And so, at the age of eighteen, I moved again, this time to Miami, Florida.

My mental picture of American high schools derived, at that time, solely from Hollywood. The reality of American Senior High in Miami Lakes, where I was now enrolled, was not at all like the friendly, well-resourced schools I had seen in TV shows and movies. It was overcrowded, with police officers patrolling the halls and parking lots. Furthermore, the staff did not understand that even though I was in eleventh grade in Costa Rica, I was a senior. They insisted that I take two more years in order to graduate, and I ended up having to attend night school in an attempt to do two years in one. A good portion of the students in the night classes were troublemakers who had been kicked out of day school for disciplinary reasons.

I also had to work for a living for the first time in my life. My mother had rented out our apartment in Nicaragua, and my father was still sending some child support money, but even with this extra income my mother's salary as a supermarket cashier wasn't enough to pay the rent and put food on the table. So I got a job at a fast-food restaurant, where I swept the parking lot, put the chairs down from the tables, and cleaned the bathrooms every single morning before moving to the kitchen to flip burgers for six hours. After work I had a two-hour break before going to night school, so my days started at five-thirty in the morning and didn't end until I returned home from school at ten at night.

Graduation was also very different from what I'd imagined. There was no prom night for me, nor did I have any friends with whom to celebrate. I just walked into the school principal's office and he handed me my diploma. I think he said "Congratulations and good luck, son." I went to the local supermarket and sat outside on a bench, staring at my diploma and wondering if this was all that happened when you graduated.

The following year, after I attended a community college for two semesters, the government terminated my federal student financial aid, claiming I made enough money at my dead-end job to pay my own tuition. I found myself without any real prospects for the future. It seemed as though I was working my butt off for a life that offered nothing at all.

It was these circumstances that led me to join the U.S. Army in Miami at age nineteen. The recruiter didn't really have to work hard to get me to sign the treacherous contract. The army offered financial stability and college tuition, two benefits that seemed tough to find anywhere else. But more than financial stability and tuition, the military held out the promise of helping me claim my place in the world. It wasn't even that I wanted to be a U.S. citizen; I just wanted to be with a group of people with whom I shared something, to acquire a sense of belonging. My visit to the recruiters' office wasn't to decide whether I wanted to join, but to decide what military branch and specialty I would choose, which turned out to be the army's infantry.

My parents were both against my signing up, not just for political reasons but because they feared war and thought I wasn't the warrior type. My mother's main argument was that the U.S. military was always invading some country or involved in some type of armed conflict, and that even if there was no war at the time, I would most certainly end up fighting one day. She begged me not to join and cried on the day I left for Fort Benning, Georgia, where I became a combat soldier.

My years in the active-duty army went by fast enough. I spent most of my time in Fort Hood, Texas, which was home to my unit, the Fourth Infantry Division. My record of good performance and discipline earned me several medals and certificates of achievement. Sometimes I let my mouth get the better of me, and I got a reputation as a bit of a rebel with my smart critical remarks, but that never became much of an issue. I always got the job done and continued to receive good reviews and promotions.

I had joined the military knowing that I wanted eventually to get a higher education, and, after three and a half years of active duty service learning the ins and outs of the infantry, I was ready to give college another try.

Before leaving Fort Hood to go home, and for the first time since I'd joined the military, the full implication of my enlisting were laid out for me by a female recruiting sergeant. She explained that anyone entering the service makes a commitment to the military for a minimum of eight years. Even someone who, like me, signs up for just three years has another five years of service to fulfill at the end of his contract, time that can be served either by extending one's stay in the regular army or by joining the Inactive Ready Reserve (IRR) or the National Guard, which requires training one weekend a month and two weeks during the summer. Whatever the case, though, soldiers are always subject to being called back to active duty until the eight-year commitment is fulfilled. Recruiters generally skate over this unpleasant fact, suggesting to those who notice it that it is a minor detail and insisting that it would take a devastating attack on the United States for non-active-duty soldiers to be called back into service from their civilian lives.

The recruiting sergeant explained that guard soldiers exist to respond to natural catastrophes in their state, which in Florida meant helping with post-hurricane relief. Her assessment of the likelihood of going to war with a guard unit was that it was almost impossible. I weighed this information together with the fact that the Florida National Guard was offering free college tuition, and decided to finish my contract with the guard, attending college as a part-time soldier.

So it was that I returned to Florida in 1998 and went back to the community college I had attended after high school, which today is called Miami Dade College. After two years there I transferred to the University of Miami. It was only when I got there that I discovered the National Guard did not pay for tuition at private schools. Fortunately, my good grades meant I was eligible for a merit scholarship covering half of the tuition fees. I took out student loans to cover the rest.

My daughter, Samantha, was born in 2000. The relationship between her mother and me did not last long, and we were never married, but I was very much in love with my daughter and did my best to be an active part of her life. I soon discovered that being a father and a student did not mix well with a military career, even a part-time one. The training schedule was demanding and I began losing semesters and, even worse, precious time with Samantha.

My feelings about the military had changed radically by the end of 2002. I felt close to my friends in the service and in many ways still regarded the military as a family. After all, I had been an active-duty soldier and in the guard for a total of almost eight years. I knew the lifestyle, the food, the mentality, the discipline and structure, the language, and even the sense of humor. But I was disappointed in the system. It preyed on the vulnerability of people, exploiting their lack of options to get them to sign up, and subsequently tied them into service with the constant promise of benefits that were just around the corner.

By the beginning of 2003 I was ready to hang up my boots. I had been undertaking research for the psychology department at the university and was working as a volunteer crisis counselor for a nonprofit organization and for a food program for the AIDS and homeless communities in the Miami area. I also was a member of three honor societies at the university. My eight-year contract with the military would come to an end in May and, if things worked out, I would get my bachelor's degree in the same month. I had decided I would apply for a PhD program in psychology and was looking forward to being a father and a full-time doctoral candidate by the end of the year.

Then, on January 14, 2003, our Florida National Guard company commander told everyone in formation that our unit had been activated in support of Operation Iraqi Freedom. Those of us who were due to get out of the military soon had just been extended until the year 2031 as a result of Congress passing a "stop-loss order." Two and a half months later I found myself in the Middle East, participating in the invasion of Iraq.

TWO

The night before leaving for the Middle East, our company had a lay-out gear inspection conducted by our company commander, Captain Warfel. The captain was a tall, slim man in his late thirties; his light brown hair, intense blue eyes, and impeccable desert uniform made him look straight out of a GI Joe box. As he walked past my gear I asked him if I could bring my Bible with me. The request was granted, but I had to leave behind my laptop computer, which I had intended to use for writing; several books I had wanted to read also had to be left behind.

In lay-out inspections, soldiers have to spread their gear in a designated area—on their bunks or the floor—in a predetermined order. Such inspections are common, particularly when a unit is about to be mobilized, but the inspection that night was mostly due to an order from battalion to strictly limit the amount of personal belongings we could bring. We had to carry our own unit supplies, including food, water, weapons, and ammunition, and with all the cargo we had, plus the weight of the fuel, there was concern that the plane would be way too heavy for the long trip.

But even after the severe weight restrictions, the plane

could still not fly the whole distance on a full tank, and we had
to stop for fuel in New York, Canada, Scotland, and Italy before arriving in Jordan, our final destination. In spite of the long
flight and the many stops, the large chartered plane was comfortable enough for the more than one hundred and thirty soldiers traveling in it, and most of us slept throughout the flight.

It was night when we arrived at the Jordanian border
with Iraq. Upon exiting the plane I saw only a big airstrip
hangar in a desolate military airport in the middle of the dark
desert. Inside the hangar, which some of us visited soon after
arriving, we encountered the first major cultural difference:
the design of the latrines. They consisted of openings in the
floor with water faucets next to them. Some within the platoon looked down on these new Arab-style toilets, and complained that from then on we would be "shitting like dogs."
This racist attitude toward cultural differences was common
throughout our deployment in the Middle East.

I felt a sense of alertness and caution immediately after
our arrival. We had traveled halfway across the world knowing that an invasion of Iraq was a distinct possibility. My first
impression of our new environment was of a desolate, unwel-
coming place. Perhaps I was just psyching myself up for the
military action to follow, but it occurred to me that we might
already be under the prying eye of our enemy. I profoundly
hoped that there would be no war, but I also knew that I had
to mentally prepare for the possibility of being part of one.

This initial impression lifted quickly the following morning when the rising sun opened a window to the modern face
of imperial war in the new century. When I awakened, I saw
that the tents we stumbled in the night before were mounted
on wooden bases and were equipped with electricity and air-
conditioning. We were in the middle of a colossal military tent
city that included two large dining facilities serving everything from bread and butter to ice cream and fresh tropical

fruit, and a PX, or post exchange store, with a wide range of merchandise including snacks and tobacco, CDs and DVDs, clothing, even folding beach chairs. The base, known as H-5, also had a Morale-Welfare-Recreation (MWR) facility, with ping-pong tables, books, and a big-screen TV for movies. Plentiful phones were located just outside the midnight mess hall so that we could drop in for a late-night snack after speaking with our families back home.

Considering we were right next to Iraq, with war drums beating insistently in the background, it was a pleasant place to be. But our standard of living improved further after we relocated to a U.S. Army Air Defense Artillery base in the mist-shrouded mountains that surrounded Amman, Jordan's capital. Our mission was to guard the perimeter of the base, which sat on top of a hill that overlooked the city. The Islamic call to prayer, a moving and mystical recitation that summons Muslims to worship, echoed throughout Amman five times a day, giving the place an air of ancient holiness, especially during the early morning hours, when the fog slowly uncovered the city before our eyes.

At the base, which was surrounded by all kinds of Jordanian army units, Patriot missile launchers stood ready to intercept Scud missiles. The widespread belief was that we were the king's guests and that we were there to protect Amman from Saddam's near misses on bordering Israel. It was said that during the first Gulf War, Saddam launched Scud missiles at Israel hoping it would retaliate and that other Arab nations would join the fight. Several of these Scud missiles fell short of their targets in Israel and hit Amman instead. In exchange for letting the U.S. military use H-5 to launch an offensive against Iraq, the United States set up air defense bases to protect Jordan.

Being guests of the king of Jordan had its rewards. A catering service delivered breakfast, lunch, and dinner every day; a dry-cleaning service operated on Tuesdays and Thursdays;

toilets, though portable, were of the Western sit-down variety and there were ample showers with running water. There was also an MWR tent with two TV sets, each with a hundred channels; we also had a beach volleyball court.

But the best thing about our time in Jordan, at least as far as I was concerned, was the fact that we were still at peace. I was pretty well alone among my fellow soldiers in holding such a view. Most of the platoon were gung ho for war and keen to put their fighting skills to the test. My platoon sergeant, Sergeant First Class Palango, wore all kinds of training tabs and combat awards from his time as a young U.S. ranger in Grenada. One day I heard him jokingly say "Give war a chance." I wondered just how much action he had actually seen in that briefest of invasions.

Back then, without yet having any combat experience, I was aware that combat was not that cleansed, pretty, *Top Gun* picture Hollywood has imprinted on young minds, where bullets fly mostly one way and friendly casualties are clean, whole, few, and heroic. I think one does not need to have actually experienced war firsthand to understand its human cost, and I couldn't possibly wish for a situation in which people I cared about would die. But my aversion to war was also very exclusive to the war in Iraq, and it was an aversion initially grounded in political reasons.

During our stay in Jordan we were able to watch the news, and even the mainstream media was reporting strong opposition to a possible invasion, not just from around the world, but also from home. Some of the biggest antiwar demonstrations ever seen in the United States took place just prior to the invasion, and I couldn't help sympathizing with the demonstrators. I didn't feel our government had made a strong case for military action. I knew that the chief UN weapons inspectors were requesting more time to try to find weapons of mass destruction, and that some of the United States' strongest allies were saying

no to the war. And the fact the most of the September 11 hijack-
ers were Saudi nationals, with no proven connection to Iraq or
Saddam Hussein, made me more skeptical still. I felt certain
that the motives behind the war had more to do with oil and
geopolitical power than with defense of the United States.

Back in the United States, before deployment, I hadn't had
the courage or clarity to openly express my doubts about participating in a war that I believed was unjustified. Besides, I didn't
want to be labeled a coward. I knew that openly expressing my
reservations could be construed as unpatriotic and treasonous,
and that I might even be court-martialed and sent to jail.

As the prospect of the invasion became more real, I tried to
find comfort in the excuses that soldiers use when fighting wars
they don't believe in. I told myself that I was a soldier and it
wasn't for me to judge the reasons behind the decisions of those
higher up in the chain of command. I had signed a contract, I
was wearing a uniform, and I had to do my duty, period. Besides, I was an infantry squad leader and my squad needed me.

But still, I had been deployed to the Middle East in support of a military effort I strongly condemned and considered
criminal. I was afraid I would never make it home to tell my
daughter that even though I participated in the war, I had
been against it. If I died, that was a part of the legacy I wanted
to leave behind for her. So, one cold night, feeling that what I
was about to do would most definitely be considered disloyal,
I secretly wrote a message to my daughter under the dim beam
of an army-issued flashlight. On a sheet of paper folded in half
I wrote the words: GIVE PEACE A CHANCE.

That night I picked a member of the squad I really
trusted to pull guard duty with me. The night was freezing as
Specialist Guevara and I stood watch on the tower overlook-
ing the sleeping capital of Jordan. We were wearing our full
battle-rattle and our Gore-Tex jackets to stop the cutting winter winds. I took my gloves off and asked my friend to step

away from his machine gun for a minute. I gave him my disposable camera and, as if about to commit a crime of treason, I pulled the subversive sign out of my pocket and unfolded it by my chest. I destroyed the paper right after the picture was taken, but not before asking Guevara, who had taken the picture with a smile on his face, not to comment the incident to anyone in the platoon or even the squad.

My secret opposition to the war was only one of the problems I had with the military. My platoon leader, Lieutenant Dominguez, and I were not getting along too well. He was an insecure person, with little idea how to run an infantry platoon. He hid his lack of self-confidence behind a mask of macho assurance, which in turn manifested itself as inept leadership. On one occasion, during training, he ordered one of my grenade launchers to engage an armored vehicle that was a thousand meters away. I had to gently remind him that the target was way out of range. Another time he almost burned a soldier by firing a flare grenade from what was clearly the wrong position. I generally tried to keep my criticisms to myself but sometimes I couldn't help calling him on his stupidities. This friction between the lieutenant and me manifested itself in a sort of abusive relationship, in which he took advantage of every opportunity to scold me in public.

But if I had difficulties with the leadership of those above me, it was clear that they too had problems with my own leadership. In particular, there were serious concerns about my decision to establish a different type of relationship with the soldiers in my squad than was customary in the army. I wanted them to follow me not because of the consequences that would befall them if they didn't, but because they respected and trusted me. This was not standard practice in the armed forces, where one of the most widely used techniques for getting soldiers to follow orders, especially when there are disciplinary problems, is called "corrective training." Corrective training is nothing more than physical punishment, which some say is forbidden in the army but which is still widespread. It is colloquially referred to as "smoking." Its most common form is making a soldier do push-ups. Ordering a soldier to get on the ground to start such punishment is called "dropping," and the position to be assumed on the ground prior to doing the push-ups is referred as "front-leaning-rest position."

I can clearly recall one of the last occasions that I dropped a soldier and I'm not proud of how vindictive I was when I did it. It was at Fort Stewart, Georgia. Private First Class Thomas was a bit overweight, and watching him eat pizza, chips, and chocolate and chew tobacco and drink beer and soda, all while being out of shape and overweight, simply disgusted me. Today I look back at how I used to be and sometimes feel ashamed. But the truth is it really bothered me to see this nineteen-year-old, insecure, out-of-shape, overweight soldier-boy in my squad. Most of the time I tried to help him as much as I could, but every now and then I couldn't help despising him, and I could be really hard on him.

One afternoon, while the squad was conducting PT, or physical training, I saw that Thomas was falling way behind everyone else during the running part of the exercise, and that the faster soldiers were beginning to pass him for the second and third time. I became furious and decided to cut through the middle of the field to run alongside him. When yelling at him no longer worked, I ordered him to stop and dropped him just off the track. I then proceeded to smoke him until he almost reached muscle failure. He raised his upper body from the front-leaning-rest position and, standing on his knees, he started to cry. His upper lip was topped with tears and snot, which he wiped with his chubby, dust-covered, sweaty right arm.

I've never apologized to PFC Thomas for that smoking, though I wish I had. That day at Fort Stewart was the last

time I ever dropped or smoked a soldier. I like to think that
abusing lower-ranking soldiers was out of character for me
and resulted from the tension between the lieutenant and me.
But I also know that my bouts of rage were the result of feeling trapped in a military effort I opposed.

When I told the oldest and most experienced squad
leader in the platoon, Staff Sergeant Ducket, about my decision not to drop my soldiers anymore, he told me that such an
approach to leadership could bring seriously negative consequences to my standing as a squad leader in the platoon. I
told him that dropping soldiers to the level of my feet was de-
grading and humiliating, and that such treatment, far from
achieving respect and discipline, only prompted resentment. I
wanted my soldiers to respect and trust me, not fear me. I also
told him that I myself would no longer drop for anyone, whatever their rank. I could tell this news surprised him but he responded by simply pressing his lips together and nodding.

Once we were in Jordan, my distinctive approach to leadership really started to raise eyebrows in the chain of command. One afternoon, while we were fortifying the perimeter
with concertina wire, my platoon sergeant, Sergeant First
Class Palango, called me aside.

"What's up, sarge?" he asked in his usual happy-go-
lucky tone.

"Not much, sergeant," I answered, wondering what he
wanted. "What's going on?"

We walked farther away from where the other soldiers
were working, which was typical of Palango, who preferred
to do only enough physical work to be noticed.

"I've noticed that you don't drop your soldiers," he said.

"Right."

"Yeah, I spoke with Ducket," he went on. "He said that
you don't want to drop your men."

"Aha, yes, sergeant."

"Well, you see the other squad leaders, they're good to their men, but they're also firm, and they enforce discipline."

"Yes, sergeant," I said. "I know, they drop their guys, and they yell at them. But you don't. I don't think I've ever seen you yelling at anyone, or even dropping anyone. You seem like a pretty calm person to me."

"Yeah, sarge," he said. "But you really can't compare. I've been in the military a lot longer, I've been to war and have shot at the bad guys, and I'm a sergeant first class. I've earned my respect."

Bad guys? I thought. *Where does this guy come from?* I knew I had earned my squad's respect, but not his.

"I have the respect of my men, sergeant."

"Well, it's not just about respect, it's also about discipline, and being the way an infantry squad leader is supposed to be."

Now we were getting to the bottom of the matter. It was not a question of my effectiveness as a squad leader, but rather of how I was expected to behave.

"Is there anything the other squads are doing that my squad is not?" I asked, shifting my eyes between him and the ground, where I was kicking little rocks with my boots.

"No, sergeant," he said, stopping for a moment, which made me look straight at him as he talked. "Your guys are doing fine, and you have two outstanding team leaders. It's just that I would like you to put a little more testosterone into your leadership style, that's all."

"A little more testosterone?" I asked, thinking what a brute I was talking to.

"Well, you know," he said. "I want to see you more in charge. Yeah, more testosterone, more infantry."

"Alright, sergeant," I said looking at him with a forced smile. "I think I know what you mean."

I knew exactly what he meant, but I had no intention of changing anything about my leadership style, and I didn't.

The main problem I had with Palango was not about the way I led my squad; it was about my overall approach to leadership and human relations. I had a hard time dealing with all the hypocrisy and backstabbing that went on within the platoon. For instance, there was a huge power struggle between Palango and Dominguez, one that one day got to an embarrassing point. It happened while we were having a command meeting in the mess hall tent, and the two "big dogs" started yelling at each other.

"You talk so much about war and battle, and all that, sir," yelled Palango at the lieutenant. "But have you ever seen war?"

Dominguez reacted furiously to Palango's question. We'd all heard him talk about war as if he and combat were old pals, but we knew that, although he had been in the military for close to twenty years, he had never fired a bullet outside of a shooting range.

"Sergeant Palango," Dominguez countered, trying to compose himself. "I don't need to have been to war to be ready for it or talk about it, and I can't believe you took that cheap shot at me. I am the lieutenant here, I am the platoon leader. Do you have a problem with that?"

"No," said Palango. "You are the LT, and I respect you, but I have a problem with you always lecturing me about battle when I am the one here who has actually fought. I was there, I was shot at, and I'm the one who shot at the bad guys."

The loud argument finished shortly after this exchange, but the friction between the sergeant and the lieutenant continued, and they used every opportunity to backstab each other. When it was my turn to go at it with Palango again, the problem, once more, involved the practice of smoking the men.

The origins of the new dispute centered on one PFC Leonard. Leonard and I had been friends for a long time, though I outranked him and we had not been in the same platoon until we were deployed to the Middle East. He was an intelligent young man, a terrific chess player who was good at math and interested in philosophical questions. But he was impractical, and often found it hard to keep his mouth shut even if it got him in trouble. On top of that, he was untidy and his personal hygiene wasn't the best. This was a combination of qualities that was almost certain to cause problems for him in an infantry unit.

Being more than a little disorganized, Leonard kept personal belongings in the same bag as his chemical protective gear. One such belonging was his CD player. One day while Leonard was pulling guard duty on a watchtower, the platoon's medic, who had the reputation of being a snitch, saw the player inside Leonard's bag while doing his rounds. The medic went straight to Palango and told him that Leonard was listening to music while pulling guard duty. The CD player was subsequently confiscated.

About a week later, Leonard and I were having a casual conversation about the condition of his boots, which at the request of his tent mates he left outside every night before going to bed. He wanted to know if I knew of a way to eliminate their nasty odor. I jokingly told him the only solution was to pour fuel in them and set them on fire, but I was probably right about that.

Suddenly he realized the time and said he had to go. I knew it wasn't his turn for guard duty and asked him where he was going in such a rush.

"I gotta go get smoked," he said with a forced smile.

"What do you mean?" I asked with a frown.

"Every day at twenty hundred hours, Sergeant Iglesias smokes me for an hour."

Leonard wasn't in the same squad as Iglesias but, for the purposes of perimeter security, reported directly to him.

"You gotta be fucking kidding me, man," I said.

"No, I'm serious. But I'm not supposed to say anything. Besides, it's cool; Sergeant Iglesias only smokes me when there are people around. When everyone leaves he tells me to recover."

Recovering means telling a soldier who's being smoked to get up from the front-leaning-rest position.

"It's not cool, man." I said this holding his arm, trying to keep him from leaving. "That shit's fucking illegal. Have you told Ducket about it?"

"No," he said. "But the order came straight from Palango, so I don't think there is anything he can do about it."

Later that night Leonard and I had a long chat. I learned that after Leonard's CD player was confiscated, everyone in his tent was ordered not to share their CD players or Game Boys with him. He was being disciplined for his irresponsible behavior while on guard duty. However, it turned out that Sergeant Iglesias agreed to let Leonard use his player on the condition that if he got caught with it, he would be on his own. One day, someone in the tent heard music coming from Leonard's sleeping bag. They found Iglesias's CD player, which Leonard had forgotten to turn off before going on duty. Instead of giving Iglesias away, Leonard said he had stolen the player. As punishment he was given a one-hour-long smoking every day for two weeks. And even though everyone knew what had really happened, they still labeled Leonard a thief and forced him to dump all of his belongings outside to make sure he hadn't stolen anything else. They also confiscated his knives "for the protection of all," an absurd measure obviously designed only for the purpose of humiliation, given the fact that they let him keep his weapon and ammunition so that he could continue with guard duty.

On another occasion, after the end of the two weeks of smokings, Leonard and I were talking again. He told me that before agreeing to return his toys to him, Sergeant First Class Palango had told him he had to memorize everything on our language card, which included some 105 words and phrases in Arabic, in five days. No one in the platoon knew more than five words. Leonard knew more than twenty; I know because I tested him. But because he had been unable to memorize the entire thing he was told by Palango he had to spend the night dumping more than two hundred sandbags on the volleyball court. He wasn't to return to his normal duties until he was done dumping the last bag.

"And no one can help me," he said, evidently distressed. "They're sending the doc," meaning our snitching platoon medic, "to supervise me."

"They're sending the medic to supervise you because they know you can hurt yourself dumping all those bags by yourself at night," I explained to him. "Have you told Ducket?"

"No."

"Okay, you go ahead, man," I said, trying hard to keep my cool. "I'm gonna go tell Ducket about this shit, and if he doesn't do anything about it, I will, because this is just too much."

Leonard thanked me and I went off to find Ducket, who was deep asleep, perhaps getting ready for our guard shift, which started at midnight.

"What's up, Sergeant Mejía?" said Ducket grumpily. When he removed his sleeping mask I could see that he was upset by my waking him hours before his shift.

"What is it now?"

"Leonard."

"Ohhh, come on, sergeant, not everyone is like you, you know?"

"No, man," I said. "This shit's gone way too far already, and if you don't do anything about it, I will."

"What do you mean? What's going on?" He was now getting out of his sleeping bag, which sat on two foam mattresses on top of an army cot. Ducket really liked his beauty sleep.

"I'm about to go tell the battery commander and the first sergeant, because what they're doing to Leonard is clearly wrong, not to mention illegal."

"SERGEANT MEJÍA, STOP!" he yelled. "Now, will you tell me what's going on?"

"They're making Leonard dump *all* the sandbags on the volleyball court at night because he couldn't memorize all the words on the language card."

"Who's doing that?" he asked.

"According to Leonard the order came from Palango, and they even got the medic watching him. They must know he could hurt himself doing that alone, at night. I'm sure the battery commander would not agree with these measures."

"Alright, sergeant, let me go talk to Palango," said Ducket, finally putting on his boots. "I'll see what I can do."

While Ducket went to meet with Palango, I went to the volleyball court to see how Leonard was doing. Before I spotted him I ran into the medic, who had made himself a comfortable sandbag seat from which he could watch Leonard dump the sandbags.

"Hey, what's up Sergeant Mejía?" He spit some sunflower seeds before saying this.

"Not much," I said, cuttingly. "Where's Leonard?"

He pointed in the direction of one of several huge piles of sandbags.

"He's alright," he said.

"Aha."

I walked toward the pile without seeing as much as Leonard's shadow. Once his profile became visible in the darkness, I saw that he had taken off his uniform top, even though it was a pretty cold evening. He was sweating profusely and had a sandbag on each shoulder, which he dropped upon seeing me. He was crying in silence.

"I'm a failure," he said, crying but with a smile on his face.

"No, you're not, man," I said, trying not to show how upset I was. They were breaking the kid down. "These people are just a bunch of dickheads," I continued. "And you're smarter than all of them."

"No." He was looking down and nodding his head, probably talking to himself more than to me. "Look at me," he insisted. "I can't do anything right. One simple task after another, and I keep failing."

"Simple!?" I asked, almost yelling. "You know more Arabic than anyone in the platoon, man; that shit ain't simple! Anyway, I talked to Ducket; I'm not sure what he's gonna do, but he said he would do something. You just be careful while you're here."

He had stopped crying by the time I started walking away.

"Hey, sergeant," he said.

I turned back to see him.

"Thank you."

I forced a smile, waved, and kept walking.

The following day Leonard got all his gear back. He told me Palango had shown up at the volleyball court shortly after I left the night before. He told Leonard he hadn't meant for him to dump all the bags, and that he just wanted to check that he could follow orders to the best of his ability, a sort of discipline test. That same day Leonard moved to my tent.

Not long after this incident my team leaders started asking me about my impending transfer. I told them, truthfully, that I had no idea what they were talking about. Then, one morning, a soldier in my squad was congratulated on his new position by another squad leader. He was told that I was about to get fired and that he would get to take my spot. The rumors became ever more intense and frequent. At first I thought little of it, but as time went by I realized the rumors were beginning to undermine my authority within the squad. I decided to confront Palango about the matter.

"Hey, what's up, big sergeant?" he said to me one morning as I approached him after breakfast. "How come you never sit with us?"

I told him I preferred to sit with my squad, which was true, but I usually sat anywhere in the mess tent. In reality I didn't like sitting with him and the other squad leaders mostly because the conspiracies and hypocrisy at their table were just too much for me to swallow along with my food.

"How do you think my squad is doing?" I asked, knowing the problem had nothing to do with my squad, or even my performance as a squad leader.

"Oh, I think your guys are doing fine," he said, pausing. The tension was palpable. "Why do you ask, sergeant?"

"Well, it's just that I've been hearing this rumor that I'm about to get fired," I said, looking at him but without smiling. "And if it's true, I'd like to know why."

"No, that's not true, but I did say I would fire whoever tries to go over my head."

"What do you mean?" I asked, though I was pretty sure I knew exactly what he meant.

"Well, somebody said they were going to see the battery commander to complain about my leadership," he continued, knowing very well that the person he was talking about was standing in front of him. "Why, was that you?"

"If you're talking about what happened with Leonard, yes, that was me."

"I'll send your ass straight back to H-5 if you ever try to go over my head again," he yelled.

"Well, I never planned to go over your head," I said, lying. "I went straight to Ducket because he is still Leonard's squad leader. But I didn't go over your head, sergeant."

"Well, do you have a problem with the way I handled Leonard? I even sent the medic, to make sure he didn't hurt himself. It was all corrective training."

"Sergeant, I have a problem with the way Leonard's been handled from the day we got here. I mean, yeah, the guy's a bit clumsy and all, but the way they're treating him is not helping him one bit. It's just breaking the guy's morale and self-esteem."

I felt like I was talking in a different tongue to a being from a different world, although in reality, compared to everyone else in the platoon, I was the only alien there.

"Whatever problems you may have, you keep them within the platoon," he said.

"Roger, sergeant," I said. "That's why I went to Sergeant Ducket. I was following the chain of command."

"And that's all you have to do, sergeant," his lips curled upward in a forced smile. "Meanwhile, don't worry about anything you hear. You're doing a good job, sergeant."

We exchanged pleasantries and by the end of the conversation we were patting each other on the shoulder. It seemed like everything was going to be okay. But the rumors about my imminent firing didn't stop; they just became a bit more discreet.

A few days after my confrontation with Palango, the "shock and awe" bombing of Baghdad started. I was in shock and awe myself, not so much because of the ruthless bombardment, but because of how the U.S. government had ignored international law and forced this war not only on Iraq, but on the entire world.

Some of the soldiers in the platoon expressed regret about missing out on all the action; others channeled their feelings in a more mature but still gung-ho way by saying that as infantrymen we should be fighting alongside our brothers. I, on the other hand, was thinking that sooner or later the trigger-happy wishes of my fellow soldiers would actually come true. Feeling more and more that combat was just around the corner, I started hoping it wouldn't last long, that it would be a quick invasion, and that we would promptly be home.

The artillery unit we were attached to received redeployment orders; they were going back to the States. We were told that we had to stay on for a while to provide security for the Kellogg Brown & Root contractors while they tore down our camp.

Just as the artillery unit left the site, Easter rolled around. Lieutenant Dominguez, now supreme chief of the base, decided it would be good for troop morale to have a barbeque. This was to be the whole nine yards—burgers, hot dogs, and even beer.

Dominguez went on a shopping expedition to get supplies for the barbeque. He took a security team with him and, against direct orders, told everyone in the team to wear their full uniforms for their little road trip. They were spotted buying beer in a supermarket by a couple of U.S. citizens wearing civilian clothes, probably diplomats or undercover agents of some kind. The civilians went straight to the general in charge of all U.S. troops in the country and reported what they had seen.

Not long after we left the site days later, once we returned to H-5, Dominguez was relieved of his command as platoon leader. Rumor has it that his shopping trip was the end of his career as an officer. The last I heard, he'd commanded a convoy en route to Iraq, and was sent back to the States soon after. Sergeant First Class Palango became acting platoon leader of third platoon to replace him.

As for me, Palango said that I was to be transferred out of third platoon to become a squad leader in first platoon.

"I hate to see you go," he said with a straight face. "But it's not up to me."

Days after I took my new position as first squad leader in second platoon, and without prior notice, the entire company was woken up at about three in the morning. We were to get all our gear ready to go. The exhilaration of going home lasted only until we learned that we were redeploying not back to the States but to what would become our new home for an indefinite period of time: we were going to Iraq.

THREE

There was something odd about Charlie Company's deployment into Iraq. Everything seemed rushed and unprepared. We had to wait for an entire day on the airstrip in order to catch a flight in a C-130 from Jordan to Baghdad International, which back then was still called Saddam International Airport. The other companies in our battalion were not able to hitchhike a plane ride in this fashion and had to travel to Iraq by land.

Rumors that someone at the battalion level forged documents to get our units into combat more quickly were reinforced when we landed in Baghdad and found there was no unit waiting for us, no orders, no place to sleep, not even food or water. My lieutenant and I had to go out the next morning, in a borrowed Humvee, to try to find another unit nearby that had extra water and MREs (meals ready to eat).

Before our departure to Iraq, all our units had returned from different sites around Jordan and assembled once again at H-5. Some people thought we were getting ready to demobilize, to go back to the United States. But I knew that this was unlikely—our battalion commander, Lieutenant Colonel Mirable, wanted us to see action. Some three months previously, on the day that our battalion pictures were taken on the parade field at Fort Stewart, he had told everyone that we were not coming back to the States without our Combat Infantry Badge (CIB). His remarks were echoed by our company commander, Captain Warfel, just before we left for the Middle East.

The CIB is given exclusively to soldiers in infantry or special operation units that have directly engaged the enemy. Our senior officers, who had spent fifteen or twenty years in the military without combat experience, knew that the award was essential to their further progress up the officer ranks. So I wasn't surprised that we were dispatched to Baghdad in such a rush. The sense that our commanders would do anything for a medal and promotion was just the seed of what later, in the heat of battle, would grow into a profound sense of betrayal.

It took about a week before the rest of our battalion started to arrive in a huge convoy from Jordan. In the meantime we roamed around the recently destroyed airport. It was evident, even in its ruined state, that the facilities there had once been very luxurious, with thick red carpets, high ceilings, and spacious lobbies.

The airstrip was now being used by U.S. military planes, assault helicopters, and Black Hawks, which took off on their missions throughout the day and night. All international flights had ceased and the airport was completely empty of commercial airliners, except for a sole passenger plane on the edge of the airstrip that had been cut cleanly in half, as if with a giant serrated knife.

Hanging around in that destroyed facility, with no sense of mission and no contact with the outside world, was enough to drive anyone crazy, so we welcomed the news of finally becoming attached to a larger unit, the Third Armored Cavalry Regiment, or Third ACR. The sooner we started the mission in Iraq the sooner we could be out of there, or so we thought. The first mission required us to travel to al Assad, an old Iraqi air force base some distance from Baghdad International.

We set off through a succession of small towns, each more destitute than the last. Barefooted children approached our convoy of sand-colored, deuce-and-a-half- and five-ton army trucks as it rolled along the road. Some of the kids tried to sell glass bottles of soda and bags of peanuts, but most just wanted to say hello and take a closer look at their latest invaders. This was the very beginning of the occupation and, even with our rifles pointed through the sides of our vehicles straight at them, the Iraqis did not appear to be angry with us; for the most part they would smile and wave, gently tapping the top of their heads in a gesture we later learned meant thank you.

The drive to al Assad shouldn't have taken long, but we ended up on the road for close to eight hours because those in charge of the convoy had absolutely no idea where we were going. During the daytime this was no big deal. At this early stage of the occupation, daylight attacks were sporadic and generally ineffective. But as night took over the sky and with no end to our drive in sight, we started to feel less like an infantry unit with a mission and more like a ship, lost in a dark, hostile sea. A reconnaissance team was sent to search for our destination and we waited for them for an hour or so, pulled up on the road in the middle of God knows where, watching a big red sun set over the desert.

We finally arrived at al Assad late that night. It turned out to be a small airstrip surrounded by a network of large domes, which in the dark could easily be mistaken for large sand dunes. But in the light of morning we could see that they were in fact concrete structures with openings at their bases large enough for fighter aircraft to enter. They were bunkers for Iraqi air force planes.

Many of the bunkers had been bombed, but it appeared that only a couple of planes had been destroyed. The rest, mostly fighter jets, had been taken out to the nearby desert where they could still be seen but were hidden from the air beneath camouflage nets. As a U.S. army soldier, I didn't know if I should laugh or be embarrassed, for the truth was that someone in the Iraqi air force had fooled U.S. military intelligence into thinking they were destroying a considerable portion of the Iraqi air force when in fact they were destroying empty bunkers.

We set up our new home in a small four-room building adjacent to one of the bunkers that were still standing, about five miles outside of the actual air base. It took us a while to clean out the building and make it livable. Since the heat made it almost impossible to sleep indoors, the majority of soldiers just took their sleeping mats outside and slept on the ground around the structure. From there we could see the camp, which was to be our area of operations for the next ten days or so and which was located in the bunker next to our building.

Our mission was to assist in the running of a prisoner-of-war camp. The unit we were relieving was led by a skinny, tall first lieutenant. Removing his shades from his bony face, he entered our building looking for Lieutenant Cerekas, our platoon leader. Cerekas had joined Charlie just prior to our deployment to the Middle East, coming from the National Guard of another state. He was short, skinny, and had the face and demeanor of a little kid. At the time the Third ACR lieutenant walked into our area, Cerekas was hanging his just-washed socks on the shower curtain pole of a destroyed lavatory. The ACR lieutenant announced that, whenever Cerekas was ready, he would give him a briefing on how to run the facility. Our barefooted lieutenant quickly found some clean black socks and hurried outside.

Upon his return, Cerekas did not seem to be in a good mood.

"They're going to need squad leaders to give you guys a crash course," he announced. "But you know," he continued, "this doesn't seem right."

"What do you mean, sir?" asked our platoon sergeant, Sergeant First Class Williams, with a slight smile and raised eyebrows. Williams was a tall, handsome black man in his late twenties, who thought of himself as always right and who hated being contradicted even on the slightest of things.

"Well," said Cerekas, beginning to show signs of agitation, "did you know they don't have an FLA around here?" He was talking about a field litter ambulance.

"Soooo?" Williams asked, in a tone that bordered on insolence.

"I don't think you can have a prisoner-of-war camp without proper medical equipment nearby," Cerekas continued. "You know what they said?"

"What did they say, sir?" Williams was now slouched on a seat made of MRE boxes.

"They said we should not call this a POW camp, but rather a *detainee* camp." He said the word "detainee" in a sarcastic tone.

Williams repositioned himself in his cardboard chair and crossed his arms. He waited, curious to see where the lieutenant was going with his line of thought.

"This place is ILLEGAL, Sergeant Williams," said the lieutenant, releasing a deep breath. "All they have for medical care is a single medic whose rank is private first class. There's supposed to be a medical facility around here. Where is it? What if one of these prisoners gets hurt?" He raised his arms in exasperation.

"So what's your point, sir?" asked Williams, though the nature of Cerekas's concern was now evident.

"The point is I'm gonna call the Red Cross, sergeant, 'cause we're not even supposed to be here. This is a job for military police, or military intelligence. We're infantry, we're grunts, and we're not trained for this. And these guys, these guys are cavalry scouts. That's why they want us to call this place a detainee camp, because it doesn't meet the proper requirements of a POW camp."

"Alright," said Williams, getting up from the stack of MREs. "First of all, it's not our job to say that this place is legal or illegal, sir."

"This place would probably be shut down if we called the Red Cross," Cerekas countered.

"No, it wouldn't, sir," said Williams, annoyed but trying to be persuasive in a low tone. Cerekas outranked him, but Williams had far greater military experience and a stronger personality. One way or another, Williams was going to persuade the LT to drop the issue; he just had to do it in a way that made it seem more like Cerekas's own decision, at least to Cerekas.

"The only thing that would happen is you would get fired, and someone else would be put in charge."

"But we can't be a part of this. I mean, I don't think we should. I think we should report it," Cerekas was beginning to compose himself.

"We just have to do our job," said Williams. "If you were to report anything, they would just point their finger at some lieutenant colonel, and who do you think is going to win? Do you really think they'll listen to a National Guard lieutenant?"

Cerekas was quiet now, listening to Williams.

"The only thing that would happen is that it would be the end of your career, sir." Williams knew he had him.

"I don't know, Sergeant Williams, I don't know," said the resigned lieutenant as he walked inside the building. He knew that, like it or not, we were going ahead with the mission.

Once Lieutenant Cerekas had left and Williams was alone with the squad leaders and a few other soldiers, he told us that he was trying hard not to step on the lieutenant's toes.

"Sometimes I want to step in," he said, sounding, as he usually did, sure of his judgment. "But I gotta let him do his job; otherwise he's never going to learn."

Cerekas, like me, was new to second platoon. While we were in Jordan, there had been all kinds of friction between platoon leaders and platoon sergeants in all the platoons in our unit; that had led to the reshuffling of just about the entire leadership of Charlie Company; Williams and Cerekas were just starting to work together.

Behind Williams a contained fire could be seen from feces burning in a metal barrel in the middle of an open space at the entrance to the bunker next to our building. The bunker, which served as detention camp, was fenced by a double strand of razor-sharp concertina wire. Another fire burned outside the camp, some fifty meters away from the concertina fence and right next to a wooden shack that served as latrine. We later learned that both fires were burning a toxic mixture of fuel and human excrement—the one inside the compound for the detainees, the other, outside, for U.S. soldiers.

We had already walked over to the camp and were about to have a crash course on detainee handling when we were interrupted by the arrival at the compound of two new prisoners.

"Oh, good," said the Third ACR lieutenant with the bony face. "Now you guys get to see the initial in-processing of detainees firsthand."

We watched as the detainees were taken to a holding area inside the wire fence but outside the bunker, where they were patted down. This body search was an additional security measure, just in case their original captors, also soldiers from the Third ACR, had missed anything that could be used either to escape or as a weapon. Once searched, the prisoners were kept in the same area, with their hands tied behind their backs and their heads hooded, until the spooks were ready to conduct an initial interrogation. (The term "spook" is used in the army to refer to people who work undercover and whose affiliation is unknown. They wear no uniform, no name tags or unit ID patches, and they generally use pseudonyms. They may be in the military—Special Forces or Delta Force soldiers, perhaps, or Navy Seals—or they may work for some other government agency, like the CIA, or NSA, or who knows what. They may even be civilians, former special ops people now working as contractors or security consultants.)

As we walked toward the interrogation room, we got our first glimpse of what was going on inside the camp. A thin, goofy-looking soldier with a big smile on his face, who seemed the type who was probably picked on by other kids all through high school, was standing next to a group of bare-footed detainees sitting on the concrete floor, hooded with sandbags, their hands tied in front of them. Another soldier— short, bald, and with tattoos all over his muscular arms—was carrying a big sledgehammer on his right shoulder. He moved around the prisoners like a boxer moves around the ring, agile, strong, mean, and ready to strike. He wasn't smiling.

We joined the spooks inside a very dark room. There were other soldiers there from the squadron we were relieving, including the lieutenant. They asked me to sit behind a desk, next to an Arab-looking spook. A lightbulb provided not real illumination but simply a lighter shade of darkness. My job was to take notes. Next to the desk was another spook who appeared to be very uptight. He was tall and had short blond hair. He asked the detainees questions in English, which the spook next to me would then translate into Arabic.

Another squad leader from my platoon was posted next to the detainees, to make sure they didn't pull any heroic stunts and did as they were told. As each detainee was brought in he was ordered to get undressed, lift up his penis and scrotum for inspection, and then turn around and bend over. I noticed a third spook standing at the very back of the room, watching everything that was going on. Despite the darkness he was wearing shades.

The interrogation started with basic questions like name, father's name, tribal affiliation, religion, place of birth, place of residence, occupation, and so on. Then the interrogator moved on to ask each prisoner how they came to be there and why they thought they had been detained. The two prisoners I saw being questioned had very little in the way of an answer to this question. They said they had been traveling by bus for several days and when the bus arrived at their stop, they got off and started walking.

Unfortunately for them there was a U.S. military checkpoint just beyond the bus stop. When the soldiers manning the checkpoint saw two individuals get off the bus just before their position and start walking away in the opposite direction, they became suspicious and quickly detained them.

"And why did you get off the bus?" asked the tall, blond spook.

"That was our stop," was the translation.

"And why did you walk away from the soldiers?"

"I walked the way I was supposed to walk." The translator stopped here for a moment, and then, looking at the other prisoner, said, "And he wants to know why he was detained."

"Tell him I ask the fucking questions here," snapped the interrogator, in a calm but deliberate voice.

The prisoner who had asked the question was visibly upset at the answer. He pointed with his tied hands at his genitals and began to speak fast and loud in Arabic.

"He says . . ."

"I don't wanna know what he says," the spook who was asking the questions interrupted.

"SHUT THE FUCK UP, MOTHERFUCKER!" shouted
one of the Third ACR guys, who clearly had plenty of practice at the job. "SHUT UP! SHUT UP! SHUT THE FUCK
UP, YOU FUCKING HAJJI." He yelled these words right
in the naked man's face.

The word "hajji" is a new derogatory term, used by the
U.S. military to refer to the enemy in Iraq, much like "gook"
in Vietnam and "rag head" in Afghanistan. Its use has expanded to cover pretty much everything Iraqi, like "hajji
food," or "hajji homes," and "hajji music." The actual use of
the word in Arabic is far from demeaning; it's used to define
those who make their pilgrimage to Mecca, known as the
"hajj," which is required of Muslims at least once in a lifetime.

The detainee finally fell quiet and started to look up at the
ceiling. His expression conveyed anger, indignation, and profound impotence.

"What did the soldiers tell you?" continued the ques-
tioner. "Did they say why you were being detained?"

"He says none of the soldiers spoke Arabic," resumed the
translator, "and that they don't speak English."

"Were there any weapons in their belongings?" asked the
spook, looking at the soldier who had almost assaulted the detainee a moment before.

"I don't know," was the reply. "The guys who dropped
them off didn't give us anything, no belongings, no paperwork,
not even an explanation; they just dumped them and left."

"Why are these guys here?" asked the interrogator, looking
down at his Arab partner, who simply shrugged in uncertainty.

The interrogation pretty much ended there and the spooks
left. Before the detainees were taken from the room they were
told to put their clothes back on and that they would be
r leased as soon as possible. There was nothing in the way of
an apology. The detainees were then classified as noncombatants and placed in a holding area within the camp, where

their hands would be untied though their heads would remain hooded. Once their numbers reached a certain level they would be taken to the nearby city of al Baghdadi for release.

Now we were told that it was time to learn how to deal with the detainees who had been classified as combatants. We left the dark room, and it took us a moment to recover from the blindness caused by a sudden rush of daylight. But right away we could hear loud screaming coming from one of the detainee holding areas: "UP, MOTHERFUCKERS, ARMS UP, I SAID. DOWN, DOWN, DOWN. Theeeere you go. ARMS UP. NOW TURN AROUND. DOWWWNNNN. UP, MOTHERFUCKERS, UP, UP, UP, UP."

Gradually, as we regained our eyesight, we could see the two soldiers that we'd met before going into the interrogation room—the goofy-looking kid and the short muscular guy, who, it turned out, was a staff sergeant. Some other soldiers were standing around but it was these two guys who were clearly the main players inside the compound. The skinny guy—a specialist, we were later told—was doing all the yelling.

"That's where we keep the enemy combatants," said the Third ACR lieutenant, pointing to a group of hooded detainees who looked confused and hesitant in the face of the savage screams being directed at them.

In our group of observers was Sergeant First Class Demarest, a tall, thin white man in his midforties and the highest-ranking NCO (noncommissioned officer) in our platoon. He was in a lower position than Williams because he was new to Charlie, which meant he found less favor with the company's leadership. He was in charge of second platoon's machine-gun squad.

"And what makes them combatants?" asked Demarest.

"The spooks decide," said the lieutenant.

"Yeah, but what kind of things have they done?"

We had walked over and were now standing much closer to the action. The skinny specialist's yelling seemed to get louder as we approached. I had the impression that he was getting meaner with the detainees, just to show off in front of us. I wondered if there was another place on earth where such a young, puny guy could get to be even half as mean to anyone.

"Well, various things," continued the lieutenant as we proceeded with our crash-course tour. "For instance, these three right here," he suspended his arm over the wire to point down at three prisoners who were sitting inside the combatants' area. "These three were caught with wooden crates that contained explosives."

"What kinds of explosives?" asked Demarest, whose blue eyes were crossed in a way that sometimes made me think he was talking to me when he wasn't.

"We don't know," said the lieutenant. "The crates were empty. They claimed they had picked them up somewhere and that they were gonna chop the crates and use them as firewood."

Demarest looked at me. He and I seemed to be wondering the same thing.

"Then why were they detained?" asked Demarest, turning his attention back to the lieutenant.

"Because they were carrying wooden crates that contained explosives," the lieutenant said in a deliberately rhythmic fashion, betraying a trace of annoyance.

"What about that guy there," asked Demarest, pointing at a detainee who looked frail and harmless.

"Oh, this guy," the lieutenant paused, and then continued in a proud tone, "this guy was caught with a sniper rifle."

"A sniper rifle?" I couldn't disguise my incredulity.

"Yes. Of course, he claims to be a shepherd, and that he needed the rifle to protect his sheep from thieves. He says he loves America. But you know, they all got a story, and they all fucking love America."

Later in the deployment we learned that most Iraqis own rifles and pistols, often from the decade-long war with Iran. Weapons were so commonplace that the new U.S.-placed Iraqi government decided to let each household keep two rifles, to be used for the protection of families from thieves and attackers as well as from rival tribes. Armed tribal conflicts were said to be widespread in some sectors of Iraqi society, particularly in agricultural towns where land was a common object of dispute. But it took awhile before the U.S. military stopped viewing every Iraqi who possessed a weapon as an armed insurgent.

We kept walking around the combatants' circle, quietly absorbing what was going on. There were periods of silence, as if the guards had decided to leave the prisoners alone, but then the screaming would start up again. In one such quiet spell, as we were listening to the lieutenant explain some detail of what was happening, a huge bang made us all jump. The entire place was engulfed by a thunderous echo. I thought at first that it must be an explosion, but everyone from the Third ACR unit seemed untroubled and carried on calmly with whatever they were doing. Before we could ask what had happened, the lieutenant took advantage of our undivided attention.

"Our job here, which will be your job as of tomorrow, does not involve determining who is or who is not an enemy combatant. Your job is just to feed the prisoners until they leave, and to keep awake those who are deemed enemy combatants."

"Those are the noncombatants," he continued, pointing to another area. "They get fed twice a day and get as much water as they want."

"What about the combatants?" someone asked.

"They also get all the water they want, but they only get fed once a day."

He showed us a stack of boxed meals that looked a lot like the MREs, but they were in yellow packages rather than the standard white. These were the meals used for humanitarian relief around the world. They were mostly vegetarian, and none included pork. Before giving the meals to the prisoners we were told to open them and take out the plastic knives and forks. For safety reasons prisoners were only allowed to use the plastic spoons to eat.

"So, you keep them awake?" asked Demarest.

"Yeah," said the lieutenant as we stood right next to the combatants' pen. "We keep them on sleep deprivation."

"GET UP, MOTHERFUCKERS!" yelled the specialist at the prisoners. "ALL YOU MOTHERFUCKERS—GET THE FUCK UP, NOW!"

One soldier who had been quietly standing around jumped at one of the detainees who was a bit slow in moving. "GET UP, YOU GODDAMNED HAJJI. DON'T YOU FUCKING HEAR WHAT HE'S TELLING YOU? UP, MOTHERFUCKER, UP, UP, UP."

My heart was racing as I witnessed all this; I found it wrong and shocking. But I didn't want to appear upset in front of the other soldiers, who seemed okay with everything that was going on. I kept reassuring myself with the fact that the detainees were not being hit, although, by the way they were shaking, you could tell their distress and exhaustion were messing them up physically as much as psychologically.

"How do they understand?" I asked the lieutenant.

"After you yell at them for forty-eight hours they get the point."

"Forty-eight hours?"

"Yeah," he answered, like it was no big deal. "That's how

the spooks get these guys to spill the beans. They sleep-deprive the fuck out of them, and then they question them."

The young specialist had by now wandered over.

"You yell at these motherfuckers to get up a few hundred times, and believe me, they'll know what the fuck's up."

He spoke to me with the familiarity of an old buddy, smiling in a way that made me want to slap him. I pressed my lips tightly together in acknowledgment.

It was clear that even with all the yelling and aggressive gestures the detainees were still not responding fast enough. Several were moving very slowly as they stumbled up and down.

"Look at them," said the short tattooed sergeant as he approached. He gestured at some detainees who were still trying to get up, while the others were already standing. "They just won't fucking listen."

No shit, I thought, *they're fucking tired, asshole.* I had disliked this guy from the very beginning, and I had mentally pictured him as a bulldog to such an extent that I was surprised by the fact that he could talk.

"Sometimes you gotta get creative with these sons of bitches," he snarled, looking at me, probably thinking I approved of his actions.

The young specialist kept yelling while the sergeant went outside the wire fence and headed toward a wall adjacent to the detainees. I saw him pick up the sledgehammer. I was truly frightened at this point. *What is this psycho gonna do now?* I wondered. I felt like I was carrying a dark secret within me. I could accept that the Iraqi detainees might be dangerous enemies, and I certainly didn't trust them. I also thought it made sense to keep them tied and hooded, since we didn't have cells to put them in and they could jump up and attack someone. But, *what was this crazy guy gonna do with that huge sledgehammer?*

I experienced horrible confusion, not knowing whether I was more afraid for the detainees or for what would happen to me if I did anything to help them. I knew that revealing the deep discomfort I felt at what was happening at the camp could only spell trouble. So what was I going to do about this guy with the sledgehammer? Probably nothing, I admitted to myself, but I didn't feel good about it.

"YOU MOTHERFUCKERS DON'T WANNA GET UP, HUH!"

The staff sergeant was standing next to the wall, and the sledgehammer looked like a baseball bat on his shoulder.

"YOU JUST WANNA DO WHATEVER THE FUCK YOU WANNA DO, DON'T YOU, MOTHER-FUCKERS?!"

The lieutenant squinted across the compound, curious to see what would happen next, and the skinny specialist giggled. I was amazed at the ease with which the sergeant swung the sledgehammer.

"ALRIGHT, YOU MOTHERFUCKERS. . . ."

Then we heard it. The entire bunker shook with the echo, which sounded much like a huge explosion. Every single detainee jumped to his feet.

"YOU LIKE THAT SHIT, DON'T YOU, MOTHER-FUCKERS?"

The noise burst forth again, now even louder. Every time the sergeant hit the wall with the sledgehammer, it sounded as if a bomb had gone off right next to the detainees, who shook uncontrollably with every thunderous bang.

"After a while," said the lieutenant, "you gotta come up with new ways to keep these guys awake." He looked at the sergeant, who put the sledgehammer back down against the wall. "But you can't overdo it, or else they'll get used to it."

"How long do you keep them on sleep deprivation?" asked Demarest.

"Well, most of these guys have been here for about a day and a half; a couple of them have been here for forty-eight hours."

There were about eight detainees enclosed in the combatants' circle, now all standing. One of them could be heard crying from under his sandbag; his low whimper got the lieutenant's attention.

"Oh, what is it? Are you tired?" The lieutenant sounded real nice. "Go ahead and let them get some sleep," he said to the guards, who smiled back.

Demarest, the other two squad leaders, and I looked at one another.

"Alright, get down, get down, motherfuckers," said the specialist in a hurried tone, as if he was about to go somewhere. "Yeah, you know what I'm saying. Get the fuck down."

The detainees all got down on the floor, and there was total silence. But none of the guards sat down or left the compound. The lieutenant studied his watch, all the time tapping his right boot and nodding his head up and down, as if keeping the rhythm of a song.

"Alright," he said after a brief period "That's enough beauty sleep; wake them up again."

"GET UP, MOTHERFUCKERS, GET UP, GET UP, GET UP," yelled the specialist and other guards, with a vengeance.

"You see," explained the lieutenant, who talked to us like we were tourists and he was our tour guide. "When you let them sleep thirty to forty-five seconds, after they've been awake for so long, you just totally fuck them up psychologically. Right now these hajjis, who slept for just forty-five seconds, don't know if they slept for a day, an hour, or five fucking minutes."

The detainee who had first gotten the lieutenant's attention was still quietly moaning. The lieutenant looked at him with annoyance but continued talking to us, explaining that the hooding of the detainees further enhanced their disorientation, because it made it harder for them to know day from night. That's when the spooks find it easiest to do their job, he explained—once the prisoners are broken down physically, emotionally, and psychologically.

"You can always come up with new ways to soften them up and sleep-deprive them for interrogation," said the lieutenant, walking over to the crying prisoner as he spoke. He stood right in front of the prisoner, almost close enough to kiss his face through the sandbag. The sobbing stopped for a moment as the prisoner sensed that someone was very close nearby, but then it started again.

"Shhhhhh," the lieuetnant's demand sounded disturbingly gentle. Meanwhile the staff sergeant had also walked over to the detainee.

The lieutenant pulled out a pack of Marlboro reds and lit one up with a lighter. The prisoner's crying was getting louder. Now the staff sergeant produced a 9 millimeter army-issued pistol and, with the lieutenant closely scrutinizing the prisoner, pressed it hard into the hooded man's temple.

"*Sukuut*," said the lieutenant, which is Arabic for "quiet" or something similar. His voice was low, and he sounded almost nice.

But the man, who probably thought he was about to be executed, continued to let out long anguished sobs and his entire body started to tremble uncontrollably. Without ceasing to apply pressure to the man's head, the staff sergeant violently pulled the pistol's receiver back, as if loading a bullet into the chamber.

"*Sukuut*," repeated the lieutenant.

The prisoner started breathing fast, now in a state of advanced panic. But his wailing had stopped and the 9 mm was now slowly removed from his temple. The lieutenant took a deep drag from his cigarette and raised the sandbag from the prisoner's head just enough to expose his lips.

"Goooood," he said. Then, looking at us, "You see? You can communicate with them; you just have to know how." He blew smoke into the man's face, and gently placed the cigarette in his mouth. The prisoner took a deep breath of smoke.

"Goooood, my friend, very good," said the lieutenant to the now silent prisoner. He smiled at us with evident satisfaction.

The following day my platoon took over from the departing Third ACR unit and we were expected to continue the sleep deprivation of the enemy combatant prisoners.

As a squad leader I had always tried to join in the work that I expected my men to do. But here I took advantage of my rank and simply watched as others abused the detainees. It didn't feel good but I didn't know how else to deal with the situation. For a time I allowed the use of the sledgehammer but then asked the soldiers to desist because, I claimed, the noise was bothering me. It was a relief that we had no pistols so the possibility of staging mock executions never arose. I spent as much time as possible inside the bunker, passing time by playing cards, mostly spades and Uno.

We only had to continue the sleep-deprivation of combatants for one day, as the following morning the prisoners were transferred to a more permanent facility, one, I hoped, that met the criteria for a prisoner-of-war camp.

The work at al Assad was one of the hardest missions I undertook while I was in Iraq, if not during my entire time in the military. On one hand I was completely against the way the prisoners in the camp were being treated. On the other, I was afraid of speaking up for them and appearing soft and weak as a squad leader, perhaps even of being charged with insubordination and court-martialed. There are standard ways of justifying the sort of things we were doing and I tried them all.

I told myself, "When I signed a contract I agreed to follow orders" and "I'm doing this for the soldiers next to me." But to this day I cannot find a single good answer as to why I stood by idly during the abuse of those prisoners except, of course, my own cowardice.

We continued to run the camp and to handle the noncombatant detainees for another week or so, until a military police unit came to relieve us. We then drove ten miles down the road to the air base's officer accommodations, a facility that included a mosque, gymnasium, and a large swimming pool, as well as air-conditioned barracks with Western-style bedrooms, showers, and toilets. It would have been nice to stay there a bit longer, but within a couple of days my unit got its next mission, this time in a place called al Hadithah.

Al Hadithah was the site of one of Iraq's biggest dams. Saddam Hussein must have been very proud of its construction, since it can still be seen on some of Iraq's old currency bills. The structure rose high above the Euphrates. From the top of the dam we could see for miles across the reservoir; at night, we could also see the lights of the nearby town, a sizeable place with a population of a hundred thousand or so.

Because of the considerable damage the place had suffered during the heavy fighting, and a lack of spare parts needed for repairs, the Iraqi engineers who had been employed at the dam before the invasion didn't have much work anymore. But despite this, and even though no one paid them to do a thing, these dedicated energy personnel showed up for work every single day. We were there to guard them around the dam on the few occasions they found something to do. I've no idea if what they were doing was of any use but they certainly took pride in their work. Once they told us that the dam had at one point powered close to 70 percent of Baghdad. Its strategic importance was confirmed by the 101st Airborne Division soldiers we relieved, who told us that U.S. Rangers had engaged in heavy fighting against Saddam's Republican Guard in order to take the place.

We were told that after the Rangers won the battle for the dam, they buried the bodies of Iraqi soldiers killed in the fight in shallow graves just outside the dam's grounds. A few days after the hasty burial, local scavenging dogs dug out the bodies and began to devour them. Finally the residents of al Hadithah decided it was time to give the dead soldiers proper burial, a matter of great importance in the Muslim tradition. We went outside as part of our relief in place tour, basically a walkthrough of our new duties. We could see the holes where the graves had been. The deepest could not have been more than half a meter.

The Iraqi workers were happy when my unit finally relieved the 101st Airborne soldiers, whom they accused of being cruel and inhumane. Part of the problem between the Iraqis and the 101st was a movie the workers had been caught watching. On one of the many days when there had been absolutely nothing for them to do, one of them had the grand idea of showing a tape of the September 11 attacks. When the soldiers heard cheering and clapping, they sent a team to investigate and discovered what looked like a party. When the soldiers realized that the celebration was in response to the footage of the twin towers collapsing, which the workers would rewind to watch over and over, they confiscated their TV and VCR, transforming an already tense relationship into a hostile one.

The fact that the workers had cheered the collapsing towers didn't help their cause with my unit either, but perhaps because reserve and guard soldiers are themselves civilians, whose primary work is catastrophe relief, it was easier for us to feel empathy for the Iraqis. Within a few days of taking over the site, our relationship with the workers improved and at times it was even friendly.

My platoon had been assigned to work inside the dam and, as at the POW camp, each of four squads worked six-hour shifts. During these hours we had the opportunity to meet quite a few of the engineers. They all spoke fluent English and told us this was commonplace among Iraqis with a college education. I noticed that the engineers related as easily to less educated workers, such as plumbers and maintenance personnel, as to their fellow professionals. Social class and status seemed to mean less to them than they did in America. On their overnight shifts they all slept in the same room in what became a kind of "guys' night out." They would bring boom boxes to play upbeat Arab music and delicious home-cooked meals that they would share, even with us. We all ate with our hands, using flat bread in the place of spoons and washing down the food with bottled sodas that looked like they came out of a 1980s TV commercial. After every meal, we would engage in long conversations, smoke cigarettes, and drink dark sweet Middle Eastern tea, which the Iraqis called "chai."

On one such night, we were talking with a Kurdish engineer.

"So, you're not a Muslim?" I asked him.

"Yes, of course I am a Muslim," he said looking at the other Iraqis sitting at the table with us.

"We are all Muslims," he continued, blowing out a mouthful of smoke, ". . . and we are all Iraqis, but these people are Arabs and I am a Kurd."

"But you all look the same to me," I said, at the risk of sounding racist.

"Well, we're not," he insisted. "I am Kurd, they are Arab."

He started to translate for the other workers who didn't speak English, probably commenting on how ignorant he thought I was.

"Can you tell the difference?" I asked one of the workers who had just heard the translation. He looked at the engineer, who in turn translated my question.

"*Nam, nam,*" he answered, which means yes, yes.

Puffing their smokes, the other workers smiled in silence as they observed me digesting the information. To make it easier for me, the Kurdish engineer explained that it was much like in Iran, where the people are Muslims but not Arab.

"They are Persians," he explained.

We talked about how some of the group had originally supported the invasion, particularly the Kurds and the Shiites. But most, if not all, were now tired of waiting for the jobs to come back, for the electricity and water to be reconnected, for the schools to open—in short, for their country to return to normal. This could only be achieved, they agreed, after the U.S. military left Iraq. I told them that we would be leaving soon and that things would be better than before. It shocks me now to recall that not only did I say those words, but I also firmly believed them. I even told the engineers that given their fluency in English and professional qualifications, they should expect to be paid a lot of money in the near future.

"In the United States," I remember telling them, "engineers like you, working at facilities as big as this, make tons of money. You will be fine, trust me."

They looked at me with evident disbelief, not arguing, but with gentle, skeptical smiles. I remembered those smiles months later when speaking to a worker in ar Ramadi who asked me for some cold water on a hot August day. He was dressed in rags and was wearing shreds of what had once been a pair of shoes. Sweat ran profusely down his dirty, sun-baked face as he mixed cement to fix some window frames in our compound. For that work he was being paid three U.S. dollars a day. He was a geologist.

I still cherish the memory of the time we spent at the al Hadithah dam, not because we were in a place that was relatively safe from attacks, nor because we frequently got to swim in the waters of the biblical Euphrates, but mostly because al Hadithah first opened the door for me to the richness of Iraqi culture. Our mission there, however, did not offer the type of combat experience our leadership was so keen to find, and in mid-May we went back to al Assad to refit for yet another mission. This next mission would take us to ar Ramadi, a city in the heart of the Sunni triangle. Little did I know that I was about to learn a new lesson about Iraq and its people: their tenacity to resist foreign occupation and fight for self-determination. This lesson, I must say, I learned the hard way.

FOUR

Life wasn't so bad for my Florida National Guard unit when we first arrived in ar Ramadi. Our accommodations, a flea-infested maintenance bay that had previously been used by the Republican Guard, was filthy and hot beyond description, but as grunts we had been trained to endure worse situations, so we couldn't complain too much. Besides, casualties for the Third ACR unit we had relieved had been limited to one guy who fired a grenade launcher at a concrete wall right in front of himself. Shrapnel from the grenade bounced off the wall and hit him in the face. By the time he was air-evacuated to a field hospital the medics didn't give him much hope of survival. It was a very unfortunate event but it didn't represent anything significant about the insurgency in ar Ramadi.

Our rooms were tiny and crowded. Grenades, rifles, claymore mines, and small antiarmor launchers were scattered everywhere, leaning up against bullet-riddled walls and stacked beneath army cots. Mosquito nets were a necessity but the bugs still got through. By the third night at the base, a combination of insect bites and the hot, sandy weather drove me to move my bed to the rooftop of the three-story building we'd occupied, where it was open enough to light up a Pepsi can full of fuel to keep insects away without poisoning ourselves. Our sleep up on the roof was occasionally interrupted by the sound of gunfire, which came from a combination of scattered attacks on U.S. troops and local celebratory fire. Sometimes we'd lie awake and watch the red dotted lines of tracer bullets arching across the night sky, a reminder that we were in wartorn Iraq. But for the most part, considering we were in a combat zone, life seemed OK.

On May 29, 2003, for reasons I couldn't quite fathom, I had been feeling strange all day. The orange-red afternoon sky was searing and unforgiving and the city was swallowed by a fog of sand coming from the southern desert. I had just received a care package from my mother, but before I could open it Sergeant Williams came to inform me that we had a mission:

"Mejía, get your squad ready, you guys are going out with the XO."

He was referring to the company's executive officer, Lieutenant Green, a short, quiet man who seemed to open his mouth only to spit tobacco.

"Do you know what we're doing?" I asked Williams.

"You guys have to provide a security escort for the mortars to the North Palace. Apparently they're getting attacked, and their guys ran out of illume rounds," he said while walking away, as if nothing he told me was important enough to warrant a stop.

"They're getting attacked?" I asked.

At this point we had been in ar Ramadi for about ten days, and for the most part, we had only been observing the Third ACR unit operate. They were an armored unit operating with vehicles, big guns, and missiles, while we were light infantry, working on our feet, so there was no way they could have trained us. We just watched what they did without saying much. We knew they thought of themselves as better soldiers because they were active duty and we were only National Guard. We, on the other hand, were infantrymen, and the infantry always thinks of itself as tougher. In any case, this was the first mission my squad had had in ar Ramadi, and the fact that it involved an "attack" made it quite significant.

"Yeah, Bravo Company," said Williams, stopping but not turning more than just his head toward me. "You'll just have to ask the XO. I really don't have much info. Lieutenant Cerekas just told me to get a squad to escort the mortars, and tonight you guys got escort."

The order for the mission had originated with Lieutenant Green, Charlie Company's XO, who apparently was coming along with us. Williams's offhand manner in passing along the order was typical. If he was directed to do something himself he would be vigorous in finding out what was involved; otherwise he affected uninvolvement in case something went wrong. He wasn't the type who liked to have his name associated with missions gone bad. He retreated back to the blown-out room he shared with Cerekas and Specialist Shanks, the radio telephone operator, or RTO.

It must have been around 1800 hours when Williams informed me of the mission. I opened my package just enough to see that there was a letter inside before putting it back on the concrete outside my dark and hot second-floor room. As I stood up to go see the XO I wondered if I would ever get to read that letter. The feeling that something bad was about to happen was hard to shake.

In the infantry, squad leaders are in charge of two four-man teams, Alpha and Bravo, which in turn are each led by a team leader. Prior to going on the mission I had a quick talk with my Bravo team leader, Sergeant Rosado, who wasn't too happy about the mission at hand.

"Man, I don't like this; there is a sandstorm, and Bravo Company is in the middle of a firefight right now. What the fuck are we gonna do there? We can't even see shit with all this sand."

The sandstorms I had pictured in my mind before we were deployed to Iraq involved raging waves of sand blasting through the desert and swallowing everything in their path. This was nothing like that. Rather, it was a thick, brown, grainy mist that hung in the air and cut visibility down to about a meter ahead.

"I know, man," I told Rosado, with my eyes half-closed, trying to keep the slow-moving clouds of sand from getting through. "But we gotta do it."

At this early stage in our deployment to Iraq I was still playing very much by the rules, trying to be a good soldier and squad leader, and to the U.S. Army that meant keeping my mouth shut and doing what I was told. Before getting to Iraq, questioning "command's wisdom" had almost gotten me fired from my squad leader position, so all I really wanted at the time was to do my job and get the hell out.

The metal plates in the back of our truck, a sand-colored raggedy old deuce and a half, didn't provide any real protection, but it still gave us a sense of security to sit behind them. I was in the rear of the deuce, using its tailgate as my shield. Behind me, with their weapons facing out on both sides, were my Alpha and Bravo teams. Short one man at the time, first squad had eight soldiers in total.

I looked back at Funez, Rosado's grenade launcher. Tall and good-looking, Hector Funez had a meditative way about him; he and I got along from the very moment I took over as the squad's leader. He was popular among the other soldiers of the company, some of whom called him Chito. He was the only one in the squad who smoked besides me.

"Hey, Chito, let me get a light, man."

He looked at me with intense eyes and pressed lips. He was probably the only member of the squad who could always tell when I had a bad feeling. He threw the lighter at me without saying a word and quickly went back to scanning his sector, even though we hadn't yet left our base, which was then known as the Eagle's Nest.

It took us about ten minutes to get to our destination, and when we arrived everything seemed peaceful. The guys at the entrance came out quickly from behind their concrete barricades to remove the spiraled strands of concertina wire that served as a gate. We entered the compound and parked just outside the palace, a good two hundred meters from the main entrance.

The mortars got out of their truck and started setting up their tubes and plates. Suddenly an explosion made the palace grounds tremble. Yelling and the popping sounds of rifle fire followed the blast. A firefight had erupted at the main entrance.

"Hey, Sergeant Mejía," said Sergeant Gallegos, my Alpha team leader, "we're getting attacked. Do you want us to get out and take positions?"

"No," I told him, "we've got friendly all around us, covering the perimeter. Just fucking lie down, I guess."

Everyone seemed happy with my decision, which went unquestioned by the XO. It seemed somewhat absurd, lying there staring at the beautiful Ramadi sky as the M-16 and AK-47 bullets flew overhead, but we couldn't do anything that would be of help and at least this way we were relatively safe.

Once the fight subsided, the mortars resumed their job, firing off their illume. Little balls of white light soared into the night and then burst, lighting up a considerable expanse of sky. Of course the enemy could use this light to pinpoint and kill American soldiers just as much as the other way around, but on this night the fight was over without any known casualties on either side. We were ordered to return to the Eagle's Nest with the mortars and Lieutenant Green.

Back at the Nest I was just opening a granola bar my mother had sent me in the care package when I was called up again. With her letter in my right hand, still unread, and the granola bar in my left, I went to find Williams.

"Us again?" I asked as calmly as I could, while thinking *What about the other squads?*

"Yeah, it's your guys' turn. Mantilla, Demarest, and Milligan will be doing it too when it's their time to do escorts," he said, referring to the other three squad leaders in our platoon.

It seemed unfair that we had just come back from a firefight and now, twenty minutes later, we were going out again. I put the letter back in its box. *I knew it wasn't over*, I thought. I had to go to the combat post, or CP, which is where the commander, XO, and first sergeant were based. Lieutenant Green was there waiting to brief me on what was required of our next mission. Before going to the CP, I looked down the corridor to where I shared a room with my Alpha team leader.

"Hey, Gallegos," I yelled, "get the guys ready; we're fucking going out again."

There was a pause, and then, in a resigned tone, "Alright, sergeant."

We were sent back to the area where the earlier firefight took place, about two hundred meters from the entrance to the North Palace. We got there at approximately midnight. The sand had cleared from the air and the night sky was starry and beautiful. But the apparent peacefulness only enhanced our wariness. The still, quiet night was keeping secrets from us, and we all knew it.

In their infinite wisdom, our battalion leadership felt it was necessary to set up a traffic control point (TCP) in the vicinity of the fight, just in case the "bad guys" — or Ali Babas, as they're called by Iraqis and Americans alike — had decided to hang out in the area. Our mission was to detain and search any vehicle circulating at that time.

Specialist Bien-Aime, one of my two Haitian soldiers and Rosado's machine gunner, had taken the south side of the perimeter and was facing the Euphrates. Hearing my steps, he turned toward me from his kneeling position.

"Hey sergeant," he said, pulling up his night-vision goggles with his right hand, so he didn't have to see me in night-vision green. "Do you really think these guys are gonna be hanging around the area after what happened? I mean, I don't mean to be a smart-ass or anything, but that's kind of stupid, don't you think?"

"I don't think you're being a smart-ass, man," I said with a resigned smile. "I think you're right, but we're not the ones calling the shots. I just hope they don't keep us here too long."

That was a hope in vain. About half an hour into the TCP we detained the one and only car circulating that night. The passengers were two Jordanian businessmen who were on their way to Amman after selling some goods in Iraq. They were carrying two huge bags full of dinars, though we later found out that, once converted to U.S. dollars, the cash amounted to less than two grand. The guys had previously been detained by the Third ACR unit, code-named "Rifles," under whose command our battalion fell. After being cleared by Rifles, the Jordanians had to delay their trip back to Jordan because of the sandstorm. Our company had verified the information with the Rifles but they still didn't want us to let the guys go.

"Combat X-ray, this is Combat two-one, over."

Combat was our company's ID, two was for second platoon, and one was for first squad. I was Combat two-one, and I was calling our company's radio operator.

"This is Combat X-ray, go ahead two-one."

"Roger," I said. "Rifles already cleared these guys. What's the delay? Can we let them go? Over."

"Negative," said Sergeant Chism, who was Captain Warfel's RTO and our company's main radio guy. "Combat seven wants to clear with battalion; just stand by, over."

Combat seven was the code name for our company's first sergeant, a tall goofy-looking man in his forties. His last name was Naugle, but must soldiers in our unit called him "The Naugulator," at least behind his back. The Rifles, which had cleared us to let the Jordanians go, ranked higher than battalion, but The Naugulator had obviously decided he could score some brownie points by being extra zealous.

"Hey, Sergeant Mejía," said Rosado, approaching me from the Humvee that was parked on his half of the perimeter. "What the hell is going on, man?"

"We're waiting for battalion to clear these guys."

The guys in question were being guarded where they sat on the sidewalk. They were calm and cooperative and hadn't been hooded or zip-tied. Occasionally they would use gestures to ask what was going on.

"What? I thought you said they were clear."

"Yeah," I replied, "but that was Rifles; now they want battalion to clear 'em too."

"Man, that's fucked up! We've been here like three fucking hours already, and these people are eating shit," said Rosado indignantly.

I generally didn't mind it when Rosado complained. He was almost always justified in doing so and, for the most part, he only bitched in front of me and Gallegos. It was only when he complained in front of the men that we had problems. I nodded my head in agreement.

By the time they told me to let the Jordanians go it was already around 0300 hours. I still had that uneasy gut feeling and I couldn't shake it. We'd been in the same place for too long, long enough for the enemy to have organized an ambush. Just before leaving I went to the lead vehicle of our two-Humvee convoy and spoke with the driver, Specialist Street, who wasn't really in our squad. He and Specialist Madsen were in the gun squad, but Sergeant Williams sent them with me because we were shorthanded. Madsen was manning the machine gun mounted on the lead Humvee.

"Hey, Street, I already talked to Sergeant Gallegos," I said. Alpha team and Sergeant Gallegos were also riding in the lead Humvee. "I have a feeling we're going to get ambushed because we've been here too damn long. If anything happens, don't stick around. Just haul ass back to base, OK?"

"Alright," said Street, with an arrogant casualness that was typical of him. Most people thought he was a total smart-ass, but I tried not to let his attitude get to me.

We started the drive back to the Eagle's Nest. I was sitting in the front of the second Humvee with Rosado. I noticed he was driving with a 9 mm pistol lying in his lap; he looked tense. I worried that he might accidentally shoot himself in the leg, but I didn't say anything. I had briefed the whole squad on the possibility of being ambushed. The standard operating procedure (SOP) for a moving ambush, as far as I could remember, was to return fire and keep moving. That's exactly what I told everyone in first squad to do.

Our two Humvees were not close to being properly armored; they didn't even have doors. Communications were a problem too. We didn't have radio contact between the two vehicles because all the small 1-26 handsets were being used for perimeter guard back at base. Worse still, only one of the vehicles had a radio that could communicate with base, and I had made the elementary mistake, as a squad leader, of riding in the other. I had no way to give or receive commands or to communicate with the base.

We had gone about two miles east on Highway 10, the main road which divided ar Ramadi north and south, and were just coming up to a curve in the road when I heard the sound of a whistle. I knew instantly what it meant and a chill ran through me. A lookout by the curb was sending a signal for others to attack.

Then we saw it: an object the size of a shoe box in the middle of the road with a wire attached to it that ran down a little slope. We could clearly see it, even those of us in the rear vehicle. Strangely, none of us said anything, even though we knew it was *a bomb*.

Both Humvees were traveling at about 50 mph, which was about as fast as they could go, and all this was happening in a matter of milliseconds, with the little shoe box creeping up on us so suddenly there wasn't much we could do, except wait. It all seemed like a set of clues in a strange science fiction movie that everyone was trying really hard to understand. And then, *the blast*.

The first thing I remember seeing was Madsen collapse out of sight as the blast from the bomb engulfed the front of his vehicle. As we slowed down a thought crossed my mind: *Could they all be dead?* It was a terrible possibility and yet I felt nothing. I was watching everything as if I were someone who was only there in spirit. I had seen it coming, called it, and even briefed my squad about it, yet my mind refused to accept it. *This just cannot be.*

I was still in a trance when I looked down at the road and saw sparks kicking up all around us. It took some moments for me realize they were caused by bullets hitting the concrete. I patted my flak vest, reminding myself that it offered no protection against a 7.56 millimeter AK-47 bullet. The structures at the side of the road were phantasmagoric skeletons of blown-out buildings, perfect for launching attacks because they provided precious high ground for shooting down at the road below. I could see the dark empty windows lighting up with what must have been muzzle flashes. I wondered what it would feel like to have a bullet fly right through my hand, or through my chest and into my heart. The ammo supply of our attackers seemed endless. Gallegos later jokingly described the event as "a rain of fire that showered down on first squad."

The awakening from my spell was sudden and loud. It came from the machine gun on top of my Humvee, which was being manned by Chito. The roar gave me a sense of security, but it also made me realize where I was. *Fuck*, I thought, *this shit is really happening.* The muzzle of my M-16 had been at the ready the whole time, but it was only after hearing the machine gun unleash hell from above me that I began firing in the general direction of the attackers. It didn't seem like I was accomplishing anything, but I kept on squeezing the trigger.

When the lead Humvee finally started to pick up speed and I saw Madsen reappear from its roof and begin firing, I felt a wave of relief.

"I think they're OK," said Rosado, with the 9 mm still in his lap. "Street is picking up speed. I think they're OK."

We made it back to the Eagle's Nest in about five minutes. The attack had lasted about a fifth of that, but when a minute seems to be the last you will ever live, eternity can fit into it. And that minute, to this very day, feels like the longest I've ever lived.

Back at the base we all got out of the Humvees in a jump.

"Motherfuckers!" yelled Madsen, "You couldn't fucking get us!"

"Is anyone hurt?" asked Rosado, looking at me.

"I don't think so," I replied, though in truth I had no idea. "Is everyone OK?" I yelled.

"Those dumb fucks didn't even hit the Humvees," yelled Gallegos.

"Yeah, I think everyone is fine," said Funez in a low voice.

"Yo, B!" said Private Estime, the other Haitian soldier and the only private in the squad. He was talking to Bien-Aime. "Can you believe that shit?"

"Man, that shit was for real," replied B.

"Alpha team is accounted for," said Sergeant Gallegos.

"Good deal," I responded, looking at Rosado and waiting for his report, even though by then I knew everyone was OK.

"Yeah, Bravo team is accounted for," he said.

"Hey, Sergeant Mejía," said Gallegos, still standing near the Humvee with the radio in it. "Captain Warfel wants us to go up to the CP to brief him on what just happened."

Gallegos, Rosado, and I slowly climbed the stairs to the second floor. They were dark and unstable, with no handrails and with rusted iron rods sticking out of smashed cement. The CP was located in the main building of the compound which housed most of Charlie Company. The commander and his headquarters platoon occupied the second floor, across from my platoon. Across the hallway from the commander's room was a room housing weapons that had been confiscated during raids. At one point it had contained a chrome-plated AK-47, but word had it that our battalion commander or some other high-ranking officer had fallen in love with it and a day or two after confiscation it was never seen again.

The commander was sitting outside on the breezeway, which was where the radio operator on shift monitored the company's and the battalion's radio transmissions. It was still early in the occupation and the private contractors hadn't yet made their entrance to install generators and air conditioners, so soldiers spent much of their time outdoors where, in spite of the occasional bullet that hit the ground nearby, the sand-laden breeze made life in hell a bit more sufferable. The first sergeant and the XO were with the captain.

"Here is Sergeant Mejía, sir," said The Naugulator.

"Sergeant Mejía, what happened?" asked Captain Warfel, looking at me as if he were both glad and amazed that we
had made it through an ambush totally unscathed.

I explained to them everything that happened, wanting to
say the ambush had been predictable and could easily have
been avoided had we not stayed at the same spot for three
hours. But I decided to keep my opinions to myself and to
limit my account to the actual events, thinking it would be a
quick briefing that would end perhaps with a request for a
written report.

"So, why didn't your squad stay, sergeant?" asked the
captain, his voice low, his small blue eyes staring intensely.

"Excuse me, sir?" I asked, directing my eyes to my team
leaders with a frown.

"Why didn't your squad fight?" rephrased the captain.

"Well, that would be the call I made, sir," I replied, sensing
something was wrong with the line of questioning. "I had a
feeling we were going to get ambushed, so I briefed the squad
and told them to return fire and keep moving back to base."

"Yes, we know you made the call, Sergeant Mejía," said
The Naugulator, whose head had been facing down but was
now upright. He was looking down at me through thick army-
issued glasses. This type of eyewear is known as BCGs, which
stands for birth control glasses because, it is said, no woman
would sleep with a man who wears them. As a married, high-
ranking noncommissioned officer in a combat zone, The Naugulator didn't seem to care much about the prospect of not
getting laid in Iraq, and he wore his BCGs proudly.

Rosado took a deep breath as he listened to our leadership
ask questions about the first well-executed ambush against
our company. Gallegos's face was expressionless.

"What we want to know," continued the first sergeant, "is
why you gave the order to leave the scene instead of fighting."

I looked at him in disbelief. *Was he joking?* The question didn't make a whole lot of sense. His lips were slightly raised, with the lower lip pressing up against the upper one. He waited for my answer with a curious frown, and for a moment I wondered if he was trying to look like Billy Idol; he kind of did, only goofy-looking, and ugly.

"I thought the SOP for a moving ambush was to return fire and keep moving," I said finally. My heartbeats were louder than usual, and my face was beginning to get hot.

"You sent the wrong message to the enemy," said the commander.

"Excuse me, sir?" I asked, half in amazement, half knowing it was coming.

"I mean, don't get me wrong, sergeant," he continued, almost interrupting me. "We are glad that your men made it out alive and that no one was hurt, but we think you could have gotten out of the kill zone, returned fire, and called the QRF."

QRF stood for quick reaction force, a fancy military term for backup or reinforcements. Usually one of the three line platoons in our company would act as the QRF while the other two conducted different missions. The QRF had been used only occasionally and had taken between twenty and thirty minutes to respond to an actual incident, which at that point had all been minor ones. The bottom line was that our QRF sucked.

"Well, we didn't know what else they had waiting for us," I said in my defense, thinking I was trapped in one of Kafka's novels, or perhaps in some kind of twilight zone. "They could have had a car bomb waiting for us, or maybe RPGs [rocket-propelled grenades]. They had all the advantage: they had the upper ground, they even had early warning, and they outnumbered us. It was a very well-organized ambush."

"How do you know they outnumbered you?" asked Captain Warfel.

"Well . . ." I looked at Gallegos and Rosado for backup. I didn't know they outnumbered us, but it certainly had felt that way. "They shot at us from buildings on both sides of the road for about two to three blocks."

"No," said Rosado. "It must have been about five blocks. Those suckers just kept shooting."

"Yeah, but how many?" pressed The Naugulator.

"It's hard to tell, first sergeant," I said. "It was dark, they were shooting from both sides of the road, and we were hauling ass."

"Well, we need to send a report to battalion, and we need to give them a number," insisted the first sergeant.

"I'd say it was between fifteen and twenty," said Rosado.

Fifteen to twenty seemed out of proportion, but it also seemed as though we were apologizing for having survived. Standard operating procedure for a moving ambush was to return fire and keep moving, and that's exactly what we had done. Staying to fight a ghost enemy of unknown capability but with evident advantage while hoping our slow QRF would respond fast would have been suicidal. It seemed as though doing the right thing had gotten me in trouble with my leadership.

"I'd say about fifteen," I finally said.

"That's the final number?" asked The Naugulator.

"Sergeant Mejía, it was more than that," said Rosado.

"I don't know how many there were," said Gallegos, looking at me. Then, looking at the captain, "All I know is that they kept shooting for a while."

"Well, Sergeant Mejía," said Captain Warfel as he started to slowly move back inside the building, putting an end to the briefing. "I think the problem here is that you just sent the wrong message to the enemy."

"I'm sorry, sir?" I asked.

"You could have moved your squad out of the kill zone

and pinpointed those guys," he continued. "You could have used your squad to hold them down while the QRF got there, and we could have killed them."

"By getting away," added First Sergeant Naugle, "you let them know that we are afraid. It was a victory for them."

Gallegos, Rosado, and I looked at one another, not saying a word. Just minutes before, we had celebrated the fact that we made it through an ambush untouched. Now we were dealing with a command that was asking us to expose ourselves unnecessarily to serious danger in order to "send the right message." They knew damn well that we had acted according to regulations, just as we knew that it was our asses on the line while they were safe back at the base. I left the command post with my two team leaders, wondering who the real enemy was in Iraq, and just how close we were sleeping from it.

The care package had Pringles, granola bars, dried fruit, a few small water bottles, and some baby wipes. After eating some chips on the dirty steps that led to the rooftop, I went into my room and dug into my rucksack to get my headlight, which I used to read the letter.

My mother was begging me to come home as soon as possible, telling me just how much Samantha needed me. "Don't try to be a hero," she wrote. "Don't volunteer for anything. Don't expose yourself unnecessarily. Never go out without your bulletproof vest, even if it's heavy." It wasn't really up to me, and the vest at that point wasn't bulletproof. It was a bittersweet thing to receive those care packages. On one hand, I got news about Samantha and the family; on the other, it made me remember a world I no longer felt I belonged to. My life outside of the war zone seemed a million years away, and the prospects of ever returning did not feel very promising.

Somewhere there had been a meeting, in some fancy office, where some grand plan had been discussed by detached people. The plan required the loss of many lives in order to reach the goals, but it was all acceptable. My life and the lives of those in my unit were all part of that acceptable loss, and there was nothing we could do about it. We had signed a contract, and we were not in control of our destinies.

My mother's letter made me feel guilty about participating in a war that didn't seem worth the killing and destruction. I felt weak for not having the strength to ensure I survived for my daughter and those who loved and needed me. But what troubled me most was not the possibility of getting killed, but the possibility of being killed *here, in Iraq.* A recurring thought was, *we have no right to be here.* But I knew I had to stop myself from thinking along those lines. I was an infantry squad leader, and my men needed me.

Specialists Funez and Hodges had laid down their mats in the middle of the rooftop. I set mine up there as well. Later in the deployment Hodges would join my squad along with his assistant gunner, Specialist Ibaugh. They were in the gun squad and were in charge of one of the M-240 Bravo machine guns. I asked Funez for a light, prompting him to cast a look of annoyance in my direction. I remembered that he'd asked me many times when was I going to get my own lighter. At least I had stopped bugging him for cigarettes. He had gotten access to a lot of the looted stuff from Baghdad International Airport: tons of cartons of Marlboros, Reds and Lights, plus Johnnie Walker, Red and Black Label. Funez was a pretty well-connected guy in Charlie Company. Everyone liked "The Funez," aka "Chito." Hodges, or, "The Hodge" was short and ordinary looking, and he still had the remnants of what might have been a beer gut. But The Hodge was a pretty smart guy with a sharp, worldly sense of humor, and he, too, was popular.

Ever since I received my package I had a feeling that something was going to happen that would prevent me from opening it. Now that I'd done so, and read my mother's letter, I reflected that though it had been a bad day, at least I had made it through. I had survived an ambush after three hours of eating shit and sitting in the open like an idiot. I was lying down and the day was pretty much over.

To this very day I can still hear the rushing sound of the RPG as it traveled from its launcher to where it landed somewhere in our base. People have told me repeatedly that rocket-propelled grenades don't make any noise until they hit something and explode in a deadly spray of shrapnel. But I can still hear that RPG screaming into our compound just half an hour after my squad and I had gone to sleep.

"GET UP! GET UP! GET THE FUCK UP!"

I don't remember putting on the first boot; all I remember was seeing it on as I slid my foot into the other. I now realize there's some point to the basic training exercises in which drill sergeants tell recruits in the middle of the night to get downstairs NOW, KNUCKLEHEADS, and two hundred recruits jump on top of one another, crawling and stepping on heads and backs as they rush to obey. But basic training was a million and a half years away, in the past; this was real. The roof was shaking violently.

"RPG, RPG. EVERYONE GET OFF THE ROOFTOP."

"Funez! Hodges! Let's go, men!" I shouted, looking back. Ibaugh had been the first one to move. He never took off his boots and, for a while, he didn't even take off his knee pads. People often gave him shit about that, but it was working well for him right now.

Hodges and Funez followed behind me. We should have been sleeping with our gear next to us; it was SOP. As squad leader I was supposed to enforce that, but I hadn't and we had to run to our rooms on the second floor to pick up our stuff, including our weapons. As I ran down I was aware of my head racing at incredible speed. I was part trying not to leave anyone behind, part trying to get to my weapon, part trying to figure out where to go next for further instructions. My mind was perhaps too frantic to feel fear but my body wasn't. I looked down and saw a circular wet patch on my desert pants. *Shit, I'm peeing myself!* My knees were shaking uncontrollably. *Fuck!* I was scared shitless, but I was still in the fight.

Then another RPG hit the Eagle's Nest, and then a third, making the building's foundations tremble. It seemed as if the insurgents had decided to go all out with this attack and the terrible thought occurred to me that we were about to get completely run over, Vietnam style.

I finally grabbed my gear and went down to the first floor, where Williams was waiting and asking squad leaders for accountability reports.

"Mejía, your guys up?" he asked.

I looked at Rosado and saw that he had all his people; then I looked at Gallegos.

"Gallegos, where the hell is Estime?" I shouted, at the same time snapping the chinstrap on my Kevlar.

"Right here, sergeant," said Estime from behind me, with a half-smart, half-scared smile across his face.

"We're up, sergeant."

Williams then looked at Milligan, who was the leader of second squad. A short, stout guy of Philippine descent, Milligan always seemed calm, even under extreme circumstances. He looked behind himself in almost slow motion, scanning the dark area for his team leaders: Macias, from Ecuador, and Moore, an African American. Moore had been a platoon commander for the marines, but some screwup with his National Guard paperwork kept him from getting his army commission, so they made him a sergeant. During training and pending approval for his commission, they had given him a second lieutenant's job. As my PL, or platoon leader, he was

the one who had recommended me for the squad leader's position prior to deploying to the Middle East. Ironically, the
army had not allowed him to be a platoon leader with
sergeant's rank, so at the last minute they deployed him as a
regular sergeant, and for a while he was a team leader under
my command.

"You guys up?" Milligan calmly asked.

Both nodded yes.

"Mantilla, where you at?" Now Williams was looking
for Sergeant Juan Camilo Mantilla, Colombian American,
prior Eighty-Second Airborne Division paratrooper, sniper-
qualified, and third squad leader. Sergeant Mantilla was the
typical army poster child: young, strong, agile, good-looking,
tactically proficient, and a soldier who followed orders without questioning.

"Right here, Will; I got all my people."

"Hey, Sergeant Williams," said Sergeant Demarest, who
had been the first one to report to Williams. "Where the hell
is Cerekas?"

"The medics got him; apparently he fell from the stairs on
his way down."

"Will he be alright?" asked Demarest, with what looked
like a smirk on his face.

"I don't think we'll ever see him again," said Williams as
he stared at nothing in particular. From that day on things
would radically change in second platoon, as Sergeant First
Class Vernon Williams became our field-appointed platoon
leader.

Later on that day, company medics started circulating the
rumor that Cerekas had jumped and purposely landed on his
own ankle, which violently broke with the fall. His alleged action was in accordance with earlier behavior during second
platoon's deployment. Once, during a scud-missile attack
drill, thinking the attack was real, Cerekas had lost control of

himself and had run desperately for cover, leaving his entire platoon behind without as much as saying "good luck," much less attempting to take charge and issue commands.

On a different mission, after being fired upon by enemy elements during a night foot patrol, Cerekas suffered a panic attack and ended patrols for the night, a decision that no one complained about. After he was gone, no one really talked about the guy, except to crack jokes about the times he'd panicked.

Some thirty minutes after the RPG attack, the order came to conduct a search outside the base area. Second platoon was soon spread in a wedge formation across the open field to the east of the base, going into an old network of bombed-out warehouses, then circling north toward a soccer field where Iraqi children often played, then around the western side of our base through a middle-class neighborhood. We searched and patrolled for about two hours, seeing the sun come up from the rooftops of the small town that spread out between the Eagle's Nest and the nearby desert.

After we finished the search, which proved entirely fruitless, second platoon dragged itself back through the gate. We were all physically and emotionally exhausted. This disheartening situation of being attacked by a resistance that we could never pin down would soon become the norm. The enemy we faced had no face, they had no units, no uniforms — we couldn't see them but we knew they were everywhere, in the homes, behind the date palm trees; they watched us through the fog and through the sand, and from dark windows. They were in the alleys and streets, and in the marketplace as well as in the mosques. They were the sons and daughters of Iraq, and they were fighting for their land.

After escorting the mortars through a sandstorm to a besieged palace, running a senseless TCP for an inept command, surviving an ambush (and being scolded for it), getting attacked by RPGs, and doing a meticulous search through the shadows of early-morning ar Ramadi, it would have been quite nice to get some sleep and some time to relax. No such luck; second platoon had patrols that day.

But before leaving to conduct our next series of missions through the city streets and alleyways, Sergeant Williams had asked to talk to me for a minute. It was about the ambush we'd gone through and the conversation he'd had, as second platoon's newly promoted PL, with Captain Warfel. Apparently, the captain was upset by the fact that the squad had celebrated its survival upon arriving to the base. He, the XO, and the first sergeant had been on the breezeway just above where we had parked the Humvees. Not only had we sent the wrong message to the enemy by driving away from the ambush, but we had also, upon returning to base, openly celebrated our escape, thus sending the wrong message to other soldiers in our unit. I listened in stony silence as Williams told me that he agreed with the captain.

FIVE

The day was clear, hot, and shiny as we left for patrols. Our first destination after breakfast was the place where, just hours before, first squad had been ambushed. We were to conduct a detailed search of the ambush area to find any clues that would help us understand how the enemy was conducting its attack and then return to our regular patrols. Tired beyond repair from the events of the previous night, we were all considerably less than thrilled by this prospect. Nevertheless, we headed out of the Eagle's Nest in two trucks.

The sun was high and the metal surface of the truck was burning hot. We drove through the streets passing mosques, schools, and the marketplace, where goats hung upside down, blood still dripping from their slit throats. The downtown area was full of life. Children roamed the streets, selling everything from peanuts and sodas to ancient Russian bayonets. Most of the women were covered in black, the younger ones with just their faces veiled. Many of the men wore traditional Arab dress, but some were dressed in sandals, slacks, and long-sleeve shirts, looking elegant and sophisticated, and quite Westernized. We saw that some held hands as they walked the street and wondered if this was just a common friendly habit or if it meant a romantic connection.

I was fascinated by how different Iraqi life was from our own back home and wanted to find out more. The cultural differences were many, beginning with the language and religion, which seemed to dominate their way of life, but another difference was the way they related to one another, even across the different clans and tribes, and the different forms of Islam they practiced. There seemed to be a unity that spread through the differences among Iraqis. I wondered if our presence had served to unite them even more. If that was the case, I didn't feel very happy about contributing to that unity, which seemed to claim most of its energy from their resistance to us and our occupation.

I was captivated by the culture and the people of Iraq, and even though I hated being fired upon, I cannot honestly say that I blamed them. And what's even more curious, I cannot say that, amid all the violence and resistance, I ever really felt hatred *from* the people of Iraq. If anything, I regretted the fact that being a U.S. soldier prevented me from experiencing the culture in any significant way. The limited interactions I did have with local people reinforced my belief that our occupation was wrong. In several conversations I had, both Shias and Sunnis openly told me that Iraqis were perfectly capable of governing their own country without the help of foreign armies. Even those who had been initially happy to see the U.S. military's arrival and who despised Saddam were now saying it was time for Americans to leave Iraq.

Coalition bombing had been severe where we had been ambushed just hours earlier. We climbed up the buildings from which we were fired upon, some two or three stories high, all just skeletal remains of residential structures. The insurgents had planned their mission well, placing themselves on higher ground on both sides of the road so they could shoot down at us from both flanks without shooting one another. The attack site was uninhabited and especially dark at night, providing both concealing shadows and protection for the surrounding sleeping town. They had conducted their ambush by the book, failing only to place a large object in the middle of the road to slow us down before the blast. Thank God they made that mistake. We also found additional wiring and blasting caps, which made us believe they might have had more explosives lined up.

The bomb they had detonated left a small crater on the road, but we soon realized that there were other similar ones nearby, an indication of other attacks in an area that was perfect for this type of hit-and-run tactic.

The homes and alleyways directly behind the buildings from which they shot at us provided quick escape routes for the attackers. All they had to do was run through the houses to their vehicles, which were probably parked on a parallel road, out of sight and out of the reach of our guns. Or they could have hidden in nearby houses, with or without consent from their residents. This line of houses just south of the road ran for about a mile before reaching the nearest friendly base. The more I thought about the attack, the more it surprised me that we weren't hurt and the happier I was about having chosen to leave the area instead of waiting for the QRF.

The patrol around the attack area ended with the raid of a seven-story office building nearby, the tallest one in that part of town. All the offices had been violently destroyed, probably by a combination of U.S. bombing—the Iraqi government officials who worked there not wanting to leave official documents behind. Looters no doubt also did their bit.

Kicking down doors and shooting locks open, we searched each floor and set a small security detail at the front and back entrances of the building. We then went to the roof, from which the entire area of downtown ar Ramadi could be seen. A myriad of low, yellow-brick structures was overlooked by tall sand-colored mosques whose minarets called Muslims to prayer five times a day. Fertile farmland next to the river stretched to the north. The vast desert swept across the south, where now and then small groups of moving dots could be seen, perhaps sheepherders searching the arid sands for grassy patches to feed their livestock.

Looking across this magnificent landscape, I reflected on the contrast between the beauty of the country and the convulsive violence we were meeting every day. It saddened me. Not for the first time, I felt a deep connection to the Iraqi people. I had already seen the pain and suffering in their eyes too often for comfort. I wanted to help them rebuild their crumbled ancient nation, bombed-out remains of a biblical land. If only we could bring peace to these people, not as foreign soldiers, but as fellow human beings, as citizens without borders.

My trance was quickly quashed by the realization that I could be attacked at any moment. Having to stay alert made me feel as if I was losing all sense of my own humanity. How could I embrace the Iraqis while holding a rifle and carrying grenades on my belt pouches? I wanted to be their brother, but I couldn't. I was an occupier.

At approximately 1100 hours we left the seven-story building near the ambush site and I found myself leading first squad up the main road of ar Ramadi. It felt surreal. One instant I was lost in the beauty of the moment, minutes later I was in deadly danger. We were all wearing our heavy and largely useless flak vests and our Kevlar helmets. We were also carrying at least 210 rounds of ammunition per soldier, plus other gear, and our weapons. All this under a merciless sun that made the water in our canteens so hot it burned our mouths when we tried to take a drink. We were headed east toward the Mayor's Cell, a walled-in three-story building from which, as evidenced by a video one of the Iraqi police had shown Rosado, Saddam Hussein had once addressed the Sunnis in the town, rifle in hand.

The Mayor's Cell was the main government building in the city and most of its offices were now occupied by newly installed government and police officials. The town's mayor and police captain had both been appointed by U.S. Army officers during a meeting, guarded in part by my squad, just days before. Other parts of the Mayor's Cell were occupied by some of Bravo Company, while we used one of its second floor red-carpeted offices as a patrol base.

As we approached the building, a radio call came through instructing us to pick up the pace.

"Hey, Sergeant Mejía," said Williams from behind me. "Something's going on at the Mayor's Cell. We've got a mission."

"What, what's going on?" I asked, trying to hide my dismay. After no sleep whatsoever for a day and a half, I really wanted to lie down on the red carpet in the patrol base, filthy as it was, to get some sleep. I was exhausted, at the point of collapse. I wanted to say *To hell with the mission, I'm going to sleep*. It didn't matter where; on the street, under the shade of a date palm tree, anywhere, I didn't care. But I did my best to keep my cool. I kept walking with a straight face and a steady pace, as if everything was fine, like a good infantry squad leader.

"There is a protest outside the Mayor's Cell," yelled Sergeant Williams, pulling the cord from the radio on Specialist Shanks's back and holding the hand mike to his ear. We didn't have hand radios at that time, so internal communication was conducted by shouting at each other.

A crowd of people could be seen some half a mile west of the Mayor's Cell. We walked past a bombed-out building next to a school. There was a headless bust of Saddam on top of an obelisk at the entrance of the building, and on the entrance walls were paintings of women wearing all black and carrying AK-47 rifles. Outside the school was a statue of a small child in a school uniform holding a stack of books under his left arm. I don't remember ever seeing any real children there.

We had to open a path for ourselves through the angry crowd of protesters, who didn't seem very impressed by our weapons. One man was holding up a sign that read, NO BUSH YES SADDAM. I remember thinking that it must have taken guts to protest like that, but I wasn't much bothered by the content of his sign. President Bush wasn't exactly a favorite of mine either.

Once inside the Mayor's Cell we were told to sit tight in the hallway. Bravo Company apparently had everything under control; they were positioned across the front yard, facing the crowd from inside the walls around the compound. We were told to hurry up in case things got ugly. "Hurry up and wait!" is one of the army's most famous and frequently used commands. But waiting wasn't a problem that day. I was so tired I didn't mind sitting on the hard, dirty surface of the building's second floor. Gallegos told me he would be on the nearby balcony, and he took Perez, his machine gunner.

Specialist Perez had a very gentle way of relating to people, Iraqis or otherwise, but the quiet and restrained manner of this kind soldier from the Dominican Republic did not get in the way of his combat proficiency. There was a running debate within the squad as to who was better with the squad automatic weapon (SAW), Perez or Bien-Aime.

Before long nearly all of the squad was on the balcony. I checked on them briefly and then went back to my comfortable, hard, dirty spot inside. I knew I couldn't sleep with everything that was going on, but I still closed my eyes, trying to rest in the darkness.

I began to relax. Soldiers from my platoon were all around, playing jokes on one another, eating whatever they happened to have in their pockets, lighting up cigarettes. I felt I could unwind, just for a minute. I knew they would call me if anything happened. With my eyes closed and legs stretched out, but still gripping my rifle, its sling coiled around my arm, I began to doze off.

I must have opened my eyes just seconds after falling asleep and, as if sensing the future, about a fraction of a second before the first blast shook the floor. A second explosion went off, and then a third. I looked at the other soldiers around me stirring themselves reluctantly, evidently hoping the problem would just go away. Then a fourth, much louder blast shook the entire building and everyone jumped to their feet.

My squad had already returned from the balcony and was waiting to receive instructions.

"The protesters are throwing grenades at us," said Gallegos.

Sergeant Williams came running back from the first floor with intel from Bravo Company. Their first sergeant had told Williams to hold tight, as they were getting ready to send out a civil affairs team to try to persuade the crowd to go home peacefully. They deployed a Humvee with an American female translator, a soldier, speaking Arabic through a bull-horn, requesting the Iraqis to leave the area. Then a grenade exploded right next to the Humvee, which was heard speeding off, out of the area.

"Sergeant Mejía, let's go," said Sergeant Williams. "We're going to the roof to pull overhead security."

Sergeant Ritz, a superb shooter who always carried his sniper scope, came with us. Sergeant Williams placed him in a strategic corner from where he could see the entire rally ground. My squad was positioned along the front of the roof. It was easy to tell when someone in the crowd was going to throw a grenade; the assembly would quiet down all at once and would move as one to the side of the street, far enough away to avoid injury from the blast but close enough to see where it hit and scream and cheer for it. Bravo Company soldiers, who were outside in the compound, were yelling at the demonstrators and trying to intimidate them with their weaponry. A black plastic bag landed near one of them and started smoking. They all ran as fast as they could away from it, narrowly escaping injury from a considerable blast. Later reports indicated that some of those throwing explosives were children.

The order came to move all friendly elements away from the immediate ground area, and for those on the roof to shoot at anyone who looked like they were going to throw a grenade. The crowd was still in the middle of the street and I sensed that they saw the withdrawal of our troops from the front yard as a victory. They returned to the area immediately in front of the main gate, yelling even louder and holding their NO BUSH YES SADDAM signs higher.

At that point the Iraqis fell quiet again and everyone moved to the side of the street. They were all looking toward an area of the street that was hidden from our view. I remembered it was a street corner where there was a shop of some kind, with a balcony right above it. It was the same building where one night there had been a short firefight between insurgents and third platoon. It was said that two little girls were shot in their sleep that night, but those reports were quickly denied by the civil affairs people. Now, from a corner of the same building, a young man could be seen emerging from the watching crowd. He was wearing gray slacks and a long-sleeve shirt of the same color. He was very young, perhaps sixteen or seventeen years of age. I followed him through the aperture of my M-16 sight. *What are you doing, man?* He continued to walk toward the walled-in yard of the compound, which was now deserted. He pulled his right hand out of his pocket and I could see it contained a small black object. He drew his arm back.

I have no memory of squeezing the trigger at the moment that a storm of bullets rained down on that young man, ending his life at once. I remember the grenade he threw exploded near where he died, far from all of us who shot at him. I also remember a couple of old men emerging from the crowd after we ceased fire, their arms held up to show they were unarmed, their heads bent. They grabbed the lifeless body by the shoulders, dragging the young man through a pool of his own blood. They moved back quietly until they were swallowed once again by the crowd, now silent, in mourning for their lost son.

The rally resumed shortly afterward, and we ended up having to call helicopters to disperse the people. The total body count for that demonstration, unofficial as usual, was four dead and several wounded. All were Iraqis.

We were told to go back inside the building after the crowd finally left. We had to get ready for more patrols around the city. I went to a dark and isolated corner of the building and sat down for a moment, away from everyone's sight, and removed the magazine from my rifle. It had nineteen bullets left, which meant I had fired eleven rounds at that young man.

Patrols resumed soon thereafter, and my squad had to cover the rear of a two-squad formation that spanned a block and a half or so. We had carried out this sort of exercise in the area several times before, but that day the streets and alleyways seemed a lot more frightening. Perhaps it was the fact that a black plastic bag had exploded inside the compound not long before and everyone in ar Ramadi, it seemed, was carrying just such a plastic bag that day.

But even worse than worrying about the potential threat

of plastic bags was being afraid of children. It was the first time since we had been in ar Ramadi that we'd heard that children were involved in direct hostile action such as grenade throwing. We found ourselves distrusting even the silliest jokes by the kids who, as always, liked to play war with the soldiers. Groups of four or five children would run alongside the formation, hiding behind parked cars and waiting to jump in front of soldiers with their arms and hands held up as if holding a rifle. *Ra tat tat tat tah!* they would yell, with smiles across their little dirty faces. It was all a game, but it was making Estime, Bien-Aime, and Chito very nervous.

The antioccupation protest and its bloody aftermath, combined with our physical exhaustion, were playing tricks on our judgment. Chito grabbed a teenager by the neck with his bike-gloved hand and slammed him against a wall, cursing him loudly in English. I thought he was about to shoot him and shouted to find out what the problem was. Chito said that the little fucker had looked at him like he was going to do something.

The young Iraqi was much smaller and younger than Chito, who was armed to the teeth with smoke and fragmentary grenades on his vest and belt and a rifle with a grenade launcher mounted on it. I felt sorry for the kid and part of me wanted to tell Chito to let him go. But I couldn't. I was angry at everyone and everything. I wanted Chito to inflict fear in the young man's heart, and to do it in a way so that all the Iraqis in the vicinity would know about it.

I could see the angry look in the young Iraqi's face, and then it occurred to me that the Iraqis who stood silently watching probably felt proud of him. Some people looked on from a distance while others stared at the ground. But everyone was aware of what was happening and I could sense their approval of his defiance. The young man had by now been released by Chito and I watched him from a distance as I walked backward with the formation. He stared at me with unwavering eyes; he definitely looked suspicious. I turned around slowly, studying my surroundings very carefully. I took a close look at everything and everyone, man, woman, and child, streets, alleyways, animals, vehicles, ice vendors by the side of the road, mosques, schools, apartment buildings. Everything, *everything*, looked suspicious.

Chicken-shit alley was the name we had given to this especially nasty slum of town, which had not only all the sewage and trash that were predominant in most areas of ar Ramadi, but also the added stench of chicken droppings that came from all the caged hens in the area. We were nearing the end of our patrol and were about to head back to the Mayor's Cell when we got a call from Combat X-ray.

"Hey, Sergeant Mejía," said Gallegos. "Sergeant Williams said to tell you that we're going straight to the bank for another mission."

"Do you know what it is?" I asked Gallegos.

"I don't know yet; I'll let you guys know as soon as I hear from X-ray," said Williams, who'd heard my question to Gallegos even though he had been walking at quite a distance from us.

"And what bank is that, Will?" I asked.

The only bank I knew of was the one that was close to the North Palace, and we were walking in the opposite direction from it.

"I think it's the bank by the gas station, downtown," he answered.

I looked at Gallegos, still not knowing where the bank was, but he just looked at me with a blank stare on his face. It didn't really matter; I knew where the downtown gas station was, so I just kept walking in the same direction, thinking

that as soon as we got close to the place we'd be able to recognize it.

By now I was so tired I was operating on reserve energy.
I could perform physical functions, such as walking and talking, but my mind was in a trance. I felt as though I was looking at things from someone else's body, the same way I had felt
during the ambush, though, unlike then, I was now well aware
of the dangers around me. I walked on, keeping my emotions
firmly in check, partly in order to concentrate on survival in a
dangerous area, partly to protect my spirits from the agony of
knowing I had been involved in killing a human being.

When the orders from battalion came through we found
out that we were to pull security on a bank that was due to receive the dinar equivalent of US$50,000 in cash. The money
was for the salaries of the local police and other officials, who
were getting paid for the first time since being appointed by
the U.S. coalition. Someone within the police had gotten
word that a group of insurgents was going to attack the bank.
It wasn't clear what the target was—it might be the bank
workers who were cooperating with the American military, it
might be the money itself, or it might be us.

What was clear, as we arrived in the area, was that a high
level of security had been set up. Elements of all three combat
companies of the 1-124 Infantry were deployed; there were
even troops from the headquarters company. Three Humvees
were in front of the bank, police cars were parked in the small
alleyways behind, and all along the sidewalk soldiers mixed
with civilians and Iraqi cops.

We went inside the bank to find out what our squad's mission was going to be. Sergeant First Class Demarest, who
had assumed the role of platoon sergeant since Cerekas's
mysterious and untimely injury, was already inside.

"Sergeant Mejía," he addressed me, "we're putting your
squad on the roof of the hospital across the street."

I didn't want to admit that I didn't have the faintest idea where the hospital he was talking about was. I knew the "Saddam's Hospital" but that was beside the river, about a mile north, through the city. I knew the route and we would have had to cross half of downtown ar Ramadi to get there. Surely he couldn't mean that one. I could already see us piling through the waves of people in the marketplace, through what we called the loop road, and then through the neighborhoods. It was not an attractive prospect.

"Roger," I said. "And what hospital would that be?"

"The psych hospital across the street," said Demarest, looking at me with his slightly crossed blue eyes. "You don't know which one it is?" he asked.

"Nope."

"Me neither," he admitted, laughing.

It was good to know I wasn't a total moron who didn't know right from left. Demarest went to ask some funny-looking sergeant major outside who liked to show off his ranger tab. I sat down on the floor next to a bed that, oddly enough, was placed in the middle of the bank's lobby next to one of the cashier counters. It was an old, roughly constructed bed, but it looked soft and comfortable, and very tempting. I was trying not to think about lying down on it when I saw a hand lift up the mattress. I looked up. The hand belonged to a young Iraqi cop who was wearing civilian clothes and a nicely trimmed beard. He looked at me and nodded his head in the direction of the bed. I looked down again and saw an AK-47 rifle under the mattress.

"Gooood," said the young cop with a smile.

I looked down at the weapon, which he was now stroking gently, as if it were an old pet dog that did not care much for its master. I forced a smile in return.

Demarest came back soon enough with the information, and we both walked outside, passing the sergeant major. He pointed out the building and showed me the entrance on the bottom floor. There were some elderly ladies right outside wearing all black with no veils. There were also cheap jewelry, CD, and DVD kiosks all up and down the hospital's sidewalk. The streets were crowded with people, many of whom were men wearing all-white gownlike shirts going in and out of a nearby mosque.

"See the building next to the bank?" asked Demarest, pointing to the building next to us.

"What, this one right here?" I asked, trying to make sure.

"Yeah, this one right here," he said. "See up there? That's Mantilla's building, those are Mantilla's guys."

"OK, I got you," I said.

Williams had taken Mantilla's squad and placed it already.

"Milligan is gonna stay with me inside the bank. You're gonna take Hodges and Ibaugh with you."

He was talking about the gun team that consisted of Hodges, who carried the M-240 Bravo machine gun, and Ibaugh, his assistant gunner. Demarest had been the leader of the gun squad, as it is customary in infantry units to give the highest ranking squad leader control of the big guns. With Lieutenant Cerekas gone and Williams acting as platoon leader, Demarest became the acting platoon sergeant, and the gun squad was split in half. I got one gun, Milligan got the other.

"Roger," I said, looking up at my position and thinking about possible avenues for enemy attacks.

I went back inside to get the teams and found them lounging around in a relaxed manner which, given the security outside, didn't bother me too much. Rosado was trying to get one of the Iraqi cops to go outside and buy some sodas. Bien-Aime was sitting on a wooden bench listening to a tall but chubby Iraqi translator talk about Saddam Hussein. The translator spoke fluent English with a distinct American accent.

"Yeah, man, that's fucked up. They're beginning to target Iraqis who help the Americans. I mean, I speak English well, but I'm an Iraqi, you know? It's fucking Saddam; he's the one behind all this shit."

I didn't know who this guy was, and I wasn't sure I wanted to. For some reason—I couldn't quite put my finger on it—he didn't seem honest. He sounded too American to be Iraqi. Plus he was overweight, which was quite unusual for an Iraqi. And though he wasn't in the U.S. Army, he was wearing an army-issued interceptor vest, the type that has ceramic plates that actually stop bullets.

Maybe I resented the fact that he was wearing a vest that even we didn't have access to at that time. The flak vests we were wearing weren't properly bulletproof. I guessed that he was stationed at headquarters with our battalion commander, most likely living at the palace. Working with the big bosses evidently had its rewards, even if you weren't a soldier.

"OK, men," I said, breaking the fun. "We gotta go pull security outside."

"What are we doing, Sergeant Mejía?" asked Gallegos.

"Hey, Sergeant Mejía."

"Hold on a second, Rosado," I said, switching my eyes from Rosado to Gallegos. "We're gonna go to the roof of a building outside and we're gonna pull security on the bank."

"I just ordered some sodas for the squad," said Rosado with a big smile.

We were all exhausted and could have used a little sugar to lift our energy levels, but we couldn't stay and wait, and we all knew it. Everyone dragged themselves to their feet, giving me a resigned smile. It wasn't my fault, but still, I was the bad guy. The translator watched everything without breaking his silence, until we started to leave.

"Fucking be careful out there, guys."

Fucking be careful out there, guys. His words reverberated

inside my head. *What kind of Iraqi sounds like that?* I asked myself. He bothered me; everything he said and did came across
as annoying, even if he meant well. But I was exhausted and
afraid, and I wonder now if he might have been a real nice
guy. Maybe we could have become good friends. Or maybe
he is dead now. I walked outside to join the squad without
looking back.

After entering through the psych hospital's dirty and crowded
lobby, we went up the stairs to the fourth-floor roof. Specialist Perez, Alpha's machine gunner, was placed at the entrance
to pull security for the rest of the squad. Everyone else was
placed around the roof's square perimeter, but mostly on the
side facing the bank with the lively street scene directly below.
    For the first time since the beginning of our deployment I
had acquired responsibility for the strategic placement of
Specialist Hodges, or The Hodge, who carried the heavy and
highly effective M-240 Bravo machine gun. The M-240
should always be positioned where the gunner can cause the
most damage, since he has what is known in the light infantry
as the most casualty-producing weapon. Specialist Ibaugh,
Hodges's assistant gunner (AG), had to be right next to him
to take over in the event something happened to Hodges.
    Assistant gunners are required to carry at least half of the
ammunition for the gunners. Part of their job is to feed that
ammo, which comes linked in belts, and to direct the gunner
so the gun's deadly bursts can kill the most people. Since the
rapid rate of fire causes the M-240's barrel to get red hot, the
AG has to also carry a spare and use it as a replacement after
a certain number of rounds have been fired, in order to prevent melting.
    "What's up, Sergeant Mejía?" said The Hodge, as he set-
tled down behind his gun, a smoke already in his mouth. "Is
this location alright with you?" I checked his position.

"Hey man, if it works for you it works for me," I said with an honest but tired smile.

I really liked Hodges. He and I had gotten to Charlie Company around the same time. We had both come from active duty and had shared the rank of specialist and the responsibilities that came with it. I remember how during classroom training days we were often both tasked as instructors. I particularly recall the time he taught a class on how to operate the radio. He had come across as funny, but also as very knowledgeable.

Hodges hadn't achieved the same rank as I had because, as best as I remember, he had taken a job that had kept him away from training for a few months and as a result had been declared absent without leave. This offense had hindered his subsequent promotion, but nonetheless he was one of the most experienced soldiers in the platoon and had served in Kosovo while things were still hot there. What he lacked in rank he made up for in experience. He kept a cool attitude concerning his superior knowledge, while I kept a cool attitude about my higher rank. Consequently he did what I told him but never hesitated to give me his opinion when he thought I was wrong.

"Man, I don't think they're gonna do shit," I said to Hodges, looking down at the moving mass of people. "We're fucking armed to the teeth."

"I don't know, Sarge," he replied. "You never know with these crazy motherfuckers."

Given the level of security we had, it really looked impossible for anyone to conduct an attack. There were U.S. soldiers and Iraqi cops everywhere, plus the Humvees with their mounted guns, and both Mantilla's and my squads pulling overhead watch. And one thing that made me think an attack was really unlikely was the sight of the sergeant major standing outside the bank, calmly talking to the soldiers around the Humvees. Someone of that high rank out on the street, not looking worried or even alert, was a strong indication that the higher-ups were just playing it safe. Either that or the sergeant major was a real idiot. But that could not be; he had a ranger tab.

Shifting my gaze from the maze of people down below, I looked across at the building Mantilla occupied. I could barely see his guys because their position was a bit higher than ours. Quickly surveying our surroundings, I realized there were buildings all around us. That made us vulnerable because there could be snipers on those rooftops, waiting and perhaps ready to shoot at us.

The street to our east, perpendicular to the main road that the bank and hospital were on, was nearly deserted. It occurred to me we weren't paying enough attention to that empty street, and that we were too concentrated on the main road. It would be difficult to attack the bank from there, but what if the target wasn't the bank but the soldiers protecting it?

"Hey, listen up!" I yelled. Everyone looked up at me from their prone positions. "Make sure you pay attention to this road below us," I said, pointing down at the deserted street. "It would be really easy for some crazy motherfucker to just throw up a grenade and fuck us all up."

The remark applied only to a couple of soldiers who were in a position that allowed them to see the road I was talking about. But I wanted everyone to hear because there didn't seem to be any awareness that we were in a position where we could be attacked. Everyone gave a half nod and went back to watching their sectors. Funez took a long drag on his cigarette.

Most of the shops were closing up for the day, ice vendors were pushing their carts with whatever unmelted ice they had left in them, street merchants of all sorts were wrapping up business in their stands. The sun had begun to set, casting a twilight shadow on the security line of Humvees, soldiers, and Iraqi cops. I heard the faint echo of laughter and saw that it came from the sergeant major, who was using his chubby Americanized translator to talk to some Iraqi cops, their AK-47 rifles resting on the sidewalk next to their flip-flopped feet. I hadn't seen any money being delivered since I got to the rooftop, but everything seemed quiet. Then, I heard the explosion.

The blast had come from a grenade but it sounded louder than that as it broke the deceitful stillness of the moment. It was followed by machine-gun fire from Mantilla's building across the street. People were running like crazy on the main road below us, but they weren't going far, just getting out of harm's way to a place where they could observe what was happening in safety. I think I was more frightened by the attack than the locals. A few seconds later a tail of fire rose up from the sergeant major's position to the rooftop where Mantilla was stationed. My first thought was that someone had fired an RPG from just outside the bank's entrance, but only Iraqi policemen and our troops were there, and neither carried RPG launchers.

"Hey, Sergeant Mejía," said Perez, looking back at me but with his gun still pointing down at the stairway. "Do you want me to move from here?"

"Negative," said Gallegos, his team leader.

"Just keep a low profile," I said to him in an easy tone, although I was really nervous. "Nobody shoot unless you have a clear target," I ordered.

Everyone listened without moving from their positions.

"I can't see shit," said Hodges. "Can you see anything, Sergeant Mejía?"

"No, man, I can't see a damned thing."

Then, more machine-gun fire came from Mantilla's position, followed by the sound of screeching rubber. I looked down and saw the Humvees taking off in a hurry. The ranger sergeant major and his entourage were splitting from the scene. As he left he was yelling out into the madness behind him:

"CHANGE OF MISSION, CHANGE OF MISSION, CHANGE OF MISSION."

The burst of machine-gun fire from Mantilla's roof had been the work of Specialist Medrano who, sitting behind a low wall observing the alleyways behind the rear of the bank, spotted a man in a window with a weapon pointed at their position. The man took a shot at him, which barely missed. Medrano returned fire but the man at the window had already left, his stretching shadow lingering for a little longer.

Just as Medrano opened up, a man walking on the street below threw a grenade at their rooftop, which exploded in midair. On hearing the blast, someone fired an illumination flare up into the afternoon's twilight, which barely missed Mantilla's position. The person who threw the grenade got away.

While some of the local people were still hanging out in the area, the Iraqi cops had disappeared, going back inside the bank without firing a single round. We were given the order to get back inside the bank as well, so we made our way cautiously down the stairs, wary of the possibility that the attackers might have set a booby trap on our only route out of the building.

We got safely to street level and went across to the bank to meet up with the rest of the platoon. Sergeant Demarest, Milligan, and I received the order to go back to the Mayor's Cell, which the battalion leadership had decided was a safer place to receive the delivery of money. Sergeant Williams remained behind with Mantilla's squad to search the house Medrano had fired at, but we later learned that they found nothing.

The bank mission was over, but we still had to conduct presence patrols throughout the city until the next morning.

There were murmurs in the crowd when we left, one squad at a time. I looked back for an instant as we started to walk through the dwindling throng; no one, as far as we knew, had died during the attack, yet there seemed to be deep anger in the distant faces. Wondering if they blamed us for what had happened I looked back again. I saw nothing; the night sky, like a coffin, had closed down on ar Ramadi.

SIX

A week or so after my squad was ambushed in ar Ramadi, and following a number of serious attacks against other squads and platoons, our company leadership decided to arrange operations into a three-phase cycle, with each platoon taking turns on presence patrols, the quick reaction force, and what came to be known as "hajji guard."

Hajji guard was by far the safest and most desirable duty in the company's three-phase cycle. Although little effort could be seen in terms of rebuilding the destroyed city of ar Ramadi, unit commanders started to receive funding to improve their soldiers' living conditions. Most of that money was used for short-term repairs, and the pocket change contracts were issued to local Iraqi companies. When the Iraqi workers came into our base they had to be searched for weapons and then escorted wherever they went. We called this work hajji guard. Other tasks during hajji guard duty included manning the different base towers that protected the compound, which was being attacked regularly with RPGs and mortars.

Much more dangerous was the QRF mission. Though most of the engagements were over by the time the QRF arrived, there was always the possibility of counterattacks, or of an ambush en route. The QRF platoon wasn't always called out when there was a problem; sometimes the platoon conducting patrols was able to handle the situation by itself. Other times the QRF was called simply to help provide security or to transport prisoners. And on yet other occasions, QRF personnel might be summoned to help secure an area and end up themselves conducting raids or search and kill.

One QRF mission that my platoon was involved in remains vivid in my mind. It was first platoon's turn to conduct patrols, and they had responded to a call from one of our informers, a man who lived with his family on the other side of the field to our east.

The informer claimed that a group of men had broken into his house and had beaten him and then raped his wife. He wanted our company to arrest the perpetrators, and said he knew where they lived. First platoon went with the man to a neighborhood just down the road from our base, where they knocked on the door of a house he pointed out to them. They then saw three men fleeing the scene. The soldiers forced the door open to go through the house and out its back door in pursuit of the suspects. Another soldier, Staff Sergeant Ciatonni, went inside to help secure the house and practically bumped into a fourth man who was carrying an AK-47 assault rifle. The man appeared to be about to slap a magazine in the weapon as he moved after the soldiers who were pursuing his relatives.

Ciatonni immediately opened fire. His first shot grazed the length of the man's forearm, leaving a small line of open flesh on the surface between the elbow and the palm of the hand. He then leveled his gun at the man's chest and fired again, killing him instantly. The other three men were all apprehended by the chasing soldiers.

Everyone in my platoon was relaxing at the Eagle's Nest when the call came for the QRF. Knowing there were no casualties on our side and no ongoing fighting, we didn't rush to get up; we put our gear on and headed to our platoon's deuce-and-a-half truck, which was parked right next to where we slept.

Our job as the QRF was to provide security as first platoon continued to search homes around the area, and to escort the truck transporting the dead body. The truck also carried the three prisoners, two of whom were the dead man's cousins; the third was his brother. Alpha team and I got in the back of the deuce carrying the prisoners and corpse. I kept my weapon trained on the prisoners, who were hooded and tied; the rest of the team pulled vehicle security.

Looking out from the back of the truck as we moved off, I could see an old man with a long gray beard watching us leave. He was on his knees and was crying with his hands raised to the sky in an imploring gesture. The sound of his anguished wail made me feel ashamed for what we had done. Something had gone terribly wrong for him that day, just as things were going wrong every day for countless Iraqis. A man like that should have been enjoying the company of his children and grandchildren in his old age. Instead he was watching us take away the body of his dead child.

On arrival at the Eagle's Nest we had to move the body into a Humvee because the gates to the hospital where the morgue was located were too narrow for the truck to pass through. No one wanted to grab the body, which was wrapped in bloodstained white sheets, so we pulled it from the floor of the truck by its feet, causing it to fall to the ground. This prompted explosive laughter from a group of soldiers from third platoon who were watching us from across the yard.

"Take a picture of me and this motherfucker," said one of the soldiers who had been in my squad in third platoon, putting one arm around the corpse's back.

The shroud had come off the body, revealing a young man,

wearing only his pants. The bullet hole in his chest was quite small but the exit wound on his back was the size of an apple. "Damn, they really fucked you up, didn't they!?" continued my former soldier, laughing.

Meanwhile, the dead man's brother and cousins were being offloaded from the truck. I don't think their hoods prevented them from seeing what was happening down on the ground right next to them. It occurred to me how upsetting it must have been for them to see their relative in the dirt, half naked and covered in blood, being laughed at and humiliated even in death.

Gallegos and Rosado volunteered to wash the blood from the back of the truck and the day proceeded peacefully enough after that. As dusk fell, the entire platoon assembled at the gate in order to go out fast and efficiently should we be called as QRF, but nothing happened that night. Around 0400 hours first platoon returned through the gate and we all went to sleep.

Presence patrols were the most dangerous of the three operations. The platoon assigned to such a mission would be dropped off by the company's old dilapidated trucks at some location around ar Ramadi. (All trucks traveled with their own security element, and no vehicles were allowed to leave the compound without at least one other vehicle.) Once the platoon reached its destination, the soldiers would walk through the area of operation, or AO, until whoever was in charge was satisfied that the patrol had gone well. The danger levels on these missions were high because foot soldiers could not physically manage to carry much in the way of body protection or firepower and, because the routes the missions took were often repeated, making presence patrols vulnerable to attack.

Most of our vehicles had mountings for heavy machine guns like the M-50 caliber or the Mark 19, a machine gun that fires grenades. But the vehicles, old and unarmored, provided big targets for the IEDs (improvised explosive devices) and rocket-propelled grenades of the insurgents. As we started to lose vehicles to roadside bombs, we found ourselves having to cram ever larger numbers of soldiers in the backs of the ancient deuce-and-a-half trucks. Riding in them became a highly undesirable task.

Despite this, we were forced to rely more and more on the use of vehicles for presence patrols, in part because the large areas we were required to cover made it impractical to walk, but also because the heat, with temperatures reaching between 120 and 130 degrees Fahrenheit, was beginning to play a role in coalition casualties.

One day second platoon was conducting patrols through the rural agrarian towns in northern ar Ramadi. Getting to this area involved traveling either on River Road, which was so named because it ran along the Euphrates, or along Highway 10, the main traffic artery through downtown ar Ramadi, which then stretched east to the adjacent city of al Falluja. Both of these roads were highly dangerous and prone to frequent attacks with IEDs.

It had been a quiet day of patrols, which was just fine by me. Unfortunately it had been apparent for some time that our recently appointed platoon leader, Sergeant Williams, was engaged in a tacit competition with the other platoon leaders to see who could kill the most combatants, get involved in the most firefights, or capture the most prisoners. From his point of view, the day, as it drew to a close, had been a failure. He was looking with increasing desperation for a prize to bring home.

Williams and I were not on the best of terms in those days. From the very beginning of our arrival at ar Ramadi, when we first started conducting patrols, I was aware of serious flaws in the way we conducted our missions. These flaws included patrols undertaken in the middle of the night through the dark alleyways of downtown ar Ramadi, without anyone knowing exactly where we were. The Third ACR unit we relieved had used phase lines, or routes drawn on maps kept at base, that they could use to report the movement and location of their patrols. They had target areas of operation they concentrated on, and their patrol routes were plotted and followed by other personnel at the Eagle's Nest. They also had specific medical evacuation lines, as well as casualty collection points. We had none of that, except areas of operation for each squad.

When I told Mantilla about my concerns, it was clear he shared them. But when I said I wanted to speak to Williams about it, Mantilla recommended that I keep my observations to myself.

"Will is a great guy," he said in a sincere tone. "But I've worked with him since I got to Charlie Company; trust me, Mejía, I know the guy."

"OK, so you know the guy. Now, what are you trying to say?"

"Will is never wrong, Mejía. Even if he knows he is, he will never admit it." He took a drag from his Mikado smoke, a local brand of cigarette. "If he thought we were wrong in the way we're doing patrols he would have said something already, and if he hasn't he's not gonna listen to you."

"Yeah, Mantilla, but I gotta tell him. This shit is fucked up."

"I agree it's fucked up, but you'll be wasting your time." Another drag. "Trust me, I used to tell him my opinion, but he never listened, so I stopped doing it."

"Yeah, but that was during training, Mantilla; this shit doesn't get any more real."

"I know it doesn't, but trust me, you'll be wasting your time."

Later that day I had a similar conversation with Funez, who every now and then acted as team leader when Rosado somehow managed to twist an ankle or come up with some other ailment.

Like Mantilla, Funez agreed with me. He too had been in second platoon his entire time in Charlie Company and knew Williams well. But he thought I should make my concerns known to him.

"Dude," he had said in a kind of sarcastic voice, "we can sit here and talk shit all night, and we can agree with each other until our faces turn fucking blue, but it's not gonna make a difference if you only tell me. You've gotta tell Will."

When I finally did talk to Williams, I learned that Mantilla was right.

"But we do have sectors," he said, looking up from the pad he had been writing on. "And we have PLGRs, so each squad can know where the other squad is at all times." By PLGRs (position lightweight GPS receivers) he meant military GPS, or global positioning satellite devices, used for navigation.

"Yeah, Will, but I'm talking about phase lines, checkpoints, either color or letter-coded sectors, you know, kind of like the Third ACR used to do."

"Well, you can work on that if you want. Then we'll talk to the other squad leaders so we're all on the same sheet of music."

He reopened his pad and began writing again. I guessed he was jotting Freestyle poetry, which I knew he was good at. The platoon had held Freestyle sessions at the al Hadithah dam, and Bien-Aime and Williams had come out as the two strongest poets. But that had been in peaceful al Hadithah. Now we were in violent ar Ramadi. And though I wasn't gone yet, this poet was ignoring me.

"Well, this would have to be at the company level," I continued, letting Williams know I was still there. "It wouldn't really be worth it if, for instance, the QRF didn't know about it, or if the company medics didn't know the evacuation routes. Combat X-ray would have to write down whenever

we crossed the phase lines, and we would stay within specified sect—"

"Well, then, why don't you go fucking whine to the
commander?"

The angry tone, the loud voice, and especially the use of
profanity were all highly unlike Williams. He had closed his
notebook abruptly and was now staring at me with a frown.

"Why are you getting all mad?" I asked, knowing he
would have a hard time admitting he was mad, since he
hardly ever was.

"I'm not mad," he said in a lower yet still indignant voice.
"I'm just saying, go whine to Captain Warfel."

"I'm not whining, sergeant; all I'm saying is we could be
doing things better, and since you're the platoon leader, I
thought you could talk to the commander and make a few
suggestions."

It was no use; the more I tried to reason with him, the more
he took it as a personal attack. But I was no stranger to being
placed on a platoon sergeant's or platoon leader's shit list, so I
continued to make my concerns known—to him and to the rest
of the squad leaders in my platoon, most of whom agreed with
me for the most part but chose not to say anything.

I subsequently found out that Williams was circulating
the rumor that he couldn't rely on me as much as on the other
squad leaders because I was afraid of the missions.

He started assigning my squad the mundane task of vehicle security whenever we undertook mounted patrols, leaving
the other squads to engage in the more gung-ho missions of
running after the bad guys. Such ill-distribution of tasks was
unfair to the other squads, but in terms of the glory that was
supposed to come with killing the enemy and raiding homes,
I couldn't care less that we were not getting our fair share.

This was one such mission. My squad had been tasked
with providing vehicle security, and we had driven through

northern ar Ramadi without catching or even seeing a single suspected insurgent. We were about to return to base when Williams gave the order to head the convoy to a group of small farms just adjacent to the Euphrates River; he then ordered everyone, apart from my vehicle-security squad, to get out of the trucks and search the fields for weapons.

All the search turned up was a few flares, an old belt of linked ammunition, and parts of a rusty old rifle. Yet these discoveries were enough to get Williams really excited and to send the squads searching every home in an area that was way too big for a single platoon to cover.

I was responsible for the heavy machine guns mounted on top of the trucks, which meant that part of my job was to use the guns to create a blanket of protective fire in the event the squads were attacked from some unexpected flank. As the squads began to spread out a long way from each other, which was inevitable given the vast area they were searching, I was forced to move the vehicles further apart in order to keep the troops covered with the machine guns. We were pretty much losing our ability to protect anything at all.

"Combat two-six, this is combat two-one, over."

"Go ahead, two-one," responded the happy Williams.

"Roger, we're stretching too thin. Do you want me to call the QRF to help us with security, over?"

"Negative," said Williams, sounding almost surprised at my suggestion. "We got this, two-one."

The QRF could have provided the entire platoon what was required to cover the area, but there were two problems with calling them out. First, the amount of arms that had been found did not begin to warrant a search of the magnitude that had been undertaken. Second, if we did in fact find more weapons and explosives, having called out the QRF would diminish the merit of the bust, especially if we called them out too soon and they found some of the stuff. Williams hated sharing his prizes with other platoons.

Time kept running as security got thinner, and yet nothing more was found. Still Williams continued to press on with the mission. Below the old, worn-out truck that Specialist Perez and I were on, a group of children had started to gather, two or three at first, then four or five. As gentle and kindly as ever, Perez ventured a few words in Arabic, but the kids only laughed at his clumsy mutilation of their language.

I generally liked kidding around with the children, but this time my area of responsibility had grown way too big and I was more concerned with carefully observing the surroundings. Some five hundred meters to our rear was the Euphrates River; to our right the fields extended for about three hundred meters before they ended in a high wall that probably marked the beginning of a whole other town. To my left the scene was almost identical, except that there was a small tree line between the trucks and the wall. Houses were scattered in no particular fashion across the fields all around us. To our front the road stretched for about two hundred meters, curving up and to the right before finally merging into the street on which we had been patrolling.

The children had moved to a tree nearby and were standing behind it; something seemed suspicious about that, but I tried to keep my concentration on the surroundings. The road we had used to enter the area was pretty much the only way out, and the wall to the left and a group of trees to the right made it impossible to see what was going on beyond a fifty-meter stretch of the road. Attacks could be in preparation there and we would know nothing about it.

The children were being called by an adult from an opening in the wall to our left. Some were already leaving the area.

"Combat two-six, this is combat two-one, be advised, we

have no eyes on the main road to our twelve o'clock, over," I said to Williams about the poor visibility to our front.

"Roger two-one, why don't you go ahead and move up to the road so you can see what's going on?" He, of course, knew what could happen if we didn't protect our only way out.

"Negative, I can't do that and provide security for the squads. Break. Can we move up the platoon line a bit, over?" By this I meant that he should leave some of the homes behind and move the entire platoon closer to the main road. That way I could move the vehicles up and provide security for the squads while keeping an eye on our exit.

"Negative, two-one, we're still searching houses back here. Out." Williams was clearly unworried by the lack of security.

The area had fallen disturbingly quiet, and every now and then a young man took peeks at us from the tree line up on the main road. I realized it was the absence of the children's voices and laughter what was creating the ominous silence. They were all gone from behind the tree and were now observing us quietly but attentively from behind the wall.

"Combat two-six, this is combat two-one; be advised, everyone is gone from the area and there is something going on by the main road behind the trees. Over."

"Roger," replied Williams in an evidently exasperated tone. "Just keep watching, two-one."

I could tell I was pushing the limits of Williams's patience, and I was worried that it would simply reinforce his view of me as overzealous about security issues. Deep inside it hurt my pride to be labeled "the scared squad leader," and I didn't want the rest of my platoon to think of first squad as a bunch of cowards. But the situation conformed with a pattern known to lead to trouble. We were in a place that had only one exit, which we couldn't see: with our squads widely dispersed, our security had been stretched way too thin and we had stayed in one place too long without requesting backup.

"Roger," I said after a thoughtful pause. I knew nothing I could say would change a thing at that point, except to further undermine my standing as a squad leader. The best route was to keep my mouth shut, but I couldn't help myself.

". . . I think we're about to get attacked. We need to get going."

"SHUT THE FUCK UP," came the angry response through the radio. "JUST DO WHAT I TELL YOU TO DO."

At that moment I felt completely impotent—the impotence that fills the heart when you know that something horrible may be about to happen and there is nothing you can do about it. I was certain that if the rest of the platoon could be made aware of what I knew, they too would appreciate the danger we were facing. But there was no way of communicating the general situation to soldiers who were intently focused on the immediate task at hand, whether it was guarding a street corner or searching a closet inside a house. And even if I had been able to warn them, getting a general agreement to refuse an order that was putting their lives unnecessarily at risk would have been impossible. I was alone.

Williams finally gave the order to turn the trucks around for load up, which didn't make sense given that we were already facing our way out and were on a narrow street. But I was done with questioning Williams for the day. I knew I had already made him not want to listen to a word I had to say. I just did what I was told.

"Why are we detaining these guys?" asked Specialist Madsen, speaking almost under his breath.

I looked behind me and saw third squad bringing three hooded men, their hands tied with plastic restraints. I knew they had found a couple of flares and some rounds, but that was hardly a reason to detain anyone, plus those had been found in the middle of a field, not in any particular house. There had to be something else I did not know. Perhaps they had found some real weapons, maybe some mortar rounds, or materiel to make IEDs. I asked the leader of second squad why we were bringing them in.

"I don't know," he replied, raising his eyebrows and nodding. "Sergeant Williams just said to detain them."

At that point Williams came up behind us with a big smile on his face. I could hear him giving Combat X-ray the grid location of the "bust," something we were required to do every time we found anything or detained anyone. He looked at Mantilla and me, as happy as he could be. I thought there might be some words of reprimand after our exchange over the radio, but everything seemed just as normal as ever.

"Hey, Will, why are we detaining these men?" asked Mantilla.

"Because of all the stuff we found in the field."

"You mean that belt of ammo and the flares?" continued Mantilla.

"Correct," replied Williams, trying to sound confident. "Even if the stuff doesn't belong to them, they *know* who the stuff belongs to, believe me, they know."

I said nothing.

On the way up to the main road, just as we were leaving, the point vehicle, in which Williams was riding, made a sudden stop. One thing you had to give Williams: unlike other leaders in our unit, he led from the front, and this time was no exception. Something was lying by the side of the road and Sergeant Macias got out of his truck to investigate. It turned out to be a mortar round that had been placed some twenty meters away from where the convoy stopped. It was clear that someone had begun setting up an ambush with IED aimed at blowing up one of our vehicles on the way out.

Macias, an infantryman, was not qualified to retrieve the mortar round, yet, showing considerable bravery, that's just what he did, cradling the explosive in his hands as if it were a baby. After that sudden stop, we continued on our way back to the Eagle's Nest ever more careful and expecting to get attacked at any moment.

In the army things work very differently from the outside world, where there's a good and a bad way to do most things. In the army there's simply the army way. We had not been blown up on this mission so, despite the fact that I felt vindicated in expressing my concerns, Williams could claim he'd been right to ignore them. Although no one ever said a word about the incident, it became known that I had complained about our lack of security and had requested that we leave the area. In the army's way of seeing things, I had overreacted.

But it wasn't just the problem with our procedures that troubled me. The mission itself seemed to me to exemplify everything that was wrong about our activities in ar Ramadi. We were out there arresting people who had in all likelihood done nothing wrong, simply because, it seemed to me, Williams didn't want to return to base empty-handed. It was all about his pride and vanity and not about the situation on the ground. I felt bad about it, but that day I was mainly relieved that nothing bad had happened to us.

Restricting first squad to vehicle security didn't last long. It was easy work, at least compared with raiding houses and doing cordon searches, and the other squads wanted their share of it. And Williams knew that, if he could deal with my sometimes insubordinate comments, he had another fully capable squad at his disposal. Soon enough we were back to performing the same duties as everyone else in the platoon.

My mouth got me on the wrong side of people regularly, but not always as a result of complaints about procedures, or lack of them, regarding the safety and well-being of soldiers in my unit. On occasion I also spoke out on the morality of what we were doing, and in particular on the way we were regularly mistreating Iraqis. This was a much more difficult issue to raise. I generally felt embarrassed to openly take the side of the Iraqis. Most of the soldiers were highly suspicious of them, and not just of some Iraqis, but of all of them. I could tell that my speaking out on their behalf was perceived as being soft and naïve, a status almost as undesirable as the status of coward. I tried to get around this by appealing to the strategy of "winning the hearts and minds" of the local population as an integral part of the mission. It worked only on rare occasions.

I recall using this argument in an attempt to change the way we were responding to the illegal sale of fuel in the town. Since the lines at the two local gas stations were enormous, and the amount of fuel sold to each individual was severely rationed, there was a thriving black market for people buying and selling gasoline. Many of those involved were children, and they used metal barrels or plastic five-gallon containers to store and then sell the gas.

The sale of fuel from such jerry cans was explicitly forbidden, but it proved difficult to stop this activity simply by issuing orders and making the odd arrest. More drastic measures were then employed, and soon enough we were opening fire on the barrels and cans, even if they were in the middle of busy traffic areas or neighborhoods. Unlike the way things happen in the movies, shooting at these containers did not cause them to blow up in the air. Our bullets simply made holes through which the fuel spurted out. So then we would throw an incendiary grenade at the pools of fuel that formed, setting them on fire. This was regarded as good sport by most of the soldiers.

It seemed to me that it must have been humiliating, infuriating even, for the Iraqis—to have a foreign army setting fire to their jerry cans wherever they were to be found, which was just about everywhere in ar Ramadi. But on the few occasions that I objected, the objection drowned in the prevailing sea of anger.

"Those fucking hajjis need to learn who's boss" was a typical response. "It's fun to shoot shit up" was another.

"Who cares about these motherfuckers; we should just bomb the entire country."

I wasn't the only person in first squad who tried to stem this tide of racist hostility. Sergeant Rosado was constantly protective of the local people, especially children. On one mission, at what must have been four in the morning, Rosado hung back at a house we had just raided. At first I was annoyed because he was holding up the rest of us, but I didn't say anything as I watched him approach a group of women and children we had herded into the corner of one room while we searched the rest of the house.

Rosado had spotted what looked like a serious burn on the arm of one of the babies. Even though the infant, who could not have been older than eighteen months, slept peacefully in her mother's cradled arms, the wound on her skin was so brutal that it pained the eye just to see it. The women evidently had had no ointment or dressing with which to treat the live flesh. Unfortunately we didn't have any medications with us either, but Rosado, who had the extraordinary ability to communicate with people regardless of language, made a point of going out of his way to look at the child and inquire about her health. I could see he made a highly favorable impression on the scared and sleepy family.

On another occasion, when our squad was pulling security at the gates of ar Ramadi's biggest hospital, we came across a young man with what looked like a machete wound that extended from between the thumb and index finger of his right hand all the way up to his elbow. The wound had been closed with big, rough stitches that seemed to be coming apart, and the poor soul had no dressing or ointment to cover it. Rosado looked into our camouflage combat lifesaver bag and was able to dig out some antibiotic cream packets and some gauze, which he gave the young man.

These basic acts of compassion and humanity were few

and far between, and we always tried to dress them up as part of a strategy of winning hearts and minds. Sometimes we tried to keep them secret. Once, after we had pretty well destroyed a home during a raid that turned up nothing, I waited for everyone to move out of the immediate area before giving one of the ladies of the house a twenty dollar bill. But this discretion did not keep us from being dubbed the "humanitarian" squad by the rest of the platoon. The title, far from being an honorable one, was a constant source of mockery and ridicule. Being humanitarian, in the universe of our infantry unit in wartorn ar Ramadi, was not seen in a favorable light.

For the most part, Rosado and I carried out our small acts of compassion separately, aware of what the other was doing, but too embarrassed to help or even publicly acknowledge them. I wasn't proud of this because I knew how hard it was to act alone.

One of the occasions on which I failed to support Rosado, knowing he was right and yet unable to overcome my own fear of ridicule, involved his protecting a young Iraqi child who had been throwing rocks at our squad while we conducted a patrol. The day was intensely hot as we rode in the back of the deuce-and-a-half truck, which traveled on the wrong side of the road in an attempt to avert possible road bomb attacks. The area to which we were being driven was not regarded as particularly hostile, but we were all aware that insurgency attacks often happened at the least expected places and times. One cannot speak of a front line in Iraq, as a roadside bomb can wait for its target on any corner of any street, in a bag, box, trash can, or in the belly of a dead animal. Everything is fair game in the land of the occupied.

Sometimes on these missions the platoon leader and platoon sergeant decided to tag along. This was supposed to facilitate the training of the squad leaders, but in fact it meant they made pretty much all the major decisions and undermined our authority. It also meant the squad had to do things strictly by the book. That ruled out dropping into the local stores where we could buy hookahs, cases of soda, and blocks of ice at lower prices than were available at the store inside the base, which had been set up by a dodgy interpreter Captain Warfel had hired. He sold everything from orange juice to Russian bayonets and Arab porn flicks, but we preferred to shop outside the base where we could get better prices and find a nice variety of Middle Eastern liquors. All that was out of the question on this occasion because Williams had decided to join the patrol.

Without the prospect of any entertaining stops, we dedicated ourselves to carefully observing every corner of the middle-class neighborhood whose streets and sidewalks we were traveling on. The homes were all behind tall, sand-colored walls that made it impossible for us to see what was happening inside. It was this type of structure that worried me during our senseless night patrols in downtown ar Ramadi, since anyone could just drop a grenade, or throw it from behind one of the walls, and then fire at us from the rooftops. There was nowhere to run, no cover, no ditch, no trench, just long roads with high walls that despised us.

The unbearable heat was putting everyone on edge. The soldiers in the rear of the squad's formation were particularly bothered by a group of small children following behind us, something quite common during patrols. Williams claimed that he had been hit by a rock thrown by one of the children. Kids throwing things at us was commonplace. I remembered that during my very first patrol in the city a child threw a rotten tomato at me which exploded all over my fragmentary grenade and compass pouch.

Every time we stopped and confronted the children, they would run like hell, leaving behind only the echo of their mischievous laughter. They were playing a dangerous game. After the protest that had turned violent at the Mayor's Cell, when our instructions were to fire at anyone who was throwing anything in our direction, including children, we'd heard that soldiers from other units had more than once opened fire on children for throwing rocks.

I liked to think we hadn't descended to that level, according higher value to human life, especially that of a child. But the heat was really getting to us. We were sweating so profusely that we had to keep patting off our shoulders and backs, and especially our bare necks, where the salt deposits from evaporated sweat really burned the skin.

We decided to take a short break by a half-built house, stretching out along the cool shade of its incomplete skeleton. Specialist Funez had a watch that showed the temperature, and according to him it was reading 120 degrees Fahrenheit in the shade and 139 out in the sun. The water in our canteens was so hot it was undrinkable. We were exhausted, but we kept our gear on, everyone except for Williams, that is. He began stripping down, dropping his armor and ammo onto the ground

"I'm gonna teach these kids a lesson," he said, taking off his flak vest. "That little one with the red shirt," he said pointing at the crowd of children, most of whom were barefoot. "That's the one that got me with the rock."

Williams was by now stripped down to his bare uniform, losing about fifty pounds. He was a pretty athletic guy, as he demonstrated when he suddenly took off, running after the crowd of kids who quickly dispersed into the side streets.

"Man, I can't believe he's doing that shit," said Rosado.

In a few moments Williams had caught the kid with the red shirt, who he dragged for fifty meters back to where we were resting. The child looked to be about eight years old and was crying pitifully as he tried to get loose from Williams's powerful grip.

"Aha!" said Gallegos, pointing at the kid with a grin on his face. "So you like to throw rocks, do you?"

Between sobs the kid spoke what little English he knew. "No, mister," he cried. "Me, no Ali Baba."

That was the phrase used by pretty much everyone in ar Ramadi who wanted to deny wrongdoing in the face of arrest, and on rare occasions it worked. But Williams wasn't having any of it that day.

"What are you going to do with him, Sergeant Williams?" asked Sergeant Rosado, looking concerned about the child.

"I'm gonna take this little motherfucker to the base and I'm gonna arrest him," answered Williams as he started to put his gear back on. "That's the only way these kids are ever going to learn not to throw rocks at us."

There was some logic to Williams's idea of making an example out of the kid; the main reaction of most in the squad was one of amusement. Of those of us who weren't laughing, Rosado was the only one saying anything.

"But he has no shoes, sergeant." Rosado's observation was greeted with laughter.

"I don't care," continued Williams. "I'm taking this one with us."

The children had regrouped at a distance and were now peering in our direction, clearly wondering what was about to happen to their friend. One thing I had noticed about Iraqis was the way they stuck together. People we detained during traffic control point missions, who clearly didn't know one another, were very soon deep in conversation as though they were family or friends from childhood. These kids were no different. Their little group continued to grow as it was joined by some angry adolescents, and even adults.

"You're not serious about arresting this kid, are you, Sergeant Williams?" asked Rosado, not minding the laughter.

"Hell yeah, I'm serious," replied our acting PL, grabbing the kid. "Let's go."

An older man then started yelling at us from the gate to one of the houses, but Williams took no notice of him.

"Man, that's fucked up," said Rosado, as we started to separate the squad into two staggered lines in order to move out tactically. "It's a long way for this kid to go without shoes."

Williams kept moving with the kid walking right in front of him, crying uncontrollably. Who knows what was going on in his young mind, but he was evidently drowning in a sea of panic. The other children were warily following the squad, and the older man finally dashed from the steps of his house to join them.

"Mister, mister, please," said the man as he got to about ten meters from us. "Child, mister, child." He gestured at the little boy's feet.

"There you go, Sergeant Williams," said Rosado. "That's the boy's father. I'm sure he learned his lesson."

"No, fuck that," said Williams, who I'd noticed was using profane language with increasing regularity. He turned to the old man. "Are you his father?"

"No, no," answered the man, trying to say more, but unable to find the words in English. He pointed at the house he came from, then at the group of children. It seemed he just knew the kids from the neighborhood and did not want any of them taken away.

"Thiiss kid," said Williams, pointing at the child, "threeww, rock, at me." Each word spoken came with its own visual translation. "I, am, going, to arrest, himmm." Williams's hands pointed at the child's hands, which he had restrained with plastic ties.

"No, no, mister," begged the man, understanding what Williams was saying. "Me, me," he said.

"You? You what?" asked Williams. "What are you gonna do?"

The older man's hands were raised to the level of his eyes, fingers spread apart and pointing upward, his mouth open but unable to speak. We couldn't understand what he was trying to say. The crowd was getting larger.

"No, fuck this!" said the exasperated PL. "We're leaving."

But before we could move off, the old man had walked up to the kid and delivered a powerful slap across his tear-streaked face. The child let out a short scream but did not say anything more.

"There you go, sergeant," said Rosado looking at Williams. "Let the old-timer take care of him; let the child go."

Williams thought about it for a moment. No one was laughing anymore. I thought, *Let him go, Williams, let the kid go.* I was all the way with Rosado but kept my mouth shut. The older man stared at Williams with a desperate expression on his face. The child was now crying quietly, not looking at either the older man or at Williams.

"No," was the final verdict.

"Man, that's really fucked up," Rosado muttered. No one else said a word.

The older man landed another hard slap on the child's head, and then a third, this time with his fist. But still Williams appeared unmoved.

"Man, Sergeant Williams, let him go man, let the kid go." Rosado seemed to speak the words more for himself than for the kid.

"No way," said the unwavering PL.

The old man now launched a flurry of kicks and slaps on the child, each one harder than the next. Even though the child screamed violently, he never looked up at his assailant, who seemed to be in more pain than the kid himself as he delivered the beating. The entire neighborhood had gathered by then, and stood in silence as they witnessed the pounding of the child. Even those in our squad who had laughed at Rosado were now quiet.

The kid was no longer crying, but the man was in tears when he tried to plead with our leader.

"Mister, please," he implored.

Williams thought for a moment.

"OK, cool," he finally replied. He took out a pocket knife and cut the kid's restraints. "You can have him."

We left the area and set up and ran a traffic control point for a while before returning to base. The incident was never spoken about again, but when I came to look back on it I remembered how my heart had cried out for me to take a stand alongside Rosado. Yet I had chosen to remain silent, to swallow my moral outrage and go with the crowd, leaving him to fight a battle he should never have had to fight alone. I comforted myself by recalling that, when we returned to patrol the same neighborhood a week later, not only did the children no longer throw rocks at us, they didn't even follow us. What Williams had done might well have saved some of those children from being killed for something as minor as throwing a rock at an infantry patrol.

The truth as I see it now is that in a war, the bad is often measured against what's even worse, and that, in turn, makes a lot of deplorable things seem permissible. When that happens, the imaginary line between right and wrong starts to vanish in a heavy fog, until it disappears completely and decisions are weighed on a scale of values that is profoundly corrupt. That day I was wrong not to listen to what my better judgment was yelling at me. By ignoring it, I failed not only my own principles but also the one person who was taking a stand for what was right and decent.

SEVEN

Toward mid-June 2003, some four weeks after Charlie Company started to conduct operations in ar Ramadi, second platoon was tasked with supporting an engineer unit from the Third ACR during Operation Rifle-Scorpion. The purpose of this absurdly named operation was to give Iraqis the opportunity to disarm by showing up at U.S. Army collection points, where they would be paid in U.S. dollars for their weapons. Rifle-Scorpion was also to include a number of raids by infantry and engineer units on suspected arms depots and insurgent safe houses throughout the city. An engineer troop, or platoon, from the Third ACR would move to the Eagle's Nest to provide Charlie Company with assistance during the operation, which had an expected duration of two weeks. And second platoon, in turn, had to move to a Third ACR for the same two weeks.

At first the prospect of joining this unit seemed promising. Third ACR enjoyed the benefits accorded most full-time soldiers in Iraq, including air-conditioned rooms, trips to Baghdad for USO concerts, and easier access to military stores. But most important, I thought, working with the Third ACR provided the protection of armored vehicles while conducting patrols with the engineers. Our expectations were soon disappointed: the cooled rooms were all already taken, the USO trips and store visits were only for Third ACR people, and, though we sometimes went out on patrols in the armored vehicles, once we arrived at our destination we had to get off and patrol on foot. We had to carry out precisely the same duties we'd had at the Eagle's Nest, but now we were also added to the guard roster to protect the engineer base, all on top of whatever raids we had to go out on with the Third ACR.

We were also responsible for guarding a local bank. For that mission we split the squad in two, with one half taking the day shift, protecting the cashiers and manager when the bank was open, and the other providing cover for the Iraqi police officers who guarded the place at night. I attached myself to Bravo team and we took the night shift. The police there did not wear uniforms and seemed more like a group of friends hanging out than a police force. As soon as we arrived at the bank for the first time, one day in the late afternoon, the person in charge of the Iraqi personnel went to the kitchen to get a large container full of food, a mixture of eggs with tomatoes and a number of spices that I did not even try to identify. The food, which was eaten with pieces of hot, flat bread that came wrapped in white cloth, was absolutely delicious. The feast concluded with sweet black tea and cigarettes.

The willingness of the police officers to share their food with us was greatly appreciated but did not come as a surprise. I had already, on several occasions, been acquainted with the exquisite hospitality of the Iraqis, which I came to understand was a central part of Arab culture, and was extended even to us occupiers.

My first experience with Arab kindness had occurred in Jordan when soldiers from the Jordanian army would show up at our post every night to share their tea and engage us in long conversations about our respective cultures. We talked in the warmth of a bonfire they would build to keep us warm during the brutally cold nights of the Amman winter. I remember with amazement how they lifted their ancient kettle, one that looked like something from biblical times, in and out of the flames using only their bare hands.

Most of the Jordanian lieutenants spoke English, which they'd learned at college and in cross training with British and U.S. Special Operation units. They appeared unconcerned about the morality of the United States invading their neighbor Iraq. Their only loyalty seemed to be reserved exclusively for their king, whom they appeared to love and fear at the same time.

On some occasions, however, I wasn't sure how much of the generosity being extended to us was genuine and how much of it was people trying to secure alliances. There were times when the hospitality seemed to extend beyond the bounds of simple kindness. For instance, on one occasion, when we were searching a large house in one of ar Ramadi's wealthiest neighborhoods, the owner offered to treat my entire platoon to dinner and asked us if we would like to move in with his family. We regularly heard about similar invitations being made to others in our battalion. Once we even heard that a squad from Alpha Company had accepted such an offer, taking up residence for a week in a fabulous mansion.

The friendliness of Iraqis brought me close to one man in particular, the manager of a propane station just west of our base, which the different company squads took turns guarding twenty-four hours a day. Guarding the station was a desired task for many soldiers of my unit because the employees there could help us get food, drinks, and ice from the city stores. Our squad even bought a TV set there. We could also use a satellite phone to call the States for two dollars a minute.

It was there that I became addicted to *tepsi*, an Iraqi stew made with eggplant and tomatoes, which was exquisite with rice or bread and perfect for a vegetarian like me. Other favorites among the troops were the shish kebabs and the baked chicken, eaten with flat bread and washed down with soda, or even beer—all of which could be bought from the station's employees.

But what I enjoyed most at the station was the companionship of its manager, whose name was Mohammed. A tall bearded man with light-colored skin, Mohammed had learned English at the university, where he had studied geology; we talked regularly and at length. Once we discussed the Holy Koran, a book of which I was completely ignorant. Mohammed explained to me that reading the sacred scripture was open to non-Muslims as long as they were clean when they read it.

"You really should take a shower before touching the Holy Koran," he told me. "But just wash your hands, and that should be enough for now, given the circumstances."

"Is it not *haram* for you to share the Koran with a Christian?" I asked him, using the Arabic word for sin.

"It would be *haram* if I didn't share it with you," he answered with a kind and honest smile. "You see, we as Muslims have a duty to spread the Holy Scripture. Whenever the opportunity presents itself, a good Muslim should always share the word; otherwise he is not doing his duty as a Muslim. As long as the people are willing to listen, a Muslim should always be willing to speak."

With that dialogue started a relationship I cherish to this day, although I have now lost touch with Mohammed. Many things that I learned from our conversations at the propane station have stayed with me. It was there that I discovered that Muslims have a deep respect for Jesus, not as the Messiah, but certainly as a valued prophet. The Virgin Mary is not only esteemed but also considered a good example of behavior and of devotion to God for Muslim women to emulate.

Mohammed was a Sunni Muslim who had worked for the Ba'ath party during Saddam's regime.

"I never much agreed with Saddam," he explained one day while we were drinking tea in his office. "But I didn't have much of a choice, especially as a geologist; I had to work for the government."

Although much of the food in ar Ramadi was cooked using wood, gas stoves were also commonplace. That meant many Ramadis had to go to Mohammed's station to get their propane. One day an elderly Shiite Muslim and his son showed up at the station to buy their gas. They were old friends of Mohammed, who did not miss the opportunity to introduce us.

"He wants to know why Americans treat Iraqis like dogs," asked Mohammed, translating for the old man.

"We don't mean to treat Iraqis like dogs," I responded. "But sometimes, when we're attacked, we have to respond, and that's when things happen."

I wasn't sure I believed my own words. Deep inside I probably didn't, but for some reason I felt like I had to defend the purpose of our presence there. The old man wasn't buying it, and he seemed pretty upset. His son, a man in his late thirties or early forties, stood with his arms crossed behind the couch where his father sat, staring at me with a serious look on his face. I glanced around the room and saw that everyone there was staring at me. Though I had taken off my helmet, I was still wearing all my gear, and I had a cup of tea in one hand and my rifle in the other. The grenades on my vest and belt made it hard for me to get comfortable. I felt as if I was being interrogated by a citizens' tribunal. Yet at no time during the whole conversation did I feel unsafe or threatened, only ashamed.

"He wants to tell you something that happened to him

just last week," said Mohammed, as he and I both watched the old man lift up his robe to uncover a huge bruise he had on his left knee.

"What happened to him?" I asked.

"He says a group of men dropped into his property from helicopters," Mohammed translated. "They held everyone in the house at gunpoint until they left, taking him away to some U.S. Army base. He injured his knee when they threw him into the helicopter."

I noticed that there was a cane leaning up against the couch the man was sitting on. Every one else present remained silent as the old man spoke in Arabic, now and then pointing at his knee, and at his son, who still stood behind him but who let his father do all the talking.

"They interrogated him for a few days, until they finally let him go. The soldiers were from the U.S. Special Forces. They thought he was some insurgent leader," Mohammed continued. I wondered how they knew the soldiers were from the Special Forces. "They finally admitted their mistake and took him back to his home, but they never paid for any of the damage they did to the house."

The old man seemed really upset, and with reason, but part of me couldn't help thinking there must have been some justification for the soldiers' actions. And they had apologized and even taken the old man back to his family. As things looked to me then, it didn't seem unreasonable.

"Now it hurts when he walks" said Mohammed, looking at the cane.

"I'm really sorry that happened," I said, switching my attention between Mohammed and his Shiite friend. "We don't really want to be here."

"Oh, I know, I know," said Mohammed. "He is not upset with you, but he wants the American army to leave Iraq."

The conversation continued in that fashion, with complaints about U.S. brutality following rapidly, one after the next, in a way that made the argument that it was all an "unfortunate and isolated mistake" not only hard for them to accept but for me to use. These were educated men, especially the old man with the banged knee, who seemed to command respect even among the Sunnis, a majority of those present. It occurred to me that the deference shown to him stemmed not just from his wisdom and advanced years but also because he was perhaps some kind of religious eminence.

I felt as though I was present at a tribunal judging the American occupation, with me cast in the dual role of defense counsel and accused, and the elderly Shiite speaking on behalf of the entire Iraqi people. I didn't feel qualified to match my formidable opponent.

In spite of his anger about the occupation, the old Shiite did not descend to personal attacks on me, engaging instead in a dignified and elegant dialogue about Iraq's right to self-determination. Though he still seemed upset, he was very cordial to me as he left. Mohammed and I continued talking about Iraq and the U.S. occupation. At one point, pressed by Mohammed's searching questions and having run out of other answers, I suggested to Mohammed that we were in Iraq to bring freedom to the country and its people.

"Freedom?" Mohammed looked at me, incredulous.

"Yes," I insisted with a straight face, not even believing my own words.

"But you said that you don't want to be here," pressed Mohammed, also with a straight face.

"I don't," I continued.

"And you said that your contract with the army was over," continued my friend, reminding me of something I had told him in the past.

"Yes, I said that," I admitted.

"Then why are you here?"

"Because the army can keep you in after the end of your contract," I explained, sensing where he was going with his questions. "At least if there is a war they can."

"Against your will?" he asked with his eyebrows raised.

"Yes," I said, quietly.

"So how can you bring freedom to us, when you don't have freedom for yourselves?"

I was unable to answer that question, but I remember thinking that Mohammed just didn't know how armies worked, even though I was aware he had been conscripted into the Iraqi army in his youth. Besides, neither freedom nor its absence had anything to do with my participation in a war that I had opposed from the outset. My misfortune was tied to a decision I had made at age nineteen when I signed a military contract and forfeited most of my rights. From that point on I had to push aside all other considerations—political, moral, and spiritual— in pursuit of whatever mission I was ordered to undertake. No, I kept telling myself, freedom had nothing to do with it.

But deep inside I felt differently. I knew that, in the end, no one could force me to do anything I didn't want to do. I knew I could say no to keeping prisoners on sleep deprivation, and to blocking ambulances on their way to the hospital. I could say no to senseless missions that put the lives of both soldiers and innocent civilians in unnecessary danger. I could assert my freedom and say no. The problem was that everyone else was doing what they were told, and the easiest thing was to keep my mouth shut and think that Mohammed just didn't understand. I hadn't just lost the freedom to think for myself as an individual with moral and spiritual values, independent from the military; I had also lost the freedom to accept the fact that I wasn't free.

The policemen at the bank we were guarding were less cultured and educated than Mohammed, and rarely challenged my views in any way. But they were still curious to know about the United States and about life in the U.S. military. I remember Rosado at one point showing the Iraqi police officers how to assemble and disassemble an M-16 rifle. They, in turn, showed him the same procedure with their AK-47s, a far easier weapon to operate. They even showed Rosado a video of Saddam Hussein giving a speech from the second-floor balcony of the Mayor's Cell.

I also remember being captivated by the beauty of one of the bank's female cashiers, even though the only thing I could see was her face. The rest had to be suggested by what few lines her green and black dress allowed my fantasy to work with. Her very intense eyes seemed blue under the dim light over her desk, but they could have been gray. Those enchanting eyes, unaware of my gaze and of their own magic, had me under a spell that for the first time made me wonder what it would be like to move to Iraq and fully embrace the culture. Marriages, it seemed, were not the product of what in Western cultures is called love. My thought was that I could go to that young woman's family and ask if I could marry her; love would be worked on after the wedding. I told myself I could easily love those intense eyes, that beautiful smile that I could only see from a distance, and the mystery of that body that I could not cease to dream about.

I knew nothing of the woman, but this seemed normal for her culture. Men and women don't date or have sex before they get married. Of course I would have to be a Muslim in order to have a chance with her family, but wasn't our God the same God? The God of Abraham? I was going crazy and I had to stop looking at her. I had been in Iraq too long. But those eyes! And why wasn't she wearing a veil? Maybe she was married already. It was crazy to think I could marry a woman I did not know, much less love her. But the possibility of it filled my heart with excitement and passion.

Whenever the bank mission was over, we would go back to the engineers' compound, where life was particularly tedious. Whenever we went out on joint missions with the engineers, we did most of the work. We were the foot soldiers and they the mounted cavalry, so they stayed in their armored vehicles and pulled security with their big guns while we stormed through buildings, breaking down doors with sledgehammers and crowbars, and rushing into dark rooms, never knowing what to expect.

We had been told that at the end of the two weeks of Operation Rifle-Scorpion, authority would start to be transferred to the Iraqi police. We would have to leave our base only if they were attacked. Meanwhile we would be able to prepare for redeployment back to the States. We'd heard these promises of a return home before. Ever since our arrival, dates for redeployment had been given out regularly, only to be postponed again and again. The difference this time was that our executive officer had confirmed the news, telling us that we were waiting for trucks so we could leave in a big convoy via Kuwait. At one point, Sergeant Williams even ordered the squads to pack some of their gear in the platoon boxes so they could be put in the supply area ready for shipping. Our hopes ran high until the operation ended and there was no dependable police force to transfer authority to. In the end it was back to business as usual, but this time the disappointment was particularly bitter.

At the end of Operation Rifle-Scorpion the weapons that people returned were few and old, and the three major raids we conducted jointly with the engineers didn't turn up any hardcore insurgents or weapons. Judging by the intensity and frequency of the attacks, the insurgency had gotten stronger and more sophisticated.

While we were staying with the engineers, third platoon was ambushed at a traffic control point. But this time the insurgents attacked simultaneously from three separate angles, which was a new development. Although there were no reported injuries on either side, the three-flank ambush on third platoon showed that attacks had gotten quite complex since we arrived in ar Ramadi, and prompted our leadership to issue the order that we should not stay in one place for more than thirty minutes, thus denying the enemy the time to prepare a complex assault. The order made sense and should have been issued earlier; however, the real issue was not whether we had the knowledge to better protect ourselves, but whether our leaders had any interest in using such knowledge.

Shortly after returning to base, we received ceramic plates for our body armor. This was the first time in Iraq that we were properly protected. Up until then we'd been wearing old flak vests from the Vietnam era that could not stop a bullet even if the enemy threw it at us by hand. All they did was weigh us down without providing any protection.

We were going out on fewer missions, for shorter lengths of time, and generally in trucks rather than on foot because, as we headed toward June, the heat was becoming insufferable. Two U.S. soldiers had died as a result of heatstroke. One had been on a mission driving a truck when, as they said, "his brain fried"; the other had been patrolling the streets under the merciless sun when he passed out and never recovered consciousness. An added reason for the less strenuous patrols was that our water supply was low, and the ratio per soldier had been restricted to two liters a day.

Patrols these days generally consisted of driving around for an hour or so, setting up a traffic control point for about thirty minutes, and then going back to the base for a break. We would do this once each day and then again at night. In addition, every morning we would patrol a stretch of Highway 10 to make sure there were no IEDs waiting to blow up our vehicles. It was one of those circular missions so typical of our deployment, where we were running patrols solely to make sure that the same patrols were not blown up. But no one thought to question it, or at least not openly.

Once Highway 10 was cleared, we would clear the Y intersection, where the road going north split east and west along the Euphrates. This area witnessed many bloody attacks on our different units and became known as Ambush Alley. These daily missions that followed the same procedure were part of the mandatory routine that started the patrols every single day. And even though platoon leaders had some discretion in how to conduct their missions, there were only so many variations that could be implemented in a mission carried out at the same time and place every single time. Luckily we did all our clearing on foot, since the insurgents who planted IEDs seemed to be more interested in blowing up vehicles than troops on the ground. And yet every time we were done clearing Highway 10 and the Y intersection, I would go back to base and thank God for letting me live another day.

Now that people were realizing bullets fly two ways in war, the gung-ho attitudes that had predominated when we were back in Jordan were seldom heard. Pretty much everyone wanted to go home. This new attitude was evidenced by rumors in the unit about how this politician or that officer was trying his best to get us out of Iraq. We called such rumors "cheese," so if anyone had supposed news regarding our departure from Iraq they would announce it by saying: "Guess what the latest cheese is?" This would generally be followed by a story about how some senator back home had written a letter to the Pentagon questioning why we'd been in Iraq for so long, and how come this, and how come that. It never amounted to anything except empty rumor.

Perhaps because of my constant proximity to death, and after losing hope that someone at home would get us out of the war,

I started commending my body and soul to God every day. Prior to going to Iraq, I had never really prayed and my faith had mostly stayed on the surface. Being in a combat environment changed things; before and after every mission, and before going to sleep, I would always say a little prayer. At first it was a simple request for God to let me see my daughter, Samantha, one more time. As time went by, however, I widened my prayers to ask for the safety and well being of the soldiers in my unit, and then I started praying for all the soldiers in Iraq and their families. Before long I was praying for the families of the Iraqis we killed during our missions. And then one day I realized I was even praying for our enemies, and for an end to violence in Iraq, and then for an end to all war.

Though I had attended Catholic schools for most of my life, and had always considered myself a Catholic, I had never been baptized. One day I heard that the battalion chaplain was offering to baptize soldiers at the palace, and even though I tried not to leave my base unless absolutely necessary, that day I made an exception and decided to make the trip with some other guys from my unit, most of whom had already been baptized but wanted to renew their vows.

After a short but tense ride through the city, we got off the trucks and went to meet the chaplain. We said a little prayer, changed into army-issued shorts and T-shirts, and walked through the backyard of the largely destroyed presidential palace. When we got to the edge of the yard we strolled along a sand-colored stone walk by the river to an area with steps that led into the water. One by one we were briefly submerged by the chaplain. That's how, at age twenty-seven, I came to be baptized in the waters of the biblical Euphrates.

Becoming closer to God brought me a renewed sense of connection to my fellow human beings, but it didn't mean I was any less able to squeeze the trigger of my rifle if I felt my life or that of those around me was being threatened. At times of extreme danger it was as if I went into a trance in which the only thing that mattered was survival, and everything else was erased from my conscience.

Attacks from the insurgency had become so intense and frequent in ar Ramadi that we became suspicious of any lapses in violence, which we took as a portent that something big was in the planning. Things got to the point where I could no longer relax unless I was out on a mission. Back at base I constantly anticipated disaster or even death, and every time I heard an explosion I was overcome by two fears: that our platoon would be called on to respond to whatever was happening or that someone I knew had just been blown to pieces. For me the most stressful moments were just before we left the base to go out on patrol. I would sit in the back of the truck, or sometimes up front next to the driver, and my mind would run wild with the horrors and hallucinations of painful death in combat.

"Don't worry so much, man," Funez would say. It seemed he had the ability to read the fears and worries on my face, perhaps because he felt them too. "We're gonna be fine."

"I know," I would say, but my stress level would not drop until we drove out of the base through the gate and locked and loaded our rifles.

Once we were actually out on patrol things got better and I regained some sense that I was in control. I could see where my squad was and if they were facing out and scanning the area with their eyes and weapons. I could see the roads and decide what routes to follow and which places to avoid. I sometimes even relaxed sufficiently to enjoy the scenery. I enjoyed seeing the people in the streets and would concentrate on trying to read the expressions on their faces. They rarely looked pleased to see us, which was understandable because, as the insurgency mounted, we adopted a number of tactics designed to minimize risk of attack to ourselves but that took

little heed of the needs and comforts of the Iraqis. For instance, we would drive on the wrong side of the highway to
reduce the risk of being hit by an IED. This forced oncoming
vehicles to move to one side of the road, and considerably
slowed down the flow of traffic. In order to avoid being held
up in traffic jams, where someone could roll a grenade under
our trucks, we would simply drive up on the sidewalks, running over garbage cans and even hitting civilian vehicles to
push them out of the way. Many of the soldiers would laugh
and shriek at these tactics, but Ramadis trying to go about
their daily business didn't see the funny side of it at all, and as
the occupation dragged on, so did their unhappiness at our
increasingly tangible presence. Even the children, who had
once run alongside our trucks, shouting and waving cheerfully, now just watched us in resentful silence. Some would
even throw their arms up in the air as a sign that they wanted
us out. We would wave back, attempting to look cheerful, or
perhaps shrug our shoulders as if to say "What else can we
do?" Every now and then someone would get exasperated
and, pointing his rifle at them, would yell, "Fuck you, kid!"

But not everyone expressed anger at us as we conducted
patrols. One very hot day, while we were feeling the strain of
being stuck in traffic in the heart of the city, a little girl appeared from between the buildings at the side of the street.
She looked up at us with an enchanting smile and several soldiers around me risked sliding a hand from their weapons to
dig out cameras and take pictures of the child. The dress she
wore, though it was old and dirty, and a bit small for her,
made her look like a little princess. She could not have been
more than six years of age but she seemed to be all alone as
she wandered the streets barefooted. In the middle of all the
violence and sadness of the occupation, seeing this little girl,
in all her innocence and beauty, renewed my sense of hope for
humanity.

Unfortunately for us, this kind of incident was a rarity. Indeed, disdain and bitterness against the U.S. Army were generally on the increase. And if the occupation itself wasn't enough, one could always rely on the ineptitude of our leadership to create circumstances that stoked people's resentment of our presence. One particular example of such stupidity remains clear in my memory.

It all began with the routine procedure of setting up a traffic control point at the end of a short patrol. Sergeant Williams decided to set the TCP next to the city's biggest mosque, a spectacular temple that rose high above the humble houses of the neighborhood it was in, between our base and downtown ar Ramadi. Though it wasn't the first time, setting up a TCP by a mosque was not something we were supposed to do. It infuriated the local people, who regarded it as insulting to their religion. This particular operation had a high profile because Sergeant Williams had insisted on bringing in the mortars with our platoon, along with an extra truck, who would be used to detain and guard people. As a result, the TCP extended the full length of the mosque.

It was early on a lively evening and soon enough there were two long lines of vehicles waiting to go through the TCP in order to be searched. Unlike the way we had run this type of mission in the past, our platoon leader decided this time to keep drivers and passengers within our perimeter after searching their vehicles, even if we found nothing that warranted their detention. A team of soldiers was detailed to park the vehicles of the people we detained, so we ended up running what looked like a valet parking service. Some thirty minutes into the operation, we had already searched a large number of vehicles that were now parked far from our perimeter, and were guarding a substantial crowd of people.

I began to worry about the overall situation, which had a number of negative aspects. We had stayed in one place for far too long; we were holding a large number of people, putting them in danger by their proximity to us; we were next to ar Ramadi's biggest mosque; and we were occupying an entire street. It all seemed to be designed to provoke a confrontation. When I finally raised my concerns with Sergeant Demarest, he replied:

"Relax, Mejía; they're never going to attack us by a mosque."

"We've already been here for over an hour," I responded. "I think now it's just a matter of how much more time we give them to continue to prep—"

"You worry too much, Mejía," Demarest interrupted me with a smile.

A group of newly graduated Iraqi police officers arrived at that moment in a patrol car. Their AK-47 rifles and the dark green of their uniforms made them look more like army than police. They found a spot near the group of detainees, who were chatting with one another, some smoking, some laughing and joking, others evidently very upset by the situation.

My job that night was to patrol the TCP to check on the members of my squad, who were all spread evenly along the trucks, providing vehicle security. As I walked up and down the street I could sense that the mood of the area was changing dramatically. The few people who had been hanging around in a park across the street from the mosque got up and left. Vehicles stopped circulating in the nearby streets, and the small commercial establishments that were open closed down and turned off their lights. From the rooftop of a nearby three-story building, a man had been observing us from the instant we arrived, but he too was now gone.

After an hour and a half of TCP, Williams had let the detainees go home, but instead of wrapping up the mission he went back to detaining more people, for no apparent reason. Specialist Simpson, who was one of the mortars, was guarding this new group, his rifle pointing at them as they sat on the sidewalk. We were both standing next to the sidewalk, between two of our trucks, when the sound of a machine gun shattered the silence of the moment.

What I saw next was something that even today still amazes me. A vehicle rolled slowly down the street and stopped near where Simpson and I were standing. The vehicle was surrounded by a ghostly aura of light, the product of the sparks that covered the vehicle's surface as a fusillade of bullets hit it. To say that my platoon had lit up that car was literally true. The vehicle was glowing from the rounds hitting it.

Simpson and I looked at each other for a split instant as the driver of the vehicle twitched with every bullet that pierced his flesh. The thought occurred to me that there might be someone else hiding inside the car, waiting for the right moment to throw a grenade. Or maybe the entire vehicle was a car bomb. None of it really mattered. Whatever had prompted the soldiers in my platoon to shoot at that man could be determined later; for the time being he was guilty by the simple fact that they were shooting at him.

It wasn't going to make any difference to the driver of the vehicle, who was already well and truly dead, but I still raised my rifle and opened fire at him. It was an automatic reaction, almost robotic, like a programmed response that involved no human emotions or thinking. The rifle moved up, the finger around the trigger began to squeeze, there was a blank stare in my eyes.

When the firing subsided I instinctively moved behind one of the trucks, perhaps seeking cover or more likely moving away from the sight of the man we had just killed, whose head hung from about a third of what used to be his neck. I then realized Mantilla was next to me, firing at the buildings across the street. I shouted at him,

"Mantilla, what the hell are you shooting at?"

"I don't know," he said with an absent voice and the same blank stare I'd had a moment before. "Over there," he went on. "Everyone is shooting at those buildings."

I looked in the direction he was facing and saw muzzles flashing with every bullet coming our way. It was only then that I realized we were under heavy attack. I pointed my weapon up and joined Mantilla in shooting back, but almost immediately the firing stopped. Thinking the firefight was over, I walked over to the beginning of our vehicle formation to look for Estime and Hodges, who had been attached to Williams for the mission, the first as a driver, the second as the vehicle's machine gunner. But when I got to their Humvee there was no sign of them.

My plan was to walk down the TCP line from front to back to make sure all the soldiers of my squad were well and accounted for. But that simple walk turned out to be more difficult than I'd anticipated. The last thing on my mind was that we were going to get attacked again. On every previous occasion that we had been attacked, the insurgents had used hit-and-run tactics, never sticking around for round two. Things would be a bit different this time.

While walking back down the line to look for the rest of my squad I saw that there was a crowd of soldiers tending to someone on the ground. It was Specialist Cardenas, a SAW gunner from second squad; he had been shot in the leg and they were moving him to safety so he could wait to be picked up by our company's medevac team.

I thought of helping to move Cardenas, but there were already four soldiers working at it, more than enough. I kept on walking, still fixed on finding each soldier in the squad as I walked down the line.

"Hey, Sergeant Mejía," said someone from the shadows. "Do you have a field dressing?"

It was Staff Sergeant Chuy, the mortar section's squad leader. He was treating an Iraqi who had been shot while waiting to be released after his vehicle was searched and cleared. I reached for the pouch where I kept my field dressing. We were not supposed to use our medical equipment on anyone other than ourselves, much less on a non-U.S. soldier, but it seemed that Chuy had already used his dressing on another Iraqi civilian casualty.

"What's wrong with him?" I asked, tossing Chuy the dressing.

"Stomach wound," he said while biting the plastic open.

The man seemed to be in a lot of pain but he was conscious and very much aware of his surroundings. He was talking to Chuy in Arabic and acknowledged my stare with a weak lift of his head. A few meters farther on I ran into Specialist Ibaugh.

"Hey—Sergeant Mejía!" he yelled. "Can you come over here? I can't get this piece of shit to work."

He was trying to get the AT-4 launcher to work. Such a weapon should only be used on light armored vehicles, not on people. But no one cared about such things in Iraq; if our unit was getting attacked, we returned fire with pretty much everything we had, and even when we were carrying less than what is considered full combat loads, we always had fire superiority over the enemy.

I tried to help Ibaugh with the AT-4 but to no avail; the launcher's sights were stuck and the trigger mechanism was malfunctioning. I told Ibaugh I would come back to help him later, after I had checked on everyone from the squad, and resumed my walk down the line.

"HEY!" yelled a voice. "HEY!"

I looked over my right shoulder and saw the man who was yelling in my direction. He was in the driver's seat of a small white station wagon, a Volkswagen Passat. Sitting next to him was an older man in what looked like a traditional white Shiite robe; his head was slightly tilted down and he seemed to be lost in his thoughts, staring at the floor of the vehicle. I could see another person in the backseat. He appeared to be a bit more aware of what was going on, but he wasn't saying a word to me or anybody else and just sat there as the vehicle's driver continued to try to get my attention.

I had recently read an intelligence report from one of the other units operating in the area that related how a soldier was shot in the face during a TCP mission. According to the report, the soldier approached a vehicle after an Iraqi man had asked for help, claiming that one of his passengers was seriously ill and needed to get to the hospital immediately. When the soldier turned his head away from the vehicle to talk to his superior, the person in the passenger's seat pulled out a gun and shot the soldier. At that moment a firefight started between the soldiers manning the traffic control point and people from two or three of the vehicles that had been waiting in line to get searched.

Now I found myself in a similar situation. My instinct at the time was to shoot this person who was calling my attention. *He wants to kill me*, was my first thought. I could no longer hear his voice, nor was I attempting to differentiate English from Arabic. I didn't care what he was saying to me. I could see that he was in distress, perhaps even great pain. But all I could hear in my head was my own voice . . . *He wants to kill me*. I raised my rifle slowly without getting too close to the vehicle. His calls continued, unintelligible, foreign, irrelevant.

Suddenly, another sound came to me, something more familiar. It was loud enough for me to hear, but not loud enough to make me react. At that moment, my only priority in life was life itself, my life. And staying alive required that I kill this man before he killed me. My eight years of infantry training always had a way of taking over in such situations and I was on automatic pilot. I looked through the sight of my M-16 with my left eye closed and my finger tightening on the trigger. Sensing the terrible danger of his situation, the man's cries became louder and more desperate but I felt no remorse, no sympathy, nothing. All the screaming would end in an instant.

"SERGEANT! SERGEANT! STOP! STOP! STOP!"

I raised my head from behind the sight and eased off on the trigger; my eyes never left the vehicle and my rifle kept pointing at it.

"They're wounded, sergeant, don't shoot them. The man is trying to tell you something."

I never knew who stopped me from killing those people. The voice was familiar because it spoke to me in English, and I have tried over and over without success to identify the person who brought me back to a state of human consciousness. Whoever it was, he saved more than the three men in that vehicle, because I know how hard it would have been for me to live with myself after killing three unarmed human beings, two of whom were wounded.

"Mister, mister," said the driver, relief spreading across his face. "Hospital, please."

"Two-six, this is two-one," I called to Williams on the radio. "I've got two wounded people in a vehicle. The driver is requesting to go to the hospital."

"Mister, mister," insisted the man, motioning his hands forward to indicate that he could drive to the hospital in his own vehicle. "Me, hospital. Mister, please, please."

"They can drive their own vehicle and seem to be requesting permission to leave, over."

"Negative, two-one," came Williams through the waves. "No one is allowed to leave the area until I say so. Have them get out of the vehicle."

"Mister, please, please."

"Roger," I said to two-six.

"Hospital, please, mister." The man's voice was desperate, but that night I was following orders.

"Get out of the car," I said to him in a firm voice, gesturing toward me to help him understand the order. But the man kept insisting. "Get out of the car," I said again, louder.

"Mister, please," he kept on and on and on. He could not understand. The person next to him was badly injured, I could see that now, and he had the means to take him to a hospital for treatment. The only obstacle was me, standing in front of him with a loaded weapon, telling him he couldn't go anywhere. "Please," he continued. "Please, please, mister, hospital."

"GET THE FUCK OUT OF THE CAR!" I yelled.

"Mister, please . . ."

"OUT, GET THE FUCK OUT." I started to raise my rifle again. "Get out," I said, lowering my voice and using my weapon instead to intimidate them.

Then it started all over again, this time with an explosion. I couldn't see the blast, but I felt the shock wave from what I later learned was a hand grenade. I started to move backward with my rifle raised, no longer aiming at the vehicle but at the building from which the attack was coming, the same building from which we'd been fired on before. Bullets were once more raining down on us, and once again we responded, this time using well-aimed high-explosive rounds fired from grenade launchers. The buildings lit up each time a grenade crashed through their windows. The targets were on the rooftops, but our proximity to the buildings made it virtually impossible to land rounds from grenade launchers there. Choosing the next best target, we opened up on the windows; if anyone was on those floors we certainly finished them off.

In the split instant it took me to move backward to cover, I was not able to identify any clear enemy positions, but once I got behind a truck I fired a few rounds toward one of the

rooftops. I simply fired in the general direction, mostly because firing was the thing to do at that moment. Someone else
was shooting next to me. It was Mantilla again.

"I fucking got shot!" he said to me, pointing at the lower
half of his vest where, sure enough, there was a bullet hole.
"The plate in my vest stopped it," he continued, referring to
the ceramic plates that we had just received.

"Did it hurt?" I asked, thinking how lucky he was to have
gotten shot that day and not two days before, when we didn't
have the new vests. An AK-47 bullet in the lower-left quad-
rant of his abdomen would have put him in serious trouble.

"No, I just felt a little tap."

The firing stopped for a second time. I saw that the man
who had asked to go to the hospital had gotten out of the car
and was sitting on the sidewalk with his two relatives. The
translator we traveled with that day was an Egyptian man who
looked a lot like the old cartoon character Mr. Magoo. He was
short, with a round face, and wore thick glasses that made his
eyes look huge. He later told us that the two older men in the
white Passat were the uncle and father of the driver. Seeing
that they were out of the vehicle and under cover behind one of
our trucks, I decided to resume my walk down the line.

There seemed to be wounded civilians everywhere I
looked. At the end of the TCP line were a couple of Iraqi police vehicles, which were being used by the policemen themselves to take cover from the attack. I was looking at these
patrol vehicles when I saw a man running toward me; it was
Sergeant Gallegos.

"Hey, Sergeant Mejía," he said, panting and sweating
profusely. "Perez and I are OK. We're up on ammo, and have
all of our sensitive items." He was doing his job as a team
leader by the numbers.

"Roger," I said. "Good job, Gallegos. Have you seen Funez
and Bien-Aime?"

"Yeah, they're at the end of the line," he gasped, still breathing heavily, "in the back of the last truck."

I continued my inspection, passing by another truck where I saw Specialist Perez, whose cover consisted mostly of a bunch of old flak vests that now lined the sides of our trucks. After receiving the new vests, our company decided to use the old ones to add some extra protection, though in truth they didn't add much. We also lined the floor with sand bags to absorb the blast of any road bombs.

"Hey, Mejía!" yelled a voice as soon as I passed the back of the truck Perez was in. "Come here and help me with this guy."

It was our platoon medic, one of the few privates who often called me just by my surname instead of addressing me as sergeant.

"What the fuck are you doing out in the open?" I asked, yelling.

"I'm trying to keep this guy alive," he said.

The medic's head was turned back toward me and he was sitting on the road facing the buildings from which the two previous attacks had come. Almost on his lap, unable to balance his own upper body in the seated position, was a wounded Iraqi civilian who looked more dead than alive.

"What's wrong with him?" I asked, getting nearer.

"Open chest wound." Then, "Talk to him, ask him what his name is," the medic continued. I momentarily thought he was addressing me but then I heard another voice right behind me.

"*Ishmak?*" It was Mr. Magoo, asking the man his name in Arabic. He received no answer.

"You definitely need to get behind cover," I said to the translator. "And you too, Sonnenschein," to the medic.

"Come on, stay with me," the medic continued to the wounded Iraqi. "We can do this, don't fucking die on me, guy."

"We gotta get behind cover," I insisted to Sonnenschein,

who appeared more concerned with the wounded man's life than his own.

The translator continued talking in Arabic to the man, who kept drifting in and out of consciousness, looking close to death. With every breath he took, air seemed to escape through several holes in his body.

"OK, let's fucking move him," I finally said to Sonnenschein. "And you," I pointed at the translator, "get behind that truck."

"OK, I got his arms," said Sonnenschein. "Grab his legs."

I slung my weapon on my right shoulder and grabbed the man's legs, but just as we started to move him, another attack began.

"Fucking hurry up, Sonnenschein, move your ass!"

"I'm moving, goddamn it," the medic yelled, crouching.

We finally got the civilian behind cover. Sonnenschein and Mr. Magoo stayed with him, trying to give the dying man some comfort. I stayed close by, positioning myself behind the truck's large tires and thinking it was probably best to stay put. There didn't seem much point in returning fire because I had little idea as to the direction I should shoot in. But heavy gunfire then broke out right next to me. It was the Iraqi police firing their AK-47s. They weren't aiming at anything in particular, simply shooting straight up in the air, above their own heads. It occurred to me that those rounds might fall back on us causing serious harm, but I said nothing.

Another loud cracking sound broke out, coming this time from the road between us and our attackers. I took a quick look and saw the first sergeant's Humvee, which had a fifty-caliber machine gun mounted on it, driving along shooting at anything that moved. At first they were firing at the wrong building, but after pretty much destroying it, they shifted their aim to the building that contained the actual targets, who soon stopped shooting.

I jumped up and dashed to the last truck in the TCP line, where I found Funez and Bien-Aime, lying on the truck's floor with the muzzles of their weapons facing through a line of old flak vests.

"Are you guys OK?" I asked Funez.

"Can you believe this motherfucker?" he answered angrily, pointing at Bien-Aime. "We're getting fucking shot at, and he starts yelling at me. I think he's fucking wounded and about to die so I stop shooting to ask him what the problem is. His fucking belt had tangled up and he wanted me to fix it."

Bien-Aime looked at me with a smile on his face. They were OK.

"You guys got all your shit?" I asked, inquiring about their sensitive items, which primarily meant night-vision goggles and weapons.

"Roger, sergeant," said Bien-Aime, still smiling. Funez nodded, still looking pissed off.

Moments later, the quick reaction force, which that night was third platoon, arrived at the scene. As they dismounted their vehicles, we got the order to load up. I went to find Gallegos to make sure he had heard the order. On my way back up the line I heard the voice of the young man whose father and uncle had been wounded.

"Mister," he said. "Please."

I looked down. He was still sitting on the sidewalk, and for the first time throughout the entire duration of the firefight, I felt sorry for him. I could tell his father was alive and conscious by the way he closed his eyelids tightly. The old man's chest was covered with blood, and he seemed to be in a great deal of pain but also in complete control of himself. His brother was wounded in his left arm, which he pressed tightly against the trunk of his body. His eyes were open but he refused to look at me. On his face was an expression that combined pain, anger, and deep pride.

"Please, mister," continued the young man, who must have been in his late twenties. He was unharmed but seemed to be in the worst emotional shape. "Please," he begged softly, almost in a whisper.

"Two-six, this is two-one. I still have these wounded people requesting to go to the hospital, over."

There was silence at the other end of the radio.

"Two-six, did you copy last?"

There were no tears running down the young man's face, but from his expression and tone of voice I could tell how upset he was. I looked over my right shoulder and saw the third platoon soldiers taking up defensive positions. Over my left shoulder I could see my own platoon loading up our trucks. Two-six was clearly occupied with something else.

"HEY!" I yelled at the couple of soldiers who were pulling vehicle security. "See these people here, they're good to go. Don't fucking shoot 'em."

"Roger, sergeant," said one of them.

"Go," I said to the man.

"Go?" he asked, moving his hands to make sure he knew what I was saying.

"Go," I said with one of my arms extended. "Take them to the hospital. Hospital, yes, take them."

He got up and helped his father walk toward their car. His uncle was weak at the knees but could walk on his own. Though I was as keen as anyone to get the hell out, I went over to their car with them. I guess I was afraid that they could get shot for leaving, or maybe I just felt guilty about the whole thing. Once they were all in I yelled again at the soldiers.

"Make a hole for this car, they're good to go."

Estime and Hodges were in the lead Humvee with Williams. Gallegos and Perez were in the same truck as me, Ibaugh was with Mantilla, and Bien-Aime and Funez were in the rear truck. Everyone in the squad was accounted for and almost everyone in the platoon had made it out unscathed. But as we moved back to base I think we all knew that the ambush marked a new level of intensity in the ar Ramadi resistance. Not only was it the fiercest and longest firefight we'd experienced to that point, but it demonstrated that the insurgency was capable of mounting attacks at very close range, and that they were willing to fight two, three, or even more rounds.

Later that night, when third platoon returned to base, we learned they had raided the buildings that the attacks had come from, but had found nothing—no dead or wounded, no weapons, not even an empty round casing. It was as if no one had ever been there.

The total unofficial casualty count from that day was seven dead civilians, all of whom had been trapped in the crossfire. The day after the firefight their blood still stained the street where it all happened. In the light of morning, a most gruesome leftover of the previous night's horror was revealed. The order had never been given to remove the vehicle that had started the firefight, the one with the dead man in it. The corpse, with its neck shot away, still sat there in the driver's seat as a reminder to all Iraqis that we were the ones in charge. I wondered which unlucky family would be called to that sorrowful sight, knowing that when they cried for their loved one who had been killed in the shadow of their city's proudest mosque, all of ar Ramadi would cry with them.

EIGHT

One might have thought that after the fiasco of the firefight at the mosque, those in charge would change the way we conducted our missions. But they didn't. We continued to stay longer than we should in a single place and made it easy for the enemy to predict our movements by following the same routes over and over. It was as if our leadership was deliberately trying to get us attacked.

As the days and weeks rolled by at the Eagle's Nest, a sense that time was trapped took hold in the hearts of most soldiers. Rumors that we were about to redeploy back to the States would continue to raise hopes in vain. Deadlines set for transferring power back to local Iraqi authorities and lowering our presence came and went, while all the time it was clear that we were actually adopting a far higher profile in the city. Meanwhile, local disdain for our presence fueled a resistance that was growing markedly.

We knew that back home, vigorous and repeated attempts were being made by our families to convince the commanding officers of the Florida National Guard to bring us back from Iraq. But they all proved fruitless. The guard force had been federalized and decisions could no longer be made at a state level.

As the prospect of going home became a flickering light in the Iraqi night, we settled unhappily into our three-phase rotation of patrols, QRF, and guard duty. There was no difference between weeks and weekends, no sense even of weeks or months, no vacations, no beginning or end to anything, just the odious three-day cycle, over and over.

At the platoon level we had a number of duties in addition to the rotation organized by the company. One such was cleaning out our improvised toilets, which were far from the luxurious chemical toilets that some active duty units used in their bases. We had to make do with metal barrels that were cut in half and had toilet seats mounted on top. When full, these had to be dragged out of the dirty trailer that served as our latrine. Fuel was then poured into them and they were set on fire. We had to stir the shit with long metal rods to make it burn properly, all the time trying not to breathe in the nauseous fumes that were given off. It took hours for the vile mess to be reduced to ashes.

Another responsibility was refueling the platoon's generator before it ran out of gas, which happened approximately every twelve hours. By this time in the occupation we had air-conditioning units in nearly every room, ceiling fans, and a freezer for each of the platoons, used mostly for cooling water before patrols. In addition, nearly every squad had its own TV set and DVD player, and some soldiers had bought computers, PlayStations, and Nintendo GameCubes on the Internet, which was available at the company's command post. So whenever power ran out, the squad in charge of refueling the generator was highly unpopular with the rest of the platoon.

We also had to provide personnel to work as radio-watch runners at the company's command post. The runners would deliver messages to people in the company whenever they couldn't be reached by radio. Although they were told otherwise, the runners used their post to gain late-night access to the Internet at the CP. Runners could also, on occasion, avoid going out on missions. These privileges made radio watch a favored task throughout the company. Soldiers with minor injuries were often given radio duty, and there were a number of people who always seemed to be posted to the radio room, much to the disdain of the rest of the company.

Although infrequent, sometimes these small tasks were all there was to do on nonpatrol days, enabling soldiers to relax and watch DVD movies and even take their chances with drinking under the cover of night. Alcoholic beverages were forbidden and impossible to find at U.S. Army stores, but soldiers always have a way of finding the good stuff, even in a combat environment. Most of the booze came from unauthorized detours during missions or from locals who sold liquor and other illegal goodies at the gates to the base. But the largest cache of booze our platoon ever got its hands on came from a most surprising source.

Our battalion commander, seeing that we had lost several vehicles to IEDs, ordered his company commanders to carry out their missions, however unconventionally, in ways that would avoid further destruction of equipment. One of the results of this directive was that we began to use the nationwide curfew to detain people driving their vehicles between 2300 and 0400 hours. After we arrested the drivers, we would choose whichever vehicles we liked, fuel them from confiscated jerry cans, and conduct undercover presence patrols in the impounded cars. Inside the trunk of one of the confiscated vehicles—an old blue Caprice, as I recall—we found a dozen cases of large dark beer cans, most of which we unofficially impounded. The next night, another platoon that decided to use the same car found the rest of the booze.

The insurgents' success rate with IEDs was increasing all the time as they improved their tactics. The first ambush my platoon encountered had failed because the resistance failed to slow down our lead vehicle in order to get the timing of the explosion precisely right, and many of the early attacks suffered similar problems. This lack of initial success had resulted in a certain overconfidence on the part of many soldiers who too easily dismissed the insurgents' skills, training, and capabilities. This underestimation of the enemy was reinforced by the discrimination and racism that drove the entire occupation. "Hajji cannot govern himself" led easily to "Hajji cannot hurt me."

Little did we know that we were not seeing the last throes of a postinvasion resistance, but rather the beginning of a widespread popular rebellion. Soon enough the insurgents got really organized, and their attacks were killing and wounding U.S. soldiers on a regular basis. The first successful IED attack we encountered in ar Ramadi took place in July 2003 on a busy road that was routinely used by military vehicles. It killed one Iraqi civilian and injured seven others, all of whom were traveling in the opposite direction of the U.S. convoy that was the intended target. Two soldiers from the Third ACR were also hit. One lost a leg in the blast, the other an eye and most of his vision. Their Humvee was damaged beyond repair. The commander of the unit involved, a colonel, decided it was time to retaliate and show the Iraqis "who was in charge."

We received orders to block all major city intersections during curfew hours. This mission came to be known as "Operation Shutdown." The thinking here was that the attackers were from outside the city and were traveling in and out to plant their bombs. But it was obvious to most of us that the insurgency did not need to import people from outside. The insurgents evidently knew the layout of the city and were able to escape into local people's homes without the alarm being raised. Everything pointed to the resistance being organized by locals. Indeed, the only way we could tell who was an insurgent and who was not was if we could find people with weapons in the immediate vicinity of an attack. But, of course, just about everyone had weapons, and those that used them against us at one moment could hide them the next and be standing there politely saluting us as we raced around looking for the perpetrators of the attack they had just mounted.

Perhaps the Third ACR commander's ineptitude in responding to the attacks had to do with the fact that very few high-ranking officers actually got out into the action, and lower-ranking officers were afraid to contradict them when they were wrong. The frustration that resulted from our inability to get back at those who were attacking us led to tactics that seemed designed simply to punish the local population that was supporting them. This became evident when we started blocking the roads during "Operation Shutdown."

The plan was for the operation to follow the same procedures for at least three consecutive nights. That was a big mistake from the outset because it gave away the element of surprise. We were to go out every night at the same hour and on the same route, to occupy the same positions for lengthy periods. The predictability of this pattern greatly increased the possibility of attacks with mortars and IEDs, especially as no reconnaissance patrols were sent out prior to the start of the mission. Because everyone in the battalion was involved in the operation, there could be no quick reaction force to effectively offer backup in the event of an attack. In short, we were exposing ourselves to great danger in order to block insurgents from entering a city they did not need to enter because they already lived in it.

Everyone in my unit, myself included, grumbled about the idiocy of the way we were to carry out the mission, which

clearly disregarded both our infantry training and our hard-
won combat experience. But no one dared say a word to our
leadership.

On the first night of the operation, the platoons assembled
at the gate of the Eagle's Nest at around 2230 hours. Each platoon had two old unarmored trucks, plus a Humvee, also unarmored, for the platoon leader, his radio operator, and a small
security element. Third platoon was the first to go out, as it
was responsible for blocking the road right outside the base.
First platoon followed, setting off to block a dark rural intersection by the Euphrates River some three miles away. My
platoon left last, heading toward a junction where five roads
converged, midway between first and third platoons.

Besides some distant explosions that lit up far away
patches of the night sky, and a few rounds fired now and
then, the first night of Operation Shutdown passed unevent-
fully. We parked our trucks across the road and posted gunners on top of them to provide suppressive fire for the soldiers
on the ground. We then placed strands of concertina wire
about fifty meters in front of our position and fastened chemical light sticks to them so that we could be clearly seen by oncoming traffic. We also placed orange traffic cones in front of
the wire as well as large signs in both Arabic and English
telling people the road was blocked during curfew hours.
And we had Iraqi cops who could yell at drivers to turn
around.

We stayed out at the blocking positions until six in the
morning, an extra two hours after the curfew. That meant going out on morning patrol without any sleep at all, but no one
really complained; we were all pretty much used to performing our duties on very little sleep and to moving from one mission to another with no rest.

"It sucks," Staff Sergeant Adams from first platoon muttered to me shortly after we returned from the first night of the operation. "But we've just gotta do it."

We were talking inside the latrine, which was baking hot as its metal walls absorbed the rays of the merciless late morning sun.

"We got patrols now," he continued, with a small box of baby wipes in his right hand. "You probably know how tired our guys are. I mean, you guys are tired as well, but that's what they want us to do, so that's what we'll do."

"Yeah," I said. "Hey, my mother tells me your wife is doing a really good job at keeping our families informed about what's going on here."

"That's right," he answered. "A group of wives, including the first sergeant's wife, are doing a good job with the family support group."

"Well, thank your wife for me whenever you talk to her. Tell her she's doing a wonderful job."

"I sure will."

My mother had told me that Adams's wife was one of the main organizers of Charlie Company's family support group. She had neglected to tell me, however, that serious political differences were beginning to create problems between her and the other military families in the company. A fledgling movement had emerged among the relatives to demand our return home. The arguments they used were that we had been deployed too long, and outside our normal duties as National Guardsmen, which were primarily to provide disaster relief at the state level. My mother made the same arguments, of course, but she added to them a condemnation of the war as imperialist and illegal and the demand for the return of all U.S. troops, not just the Florida Guard. Most of the other families, including those of Sergeant Adams and the first sergeant, were staunch supporters of the war.

I finished smoking my cigarette, cleaned the sweat off my forehead with a baby wipe, and left the sizzling latrine for my platoon area. We were on QRF duty that day and waiting to see if we were to be called out to support the patrols.

We didn't have to wait long. We were watching a movie on Hodge's portable DVD player, which had been hooked up to the TV set our squad had bought at the propane station. *Black Hawk Down* was about halfway through when we got the order to gear up. The report coming in was that first platoon was taking enemy fire from a large group of people and vehicles in downtown ar Ramadi. This was bad news because the fiercest resistance until then had been from hit-and-run attacks. Now, apparently, a large group of attackers, including several vehicles, was firing at an entire infantry platoon from out in the open. The insurgency was evidently escalating.

My heart was racing as I climbed up on to our truck. The rest of the squad had already mounted and were pointing their weapons out, waiting to lock and load before going through the exit control point, or ECP, which is just a fancy term for the word "gate." Milligan was up front in the cab next to the driver. I had found a place at the back by the tailgate. I was about to light up a smoke when the first sergeant showed up, a big smile on his face.

"Stand down, second, stand down. It was a false alarm."

"What's going on, first sergeant?" asked someone.

"First platoon is NOT under attack," he said, smiling. "They thought they were under attack by a big crowd, but it was just a funeral."

It is the custom in ar Ramadi, as it perhaps is in most of Iraq, to fire weapons during funerals, weddings, and other social events. It was an activity that had almost translated into tragedy. Fortunately, first platoon had realized what was happening before opening fire. At the news of their mistake, uncontrollable laughter broke the tension that had plagued the air just moments before.

"Hey, first sergeant!" somebody yelled from one of the other trucks.

"What's up?"

"What's the matter, first platoon can't get a kill so they're going after dead people?" Everyone laughed again.

"Are they that fucking desperate?" asked another.

We all got out of the vehicles and went back to our rooms, lighting cigarettes before restarting the movie. By the time first platoon returned from patrols everyone in Charlie Company had heard about the funeral. A clown's welcome was their due, and they received it cheerfully, with smiles and deep bows.

To everyone's surprise, the second night of the operation went peacefully enough, the only remarkable thing being that we denied ambulances passage to ar Ramadi's main hospital, or to any hospital, as the entire city had been sealed off by our battalion. The Iraqi cops standing guard with us could not understand it. We explained to them that according to our reports, ambulances were being regularly used to transport explosives and carry out attacks against coalition forces, and that we couldn't take any chances. All vehicles had to be turned back or be fired upon.

This no-risk policy made perfect sense to me at the time. When I was approached by an Iraqi policeman who wanted to allow through an ambulance taking a pregnant woman to the hospital, I didn't even have to ask my platoon sergeant for advice.

"No!" I yelled to the cop.

"But mister, child, please."

"No, I already said no."

"But, mister, look." He wanted me to understand what was happening.

"I know, child, yes." I moved my hand in front of me forming the curve of an imaginary belly to show him I knew the woman was pregnant, even though I had not seen her.

"Hospital," he said as he started walking back to the ambulance, perhaps thinking I meant, "Yes, they may pass."

"NO!" I yelled at him. "I know the fucking woman is pregnant."

The Iraqi policeman waved at the paramedic, who stood outside the vehicle the entire time, to start moving our way as he kept walking toward them. The paramedic got back inside the cabin and started the engine. I raised my rifle and pointed right at the ambulance, ready to shoot if it moved an inch closer. The cop realized I was about to shoot and got between the ambulance and my rifle.

"No, no, no, no," he said, his arms extended, the palms of his hands motioning "No, don't shoot, please."

He yelled a few words at the driver and sent him on his way to who knows where before joining us back at the blocking point. I felt terrible, but I couldn't shake off the mental image of an ambulance blowing up in the middle of our blocking position. Part of me wanted to inspect the vehicle to make sure it did not contain explosives, but I was afraid of even that. What if, knowing they couldn't kill half the platoon, they decided to kill just me? Besides, I was a squad leader and the proper thing would be to ask one of my teams to carry out the inspection, and I didn't want them to be exposed to that risk. And if we let the ambulance through we would have to radio the other blocking points to let them know it was on its way and they would know we broke procedure, and that we were weak. This was all under the assumption that Demarest would allow it, which was unlikely. I wondered what would happen to the pregnant woman, if there was one. Where would she go to have her baby? The question kept returning, but so did the image of the ambulance blowing up. I was deeply conflicted, but I was alive and that was enough for the time being.

The next morning we were out on patrol, happy to keep a low profile and certainly not about to go arresting people without good reason. Demarest had taken over the platoon while Williams and a couple of other soldiers who were police officers back in the United States were at one of the palaces training young Iraqis to become cops. Demarest encouraged a sense of basic respect toward the Iraqi people we interacted with. We basically did our job and moved out. That's the way Demarest liked doing things, and I was all for it.

The patrol day was going fast and without any fuss when, in one of the neighborhoods between our base and downtown ar Ramadi, we saw a couple of youngsters take off running upon seeing us. We got down from the trucks and gave chase, but it soon became clear we couldn't catch them. As was often the case, we decided to search a couple of nearby homes. The procedure was always the same: a team would stay outside securing all entry and exit points of the house, another team would go in and set up internal security, and maybe two soldiers would search every corner of the house.

Even some of the humblest of dwellings in ar Ramadi had two or three floors, and every rooftop was a common area where people would sit and drink tea, smoke cigarettes, talk to friends, and even spend the night when the temperature was too high, which was pretty often. Before any searches were conducted, all the members of the family would be ordered to gather in one of the first-floor rooms, children and the elderly included. In our squad, the soldier chosen to watch the families was always Sergeant Rodriguez, who at fifty years of age was by far the oldest among us.

As squad leader I generally moved around between the soldiers who were doing the searching and those pulling security inside and outside the house. Sometimes, when we had

been out during the hottest hours of the day, I would go to the
refrigerator of whichever house we were searching and find
the ice-cold water that Iraqi families kept in metal bowls or
big plastic bottles. I would take a drink and pass the water
around to the rest of the squad, without asking anyone in the
family if this was OK. It seemed like our right, and I never
gave it a thought, not back then.

I would often sit in the living room in an area from which
I could observe the cornered family. Choosing the most comfortable chair to sit on, I would ground my helmet on the
floor, never letting go of my rifle. The entire family would
stare at me from the floor where they usually sat on a blanket,
but I never wondered what they were thinking. I simply sat
there and drank their water, tired, hot, and ready to move on
to the next house. And it never really bothered me to see
grandmothers and wives evidently terrified by our taking
their men away, though I sometimes tried to calm them with
words of reassurance that they would be well treated and, if
they were innocent, back in no time.

I never doubted those words, not at the time. We were the
U.S. Army, after all, and we did not mistreat those who were
innocent. Sure, there had been the sleep deprivation and
mock executions at al Assad, but those had been isolated
events—the exception, not the rule. It wasn't until nearly a
year later that I would learn that my experiences of detainee
abuse paled in comparison with what occurred at Abu
Ghraib prison in Baghdad. As it turned out, the families
whose terror I so readily dismissed knew my own army much
better than I did.

To our surprise, the third night of Operation Shutdown
passed without attacks on our positions. A soldier in my old
platoon opened fire with his machine gun on an eighteen-
wheel truck that failed to halt at the roadblock just outside of
the Eagle's Nest, killing the driver. The truck had reached a

full stop but had then started rolling slowly forward. That, together with the fact that a subsequent search of the shattered
cab did not turn up any weapons, made simple brake failure
the most likely possibility. But this sort of mistaken killing of
civilians had long ceased to arouse much interest or even
comment.

On our return, I ran into Rosado, who had stayed back at
base working as a radio runner while the rest of us were out.
While in the radio area, he had overheard a conversation between Captain Warfel and Lieutenant Colonel Mirable. The
latter had apparently told the captain that we were going to
be sent out again, for a fourth night, in order to draw the enemy out.

"Man, it's fucked up," said Rosado. "This motherfucker
didn't have enough with doing this shit for three straight
nights, now he wants us to go out a fourth. He's not gonna
stop until somebody fucking dies in this battalion."

Rosado was right. It seemed pretty clear that the colonel
was trying to instigate a firefight and we were the bait. We
were to follow the exact same procedure we had followed for
three consecutive times a fourth and fifth time.

By the fourth night of Operation Shutdown much of the
initial lamenting and grumbling had been replaced by a silent
mixture of terror and resentment, which floated in the air as
we sat in the trucks waiting to move out. Although we felt our
chain of command was playing Russian roulette with our
lives, no one dared say a word. Two loud explosions were
heard just after first platoon followed third outside. The explosions came from mortar fire aimed at the road we all traveled to get to our final positions. But the mortars had missed,
first platoon had been told to push forward, and the mission
had continued on as planned. We all just continued to stare at
one another in dead silence, a silence that, sadly, would not
last too long.

"First platoon got hit, they're under attack," Demarest came through over the two-way Motorola radios we used for internal communication, and which had been sent by our relatives. "We're moving out."

"Roger," came the replies from each of the squad leaders.

"Do we have any more information, over?" I asked.

There was no response, probably because the Motorolas were hard to hear a lot of the time. We set off for first platoon's position, bypassing our own five-road intersection and driving down roads that seemed perfect locations for IED attacks. Our stomachs were in our mouths, knowing we were heading straight into the belly of a raging gun battle.

The traditional sounds and visions of war announced the firefight minutes before we arrived at the scene. The powerful rounds of a fifty-caliber machine gun streaked across the night sky, leaving traces of light along their deadly trajectory, and the rattle of small arms fire could also be heard in the near distance. Ahead of us the sides of the road were occupied by first platoon soldiers lying in prone positions behind low mounds of broken bricks and scrap, the kind of trash that lined the streets all through the city and nearby desert.

With first platoon spread out across our front, countering the enemy's attack, it was impossible for us to fire our weapons without endangering our own people. All we could do was to secure the rear of the formation and wait for the firefight to subside.

As the battle raged, reports came in that there were at least two serious injuries. First platoon's lead Humvee had been hit upon arrival by a blast from either a rocket-propelled grenade or a mine, no one knew for sure. The vehicle's gunner, Specialist Recio, had taken shrapnel and bullet wounds on both his legs, losing most of the flesh from one of his calves and nearly dying from blood loss. Specialist Mayorga, the platoon's medic, was riding in the same vehicle and lost three

fingers. Other casualties included Sergeant First Class Mateo, the platoon sergeant, who took shrapnel wounds to one
of his arms, and first platoon's PL, Lieutenant Barr, who was
hit by shrapnel on the back of his neck. The only person unscathed was the lieutenant's radio operator. The vehicle was
destroyed.

When the gunfire finally stopped, I heard a voice on the
radio requesting Demarest to send one of our squads on a
search and kill mission into nearby woods where someone in
first platoon thought we would find injured enemy personnel
waiting for us. I knew the area. It was located next to the Euphrates, covered with low bushes, and with little light; a perfect spot for booby traps and IEDs. I could hear an urgent
inner voice pleading *Not my squad, please; don't let it be my squad.*

"First squad!" yelled Demarest.

Fuck! I thought. *Why did it have to be us? Don't fucking say it,
Demarest, don't you dare. . . .*

"Get your squad together, Mejía, we're going on a search
and destroy mission."

"Roger, sergeant!" My reply surprised no one more than
me in its conviction and fearlessness. "Rosado! Gallegos! Get
your teams ready. We're going to search for enemy dead and
injured."

"Milligan!" continued Demarest. "You're coming with
us too."

Great, I thought, feeling very relieved that we weren't going alone. By the time we left for the woods we had both first
and second squads, plus Demarest and the XO, all going on
the mission. On our way to the low ground we walked past
the dead body of a large man on the side of the road. First platoon soldiers, who were carefully guarding their perimeter
with their weapons facing out and away from the dead man,
turned their heads to get a quick glimpse of us as we moved
stealthily toward the dark bushes. What little we could see of

their expressions was not encouraging; it was a familiar look that expressed sympathy and concern but above all the message *Better you than me.*

A small person stood next to the dead man, who appeared to be covered from head to toe with a white sheet. Several people later told me that this was a young child standing next to the corpse of his father. I subsequently tried to remember the boy's face, whether he was crying or looked sad, but the more I tried to remember the more I realized that there are moments my memory will just never let me revisit.

We walked on, fear stalking our every step, combing the small creeks and undergrowth next to the river but finding nothing. As we returned to relative safety I was aware that something was preoccupying me, something that would not allow me any measure of peace but that I could not quite identify. It occurred to me that it was connected with the corpse we had walked by on our way to the river and had passed again, moments before, on our way back. The child who had been standing next to the body was gone by then.

I retraced my steps, telling myself that I was going back to collect Funez, who had stayed behind talking to soldiers in first platoon. In fact, I wanted to take another look at the corpse. I was curious about where the white sheet that was covering it had come from. I knew we didn't carry them.

I paused next to the body and stared at it for an infinite moment. What I had convinced myself was the sheet that covered the corpse was just the white robe the man had been wearing when he was killed. The robe had looked like a sheet that covered the whole body because the man no longer had a head. The fire from the fifty-caliber machine gun had decapitated him.

"Didn't you see it?" someone would ask me later.

"Didn't I see what?" I asked back, fearing the answer.

"His head. His head was right next to him, by the curve."

The widely circulated story following the incident was that immediately after the initial attack a vehicle had approached first platoon's blocking position at high speed. When warning rounds failed to stop it, the order was given to destroy the vehicle, and that's when a machine gunner had opened up with the fifty-caliber machine gun, decapitating the driver but miraculously missing the child who was in the passenger seat.

Thinking about the matter further, and after speaking with a number of people who filled in missing details, I tried to reconstruct my own version of this horrific scene. Perhaps I did see something next to the body, but my mind had told me it was a rock. But had it been that close to the corpse? Had I seen anything at all? And why, when everyone else had recognized that it was a child standing next to the corpse, had my mind erased all traces of his face and clues to his age? Perhaps my memory was playing tricks on me in an attempt to repress images of a story that wasn't just painful to tell, but also to remember.

Before the end of that awful night, another event took place that changed what had been my more-or-less passive acceptance of fate into a rebellious protest. It was a conversation I overheard by mistake. We had just returned to the Eagle's Nest. We had suffered four injuries, two of which were serious, one life-threatening. One of our vehicles had been destroyed. As if this was not enough, an innocent civilian had been decapitated in front of his child. It was therefore hard to stomach the dialogue I witnessed between Sergeant First Class Demarest and Captain Warfel:

"Yeah," said the captain. I wondered if it was the first time I had ever detected concern in his voice. "The medics are saying Recio could have died from the loss of blood, and that he will probably lose his leg."

Demarest looked down at the ground for a moment, evidently unable to say anything.

"And Colonel Mirable has told me we're doing the same thing tomorrow night," continued the captain. His voice was flat, without emphasis.

"The same exact thing?" asked Demarest, looking up.

"Same thing," Warfel replied.

"But that's just crazy," said Demarest, even though it was unusual for him to voice criticism of his superiors.

"I know," continued the captain, with a very serious look on his face. "But he's saying we've gotta let the enemy know we're not afraid."

It was typical of our leadership to place concerns about how the enemy felt or what they thought over the well being of soldiers and innocent civilians. The fact that the appalling events of the fourth night of that senseless mission could have been avoided by simply doing what we knew we should do seemed to mean nothing to our colonel. Now he wanted us to do the exact same thing again.

"No way!" I said to Demarest after Warfel left. "I'm sorry, sergeant. I have all the respect in the world for you, and I hope you don't take this personally, but I'm not going on the mission tomorrow."

"You have to," replied my platoon sergeant in a calmed voice. "You're a squad leader and your men need you."

"What the fuck can I possibly do when this dickhead colonel won't let us do our fucking job!?" I asked, furious.

"I know what you mean," Demarest's voice was sympathetic. "I even told the commander I though it was crazy. But the order came from the BC, and we just have to do it."

"Man, fuck the battalion commander!" I said, almost yelling. "Why doesn't Warfel do shit about it?"

"He can't," continued Demarest. "We just have to do

what we're told and make the best of what we have. That's why you have to go out there and provide leadership to your squad the best way you can."

"Well, I'm not going, sergeant. And I hope you don't take it personally, but this motherfucker is using us to get medals and promotions, and I'm not gonna be a part of it. Why doesn't he come with us if he's so interested in showing the enemy we're not scared? I have never seen his ass out there."

Demarest looked at me in a manner that suggested he agreed with most of what I was saying but was unable to let go of some twenty years of military training and the misguided sense of blind loyalty that came with it. I felt as though I was punching through imaginary walls of hard concrete with my bare fists as I confronted my deepest fears and insecurities. I did not want to disobey my orders and I was terrified, but I felt like I had to do it.

"I promise you," I continued. "I won't try to start a revolution or anything, but I'm gonna talk to my squad and I'm gonna explain to them why I'm not going out tomorrow, and I hope they follow my lead, because we don't have to do this shit."

I left to go back to my room, still on good terms with Demarest, who told me he would wait until the next day to tell the captain of my position. When I subsequently talked to my squad, though none of them held it against me, not one of them wanted to follow in my footsteps.

The following morning Williams returned from the palace, where he had completed his work as a police instructor. Some six hundred young Iraqis had been trained as police officers by Williams and the other soldiers of our battalion. The excitement that accompanied their graduation vanished very quickly after the ceremony when a bomb placed right outside the police station claimed the lives of seven of the new graduates, sending sixty-three others to the

hospital with severe injuries. Of the five hundred or so unharmed survivors, more than four hundred resigned straight
away. In any event, the training was over, Williams was back,
and he wanted to see me about my refusal to go out on the
mission.

"If you don't go out tonight they're just gonna slam you,"
said Williams. "They're gonna make an example out of you."

"Well, I'm gonna request an IG investigation into the way
the colonel is exposing us just to get medals," I replied, referring to the inspector general, which is the legal body in the
military that conducts investigations whenever wrongdoing
is suspected.

"And how are you going to prove that?" asked our recently returned PL. "How are you going to prove he's doing
it for medals?"

"How else can you explain that he's violated every rule of
the infantry? How will he explain giving up the element of
surprise? And doing the exact same mission, in the exact
same manner, over and over and over?"

"He doesn't have to explain it," replied my PL with a
frown. "All he has to do is blame it on the next higher person,
and then the next higher, all the way to the general, if it even
gets that far. Now, do you really think they're gonna listen to
a staff sergeant over a colonel? You're out of your mind. You
might as well just say you're too afraid to go out; they'll go
easier on you."

"It's not a matter of being afraid, Will." I was annoyed at
him for giving up on me so easily, without listening properly
to what I was saying, but at least he seemed concerned about
the course of action I was about to take. "I mean, I am afraid,"
I continued, "but I would go out and do my job if they let me.
They won't let us, they just keep setting us up for failure."

"I'm telling you," he insisted, raising his eyebrows as if he knew he was right beyond anyone's opinion, "you might as well just say you're too scared, or they're going to throw your ass in jail for everyone to see."

"I'm not gonna do that," I continued. "Even if I go to jail, I'll have a lot in common with the boys at the brig, and I'll be alive and able to tell the story."

"Just tell them you're scared, Mejía, just tell them you're scared," he pressed, making me think he probably did think I was refusing out of plain fear. "They'll go easier on you, and you might even get off without punishment."

"No, Will," I said, stubbornly. "I have to let them know I value my life more than anyone's promotion. I'd rather go to jail than die, kill, or be injured for someone's personal glory. You tell them that's why I quit."

Williams said he would, but he didn't. When he went to the platoon leaders' meeting with the commander later that day, he found a most unexpected situation. The soldiers of first platoon had gotten together upon returning to base after the fourth night of Operation Shutdown. They were very angry about what had happened and at how they'd lost four people in one night, plus a vehicle. On hearing that we were being ordered to follow the same procedure for a fifth consecutive night, they decided they would refuse to go unless the mission was reorganized in a way that was sensitive to our safety and that let us regain the element of surprise. A group of squad leaders from first platoon, led by their new platoon sergeant, Staff Sergeant Adams, delivered this news to the commander and first sergeant.

When Williams summoned the squad leaders to give us the briefing for that night's mission, he called on me as if nothing had ever happened. But important changes had been made. We were to go out during daylight hours to check out our positions before we occupied them, and we were to conduct presence patrols throughout the roads and alleyways of our area of operations, where attacks were likely to be set for us. In addition, the presence patrols would not stop during the roadblocking of the city, but would continue throughout the curfew, making it harder for the insurgents to ambush any elements that had stayed in one place for too long. And instead of returning to base at 0400 hours, we left two hours earlier, which increased the likelihood that any plan of attack set against our retreat would be thwarted.

The final night of Operation Shutdown went off without any incidents or injuries whatsoever. I went on the mission with the rest of my platoon, as first squad leader, and my original refusal to participate in the mission was never again spoken about, at least not in Iraq.

NINE

For some time after the end of Operation Shutdown our company continued blocking ar Ramadi's main intersections every other night. My pleas for the missions to be conducted using the element of surprise were taken to an extreme, making me think I should have been more careful about what I wished for. Instead of setting up the usual high-profile blocking positions with signs, chemical light sticks, military trucks across the roads, and soldiers manning the positions to turn traffic around, we were told to hide behind the bushes next to dark roads. The only thing we were to set up in the road to indicate it was blocked was a single strand of concertina wire, which we were to place some fifty meters ahead of our position. My platoon was given a location near where first platoon had been ambushed on the fourth night of Operation Shutdown, right alongside River Road.

"Any vehicle reaches the wire, you open fire on it," Williams had said during the squad leaders' meeting.

"Did you say the only thing we're using to mark our position is a single strand of concertina wire?" I asked our PL.

"Correct."

"And we're setting up right by River Road, just off the Y intersection, right?"

"Correct, that's what the commander said."

Anxious looks darted around the room as we digested the implications of the order we had just received. We were to set up a blocking position on a dark road that led to the city's biggest hospital, without marking or manning it, and we were to shoot at anyone who reached it. Any parent taking their child for medical treatment could easily reach the wire. The mission did not directly require us to kill innocent civilians, but it certainly did not leave much room for averting a tragedy.

Yet not one of us said anything to point out the inherent immorality of such a command. We all just raised our eyebrows and went on with the meeting, taking copious notes on everything our platoon leader told us. Without it ever being discussed, let alone challenged, we had adopted an unofficial "shoot first, ask questions later" policy.

When it was time to relay the details of the operation to the members of my squad, I wasn't sure of what to say. I was conflicted about these orders, but I also knew that telling my squad not to follow them would put all of us in danger of being criminally charged, and I was terrified by that idea. I realized I needed to come up with a safer way of keeping the squad from making a terrible mistake that could haunt us for the rest of our lives, but I had to do it without overtly promoting disobedience.

"I will not shoot," I finally said, after a long quiet stare at the ground. "I will not shoot unless I can tell they have a weapon and I feel threatened."

This was by no means a foolproof plan. Iraqi policemen, for instance, were armed and rode in the back of civilian pickup trucks without uniforms. I felt like a coward for not speaking more loudly against an order that could result in the killing of unarmed civilians. We had every right to refuse that mission and I knew I should have done so at the squad leaders' meeting. It was too late now.

"But why, sergeant?" asked one of the soldiers.

I was glad someone asked the question.

"Because we don't know if there will be women and children in that car. Just for reaching a wire that they can't see in the first place, we're gonna fucking shoot'em? We're the ones who are gonna have to live with the shit if we kill innocent people. It won't be the captain or the colonel squeezing the trigger, men, it will be you, and you, not they, will have to live with that shit."

Other platoons set their positions in less obscure areas, where their wires could be seen even if they kept a low profile and, to my knowledge, they never had to decide whether or not to shoot at unknowing and unarmed civilians.

Fortunately, we never actually had to make that awful decision either. My perception was that word had gotten around that we were setting up traps by the river, and that most locals avoided the area while we were there. The worst thing that happened during that and subsequent nights was that, on a couple of occasions we had to guard explosives, old 155-millimeter artillery rounds left for us by young Iraqis, and wait for explosive ordnance disposal personnel to arrive in order to get rid of them.

After a couple of weeks we dropped the blocking positions by River Road, but our command continued to order us to conduct missions that were entirely predictable to our enemies. We cleared the same stretch of Highway 10 in the exact same way, at the exact same time, every single day. And we were attacked almost every single day. We all knew the inevitable was bound to happen, and soon enough it did. One awful day, as first platoon cleared the road, an improvised explosive de-

vice went off, destroying Staff Sergeant Adams's Humvee
and sending shrapnel through his Kevlar helmet and into his
skull.

We were on QRF that morning and rushed to the attack
site as quickly as we could, which, as usual, turned out to be
too late; the perpetrators had already fled. We returned to
base to find a demoralized company and what was left of
Adams's destroyed Humvee. Splattered blood lined the vehicle's interior and stained the green bandana Adams wore
around his neck and which was now lying on the sandy floor
of the vehicle. Adams had received severe head injuries that
might permanently affect his motor and intellectual skills. He
was the most serious casualty suffered by our company up to
that time.

But there was no cessation to the senseless missions; our
soldiers continued to be injured, and our vehicles continued
to be destroyed. A friend of mine, Sergeant Mario Vega, was
injured by an IED explosion that threw him against a wooden
bench in the back of the truck he was riding in, injuring his
lower back and right arm and causing temporary blindness.
He was evacuated to a nearby medical facility and should
have been transferred from there to a proper clinic for reha-
bilitation. But instead he was returned to our base, too weak
and blind to get out of the truck without help. Later in the
mess hall I had to feed him because he couldn't eat by himself.

"If your injury is severe enough for them to send you
away from your unit to get treated," he complained, "they're
supposed to send you out of the combat zone to convalesce,
not send you back to your base. At least that's what the
medics there said."

"So what happened?" I asked him, holding a spoonful of
scrambled eggs in front of his face. "How come you're here
and not in some air-conditioned hospital getting better?"

"Well," he said, able to smell but not see the eggs, "as I

was about to leave for a more permanent facility, one of the medics came and told me my commander had radioed and said that I wasn't allowed to go anywhere, and that I was to return to duty."

I rewarded that bit of information with the eggs and even threw in some cold ham. I let him chew.

"And then what happened?" I asked, even though he hadn't swallowed the mouthful of food I'd just fed him.

"Then I went to ask a major who was there. He was one of the doctors who worked at that facility."

"And what did he say?" I asked, without offering any more food. The huge black goggles he was wearing looked ahead in an empty, blind stare.

"He said that yeah, you're supposed to go someplace else to get better."

"So why didn't you fucking leave, Mario?" I dropped the empty spoon on the plate.

"Because! This colonel, our doctor, came and got me," he responded defensively.

He was referring to our company doctor, a lieutenant colonel who was a plastic surgeon in the civilian world. I remember how I once told him I had handled a bottle of liquid mercury, which the insurgents use to set up improvised bombs. I was worried it might have poisoned me. He told me that he liked to play with the stuff and see how the liquid metal flowed and that I shouldn't worry unless I had taken a sip of it.

"So what exactly happened?"

"So he fucking came and asked me why I was asking other doctors questions. And then we came back here."

Vega's case wasn't one of a kind; in fact, we had several soldiers who had received wounds serious enough to be sent home to recover but had returned to the company. If soldiers were let go, there was a risk that the size of the company would fall below combat strength. In that case it would be disbanded and the commander would lose his post.

Another soldier, José Mangual from the Puerto Rico National Guard, had major surgery on hemorrhoids and could hardly move afterward. Instead of going on leave to recover, he was kept in ar Ramadi, where occasionally he pulled radio watch.

According to what they told us, the entire Puerto Rico Guard unit had been royally screwed from the beginning. Their units had been sent to Florida at the request of Florida's governor on the understanding that they would pull security on the ports and airports while we deployed to the Middle East. But once they arrived, they were immediately attached to our unit and sent to war. Word among the Puerto Ricans was that their governor was very irate about what had happened and, along with the commanding general of the Puerto Rico Guard, was trying to get them back home.

This wasn't the only incident that upset the Puerto Ricans attached to our unit. During training in Jordan, Alpha Company's executive officer, a white man, had taken digital pictures of Puerto Rican personnel and of a couple of black troops and pinned them to silhouettes for target practice. Such a blatant display of racism did not have serious consequences for the officer: he was merely transferred to an administrative position, probably more for his own safety than anything else.

In our company, racism was generally less obvious, but it surfaced there too. When a white soldier accidentally fired a round while riding in the back of a Humvee, the bullet ricocheted against a hard metal surface and hit the soldier in the vest without injuring him. A similar mistake had resulted in the serious reprimand of two Latin noncommissioned officers

in our platoon. Not only did the white soldier escape reprimand, he was awarded a Purple Heart.

The casual racism of our leadership, combined with their
determination to repeatedly send us on what we regarded as
senseless missions to further their own careers, began to en-
gender serious resentment in the ranks.

One night, after denying his earlier statement that he
would not return to the United States without the Combat
Infantry Badge (CIB), Captain Warfel was summoned by
Sergeant Williams to meet with our platoon to discuss the issue. The meeting took place in my squad's room, where our
entire platoon, about thirty-two soldiers in all, sat on army-
issued green cots.

"I never said that," Warfel protested. "I never said that
I did not want to return without a CIB. I would like to
get the award, as every officer does, but I never made that
statement."

Sergeant Williams was standing next to him, glowering at
all of us. It soon became clear that he was angry that, despite
widespread complaints about Warfel's initial comments, no
one in the platoon was prepared to challenge the captain.

"Well, now you have him here," Williams said. "Are you
guys going to tell him all the things you told me?"

Even though I give Williams credit for standing up for
the platoon like that, it had been obvious for some time that
there was something personal between him and our company
commander. The problem was that Williams wanted to do
things his own way and regularly second-guessed Warfel,
who asserted his authority over Williams every time. The latest brush between them concerned a soldier in our platoon
named Carrasquillo, whose grandmother was in critical
condition with a respiratory disease. Carrasquillo had been
brought up by this woman and that entitled him to emergency
leave to go visit her. Williams made several leave requests to

Warfel on Carrasquillo's behalf, citing two emergency notifi-
cations from the Red Cross confirming the advanced state of
the old woman's illness. But Warfel continued to refuse to approve the request for leave, even telling Williams that he
thought Carrasquillo was a liar. The dispute had become well
known in the platoon.

Now it was Carrasquillo, appropriately enough, who
spoke up against Warfel.

"You did say that, sir," he said. "You said to all E-4s and
below that you did not want to return without your CIB."

"Yes, you said that sir," reiterated another soldier who
was sitting in the back of the room.

Soon more voices of reproach made themselves heard,
until the room was filled with a loud murmur of criticism.
Though no one was overtly critical of Warfel, or accused him
directly of serious wrongdoing, it was clear that there was
much unhappiness about his failure to protect his troops from
what was widely regarded as the cruel and unscrupulous am-
bitions of a glory-obsessed battalion commander.

"I never said that," Warfel insisted again, nodding his
head with his eyes closed. "I never said that I wanted the CIB
to the point of not wanting to return without it."

"Well, what is it that you do want, sir?" asked an anonymous voice from the back of the room. We all fell quiet.

Warfel replied without hesitation: "My dream in life is to
be the commanding general of the Florida National Guard,
that's what I want."

So much for wanting everyone to return home alive and
in good spirits, or for helping the Iraqi people to build a
democracy and a decent society. It was the wrong answer but
no one questioned the hollowness of such naked ambition.
The room fell silent until Warfel left.

But the majority of our company's anger was not really
directed at Warfel; it was instead aimed at our battalion com-

mander, Mirable. The rumors that he was doing his very best to get the worst missions in order to expose his battalion to combat, and to even create that combat, had started at the very beginning of our deployment, but they had not meant much to anyone until we got to ar Ramadi and began experiencing combat. The message I understood from my fellow troops was that statements such as, "We've gotta send the message to the enemy that we're not afraid," or "We've gotta draw the enemy out," were all beginning to sound increasingly macabre, as they started to translate into fierce firefights and roadside bomb attacks, most of which could easily have been avoided.

As tensions and resentment mounted, I heard rumors that soldiers in our unit were plotting Mirable's assassination.

"I've heard that someone is thinking about cutting the bottom of a water bottle and taping its top to the muzzle of a rifle and use it as a silencer," said Rosado to me one day, after coming back from radio watch. "I'm telling you," he continued, "they want to kill his ass."

I didn't take Rosado seriously, at least not until a few days later, when we were called to a company formation, a highly unusual occurrence in a combat environment. Standing in front of us, Captain Warfel held up a piece of paper and showed it to us. It was a letter that had been sent from inside the Eagle's Nest and it contained a threat to harm not only Mirable, but also his family in the United States if we weren't redeployed as soon as possible. Warfel wanted any information leading to the letter writer, and warned that anyone making such threats could and would be punished by the Uniform Code of Military Justice. No one came forward, not that day, nor ever.

Soon after the formation we heard the news that we had been awarded our Combat Infantry Badge. The badge itself bears an emblem of a musket with the hammer dropped, resting on top of an oak wreath that represents strength and loyalty. Local Iraqi tailors were brought in to make the badges and sew them to the top of the left breast pockets of our desert combat uniforms. Wearing the award was optional, but the insignias were distributed to all soldiers, and our leadership put out the word that we were highly encouraged to make use of them. This was one occasion when our leaders led from the front: they were among the first to visit the tailors to get their little patches of glory sewn next to their hearts.

Once the badge had been awarded, the attractiveness of life in ar Ramadi paled pretty quickly for our officers, as it had for the rest of us. But it was too late for our lieutenant colonel to say "I've had all the combat experience I need; now I want to bring my unit home." Events in Iraq were not going as planned and the military was in dire need of all the infantry it could get its hands on. The Third ACR unit we had been attached to was to be replaced by one of the most decorated elite units in the army, the Eighty-second Airborne Division. The inheritance of these new masters of ar Ramadi included two presidential palaces, the government buildings, the local police force, the military stores, the Kellogg Brown & Root dining facility with all its foreign employees, and the old, raggedy, ill-equipped, combat-tested 1-124th Infantry Battalion of the Florida National Guard. We weren't going anywhere.

Although formally attached to the Eighty-second Airborne, we were to report directly to a unit of the First Infantry Division, known as "the Big Red One." This very peculiar situation reduced us to an uncertain state of military homelessness, where both the Big Red and the Eighty-second could point at the other when it came to providing us with much-needed vehicle parts, new tires, and ammunition. No one took responsibility for supplying us, but everyone, including Third ACR units, wanted to use us for joint missions.

Initial relations with the newly arrived gung-ho elite warriors of the Eighty-second were not without some strain. Their officers regularly took offense when we failed to salute them, though we actually did this to protect them from possible sniper attacks. They also reprimanded a few of our soldiers for not having military-standard haircuts, and for wearing short beards even though we explained that this was to help us blend in with the locals on our undercover patrols in civilian vehicles at night. The Eighty-second's command put out an order forbidding National Guard units from using the military store and dining facility at the main palace. We were relegated to the third-class facilities at the smaller palace, a move that was much resented throughout the company. But as a National Guard unit, we were used to being treated as the unwanted adopted child of the military, so we got over the humiliation soon enough.

The combination of having received the CIB and the snobbery of the Eighty-second Airborne produced an extraordinary turnaround in the attitude of our battalion commander. Having seemed gung ho about sending us into action wherever it could be found, Mirable suddenly turned to us for help in trying to get the battalion sent back home. The occasion was a speech that he made to our company on the second anniversary of 9/11. We were expecting a remembrance of those fallen from the terrorist attacks and a patriotic justification of our continued presence in Iraq. Instead, as I remember it, our commander shocked a room of battle-weary grunts:

"We are soldiers," he said, "and we are not to question our orders or our missions. We cannot say that it is time for us to go home; we can only fight and do as we are told." He paused and appeared to reflect for a moment on what he was about to say. "But our families can request our return. They have that right. My wife, right now, is working with a group of family members in Florida, collecting signatures to put pressure on our politicians to do whatever they can to get the 1-124th Infantry back home. Your families can do the same, and you can encourage them to join the effort for our redeployment."

It was clear to me from his speech that not only had Mirable seen enough of ar Ramadi, but he also had no clue as to when our unit would be redeployed and he no longer had any say in the matter. It was the first time I realized how powerless he now was. Though I was still convinced that he had used his influence to get us into Iraq quickly, and that he had fished for severe combat assignments in pursuit of his own career, I now also knew that he had gone too far and that there was nothing he could do to get us back home.

Not long after listening to Mirable's speech, I wrote a letter to Captain Warfel requesting to be sent home. The letter explained in detail my legal status as a soldier in the U.S. Army without American citizenship—that prior to our deployment I had been in the military just short of eight years, and by the army's own rules and regulations, eight years represented not only the end of my contract, but also the maximum amount of time a non–U.S. citizen could lawfully be in the armed forces. I also pointed out that my green card was about to expire.

With these same arguments, I had unsuccessfully tried to get out of deployment on a number of occasions starting as early as January 2003, but the answers I received from the different personnel I spoke with were always the same: "Don't worry, sergeant, you'll be a hero and a citizen when you get back home." I wanted to be neither a hero nor a citizen, I just wanted to get out of a war I considered illegal. But every time I got turned down, I accepted whatever reasons

legal personnel gave me, and soon enough I was back with
my unit. The people I dealt with seemed ignorant of the
army's own regulations, but I came to see that not as a flaw in
the system but as an integral and necessary part of it.

Trying to get out of the war felt more like the quest of
Sisyphus as he pushed the boulder up the hill than like realis-
tic attempts to get out, particularly now that we were in Iraq.
Soldiers' requests to go home to see dying relatives or newborn babies or to bail out businesses going bankrupt without
them were repeatedly rejected. Every time I thought of asking to be sent home I laughed at myself for even allowing the
thought. But every now and then I felt as if I had to at least
try to get out, even if I knew the military would simply laugh
in my face and send me back to the lines.

Upon reading my letter, the commander and the first sergeant tried to fix the problem by downloading immigration
documents from the Internet. But all they could come up with
were forms to prolong tourist visas for a week or two. Fortunately, Sergeant Williams saw my case as another battle in his
ongoing war with Warfel and, by applying continuous pressure, finally reached an agreement that allowed me to take a
three-day trip to al Assad to meet with an officer from the
judge advocate general, or JAG, the military department that
deals with legal matters.

Al Assad was very different from when I was last there. It
had been transformed from a desolate network of blown-up
airplane bunkers in the middle of nowhere to a thriving military town with a well-supplied store, an AT&T call center, a
swimming pool, a finance department, a post office, a chapel,
and a JAG office.

After an initial interview I was passed on to a Captain
Mohammad. Tall and dark, perhaps of Arab descent, Mohammad was a criminal defense attorney for the Eighty-
second Airborne, the kind of guy who defends GIs who are

charged with things like cruel treatment of prisoners. He had
worked for the Immigration and Naturalization Service before joining the army. After quickly reviewing my case he
concluded that I should apply to renew my U.S. residency
through the Internet. He told me that it might be necessary to
send me home at some point during the process of renewal
but added that doing so now would be premature. And in any
event, that decision would be entirely up to my leadership.

I asked him about the rule preventing extensions after
having been in the army for eight years without being a citizen, but he claimed not to know about it and reassured me
that there wouldn't be any negative repercussions for me,
even if such a rule existed.

"And don't worry," he added with a reassuring smile,
"you will continue to get paid and you will have all your benefits while you're here."

By then I was overtaken by that familiar sensation that
the military machine is not programmed to help soldiers get
out of war, especially when they are infantrymen. The one
and only hope I left that place with came after asking Mohammed one final question:

"What if my U.S. residency expires? Could the army still
keep me then?"

This time Mohammad was clearer.

"No," he responded. "If your residency expires the army
would have to let you go."

With this bit of information I returned to ar Ramadi and
reported what I had been told. I was ordered to attend a
meeting in Captain Warfel's room where, besides the commander, Williams and I were met by the first sergeant and
Lieutenant Green.

Upon entering we saw Captain Warfel sprawled on his
cot, with the demeanor of a despotic Roman emperor, but
without the grapes. He looked to his right where The Naugu-

lator was standing and gently smiled at him. Once more it felt
as if I was being tried for a capital crime; Warfel was presid-
ing over the court, The Naugulator was the prosecution,
Green the jury, and Williams was my defense attorney.

"Why can't you just apply for a renewal of your residency
from here?" asked the prosecution.

"Well, first sergeant," I responded, "I have a custody trial
pending at home, and I want to resolve that before renewing
my residency card."

My letter to the commander had explained that I had initiated a legal action to establish paternity of my daughter,
which had initially been contested by her mother. In the end,
the judge gave me parental rights but ruled that I had caused
unnecessary litigation for the mother and ordered me to pay
part of her attorney's fees, which I had not yet done. At the
time I worried that this debt could work against me when applying to renew my residency status.

"Why didn't you take care of that before we left?" asked
Judge Warfel.

"I was going to school full time sir," I replied. "I was not
sitting on thousands of dollars; I depended on scholarships,
loans, and the army's GI bill to subsist."

"Yes," said the captain, almost interrupting me, "but why
didn't you bring up the issue before we came to Iraq?" The
gentle smile was gone.

"I did sir; you can ask the first sergeant."

I exchanged a quick glance with The Naugulator, who
looked annoyed at the fact that I was using him to make my
case, but he didn't deny the claim.

"He even picked me up once from a legal aid office at
Fort Stewart," I continued.

"And what happened there?" asked Warfel, this time
looking at something in his hand.

"They said not to worry, that we would probably only be deployed for six months, and that upon return I would be a hero and get my citizenship right away."

"I know there is a way to extend your residency," said the first sergeant. "I think we can do that without you having to go back."

"Yes," intervened Williams, "but that doesn't solve the problem of his residency when he gets back. Even if he can extend it, he is still going to have to clear the issue of not having paid the attorney's fees, as the judge ordered him, or he may be held in contempt of court."

I got the distinct impression Williams had no idea what he was talking about, and for a moment I almost laughed, but he spoke with the confidence of an American Civil Liberties Union lawyer.

"He really could be deported, sir," continued Williams, ignoring the prosecutor and looking at the judge with severe eyes. "And he has a little girl to support."

Williams's mistake was to think these people cared about the soldiers and their families. I knew the only real solution was to make them see the possibility of permanently losing a soldier.

"Right now I'm just trying to keep him here," said The Naugulator. "When he gets back he can take care of whatever issues he has."

"How about this, sir," I finally said for myself. "Why don't we forget about all this and you just let me go in January? My residency expires in March of next year, which means that by then I have to be completely out of the military."

I figured if I could make the captain understand he could lose me for good, he would send me home, at least for a couple of weeks. I could work there on making it permanent. The main objective was to get out of Iraq.

"You give me a few weeks to out-process, plus a month of terminal leave," I continued with my eyes wide open and not looking at anyone in particular. "I'll be out by March 6, sir, which is when my green card expires. Just let me go in January."

The captain grimaced at the prospect of my leaving the army altogether.

"We'll think about January in January," he said. "What we'll do now is call Florida on my satellite phone and talk with the top state JAG officer."

Before receiving command of our company, Captain Warfel had a full-time job in Florida's National Guard headquarters, where he performed administrative duties. He knew all the bureaucrats in the administrative ranks. This officer he was talking about was not only his co-worker and friend but also his next-door neighbor; her name was Colonel Masters.

"If anyone can help you," he continued, "it's gonna be her."

The captain's satellite phone looked like a cell phone from the nineties; it was big and boxy, with a huge antenna. As Warfel dialed the number, he looked at me searchingly.

"If you had the opportunity to leave this war tomorrow, would you do it, sergeant?" he asked.

"Yes, sir, I would," I answered without hesitation, wondering what his reaction would be if I told him I was against the war.

"Even if we all stayed here?"

"That's right, sir."

"I don't know how you could do that," he said, nailing his eyes on mine. "I couldn't live with myself."

It's hard to say precisely how I felt at that moment. On one hand the thought of leaving the unit made me feel guilty, mostly because of my squad. On the other, I knew the war was wrong and that we were brutalizing the Iraqi people by being there. But I also felt an impulse to tell Warfel that want-

ing to stay in combat, issuing orders from the safety of the
base, was quite fitting for an officer whose goal in life was to
be a general, but that I had other goals in life.

"You have to promise me that if I let you go, you'll take
care of all your things and then return," he said, waiting for
someone to pick up on the other end.

"I'll give you my word, sir," I said. "But you have to give
me yours that if, by regulation, I am to be discharged from the
service, then you'll let me go."

"If by regulation I'm supposed to let you go, then yes, you
have my word."

Someone on the other end picked up the phone.

"Yes, Kathy? Hello, Kathy, this is Tad. I'm calling you
from ar Ramadi."

From what I could make out, Kathy was pleasantly surprised to hear "Tad" calling from wartorn Iraq. But formali-
ties were completed briskly, probably because Warfel knew
each minute was costing more than two dollars. He turned to
more serious matters.

"Yes, Kathy, I was wondering if I could talk to Colonel
Masters. No, she's not there?" he turned to look at me. "Well,
then maybe you can help me. There is a soldier in my company who's having some immigration issues. What? Mejía.
Yes, you know him?"

The captain frowned at me and covered the phone with
his hand.

"Do you know anything about a congressional inquiry
into your case, sergeant?" he asked.

"No idea, sir," I replied, not even knowing what a congressional inquiry was.

"Well, yes, yes," he continued, to Kathy. "He's right here,
let me put him on."

He handed me the phone.

"Yes, Sergeant Mejía?" asked the voice a world away.

"Yes," I said.

"Sergeant Camilo Mejía?"

"Yes," I said, wondering what was happening. "That's me."

"Hello, sergeant, my name is Kathy Tringially; I work at the Florida National Guard headquarters," she said, without mentioning a military rank, which made me think she was a civilian. "I'm going to ask you a few questions."

"Yes, ma'am," I said. "But how do you know my first name?"

"Well, there is a congressional inquiry on you. Your mother sent a letter to Senator Bill Nelson, from Florida, and he requested an investigation of your case. Now, let me ask you, sergeant . . ."

"Yes, go ahead, sorry." I was really eager to hear what she was about to ask.

"Have you applied for your citizenship?"

"No, I haven't."

"And when was the end of your eight-year contract with the army?"

"It was May of this year," I said, thinking that she had looked at the regulation I had mentioned in my letter to the captain.

It was the third week of September, and my contract with the military had officially ended almost four months earlier.

"Well, then you have to be discharged from the military immediately," she said.

"What about the stop loss?" I asked, referring to the military term for involuntary extension during war.

"You cannot be extended," she said, "unless you have applied for your citizenship and have a court date for becoming naturalized."

"What about the fact that there is a war?" I was both excited and in denial simultaneously.

"The regulation is very clear, sergeant. You have to be discharged from the service. Once you become a citizen, you may reenter the military, but right now you have to be discharged."

"Well, can you say that to my commander?" I asked my beloved Ms. Tringially.

"Yes, sure," she said. "Put him on the phone."

"OK, thank you." I wanted to kiss her. "She says I have to be discharged," I said to the captain, handing back the phone.

"What?" he said with a still deeper frown. "Hello, Kathy? Hello, hello. Kathy, are you there? I lost the signal," he said to me, turning the phone off with his thumb and putting it in the right pocket of his desert pants.

After speaking with Tringially without a problem the entire time, it seemed odd that he'd lost a good signal.

"Well, sir, she said that I have to be discharged immediately."

"Well, that's not what she said to me," the captain snapped. "We're gonna try again tomorrow, when Colonel Masters is in the office. She's the top legal officer in the state, and she'll know what to do."

"Roger, sir," I said, walking away from the captain.

I later learned that the letter I wrote to the commander, and which I had e-mailed home for record keeping, had then been given by my mother to a U.S. senator to try to get me out of Iraq. Because of that letter there had been a congressional inquiry (an investigation initiated by a member of Congress), which had determined that I was to be discharged from the military. I felt that whatever Colonel Masters had to say couldn't really matter much. What could be more powerful than a congressional inquiry? With more than eight years in the army, I still had no accurate idea of how powerful the military really is.

The following night, sure enough, about an hour before our scheduled meeting, the captain sent for me again. He passed me the phone to speak to Colonel Masters.

"I am familiar with your case, Sergeant Mejía, and I think we can help you become a citizen. I am going to send your commander the forms for you to fill out."

I usually feel more comfortable speaking with women than men, especially in the military, but I realized immediately that Colonel Masters was an exception.

"Yes, ma'am," I said. "Thank you, but about the regulation? Ms. Tringially said that there was a congressional inquiry and that an investigation showed that I'm supposed to be discharged."

"Well, I haven't seen that regulation," said Masters in a slightly exasperated tone. "Besides, we also discharge fat people from the army, but we're not doing that right now, are we sergeant?"

"I don't know, ma'am," I replied, momentarily confused. Why was she talking about fat people?

"Well, we're not!"

"But what about the congressional inquiry and the fact that I've been in the military past my time without having applied for citizenship?" I asked, falteringly.

"Well, if you're serious about becoming a citizen you'll fill out the forms that I will send you and return them to me as quickly as possible," she said in a hurried voice, which made me wonder what her rush was. "Then, Captain Warfel should call the G-1 office in Baghdad to find out what they are doing with people in the same situation as you."

"The G-1 office?" I asked.

"Yes, I'll tell him all about it. Meanwhile, you just send me back all the paperwork I send you, and we'll help you become a citizen."

I didn't want to appear unpatriotic, but I had started to wonder why they were so hell-bent on making me a citizen. My request from the beginning had been to be sent home to renew my soon-to-expire residency card. Now everything seemed to center on my becoming a citizen right away.

After the conversation with Colonel Masters I went back to my room, not really wanting to ever again push the boulder up the hill. All I could do was to try to keep my body and spirit together until the end of my war experience. Though I was disappointed that I had to stay, I was also glad it was all over. At least I'd tried, and I could now go back to my squad and let them know I wasn't leaving. I had shown the letter I wrote to a couple of the squad members, and they all knew I was trying to get out. None of them expressed anger at me for wanting to leave, but I could tell that they would rather I stayed.

A couple of days later, in the final week of September 2003, the radio watch runner delivered a message to Sergeant Williams. Captain Warfel had radioed in from the North Palace, where he was having his command meeting with Colonel Mirable and the other company commanders. The Department of the Army had approved a rest and relaxation program that allowed soldiers staying in Iraq for a year or longer to go home for two weeks. Our battalion had received twenty such slots.

"The commander wants you to be in that first batch," said Williams, as he stood at the doorway to my room.

The squad members had been really successful at block-ing outside light from our sleeping quarters. With Williams holding the door open, the light flooding the room was blind-ing me, and my eyes instinctively searched for Williams's shadow to reclaim their vision.

"Shouldn't you send somebody else?" I asked, in shock at the surprising new development, but acting calm. "I'm prob-ably going to end up staying over there, Will."

"So, stay," responded the dark silhouette. "What the hell are they gonna do? You're residency is expiring."

"Yeah, but this is only for two weeks. They're gonna want me to return," I insisted.

"Don't worry about that."

I wondered if Williams was being a nice guy, or if he was just siding with me to have another go at Warfel. Whatever it was, he didn't seem to mind the possibility of me leaving for good. Perhaps it had occurred to him that this was a good way to get rid of the one squad leader who had the bad habit of questioning his authority.

"What the hell are they going to do?" he pressed on. "If your green card expires, and you're supposed to be out of the army, tell me, what the hell are they gonna do?"

"Alright, Will," I said.

"Well then, hurry up. You gotta be ready to go in about an hour." He closed the door, leaving me in the darkness to reflect for a few minutes.

I gathered up a few things to bring with me, the bare basics. For munitions we were only to bring one full magazine, no grenades, and no special equipment. Once I had everything ready I looked for as many squad members as I could find to say good-bye to them.

"Will you be returning, Sergeant Mejía?" asked Estime.

"I don't know, man," I said to him. "Maybe not."

He wished me good luck and we embraced for a brief moment. Then Mantilla came running up with a yellow envelope.

"Do me a favor," he said. "Give this to my wife; here is the phone number."

"Alright, man, don't worry, I will."

"OK, take care."

"I will, and you too."

On my way out I was met by The Naugulator, who had leave forms for all Charlie Company personnel to sign. As a staff sergeant, I was the highest-ranking soldier going from the company. I was under orders to send an e-mail back to the

first sergeant upon arrival in the United States, confirming
that we had all made it safely back, and detailing the date of
landing, which would officially initiate our two-week R&R.

As I was climbing on the truck Captain Warfel arrived
from his command meeting. He looked up at me.

"I made sure you were on this trip because I want you to
take care of your issues at home," he said smiling. "I expect
you to have those issues resolved when you return."

"I will take care of everything, sir."

Those were my final words to Warfel as I began my departure from Iraq.

TEN

I was one of about twenty soldiers from the 1-124th Infantry riding in two old five-ton trucks en route to al Assad air base, on the first leg of our trip home for the two-week R&R. In addition to the twenty lucky soldiers going home, the convoy included two Humvees armed with fifty-caliber machine guns to provide security for the return journey after we had been dropped off. Because the most direct route to al Assad had recently been the site of many IED attacks—one killing a soldier and injuring another just the day before—it was decided that we should take a less-traveled road. This took us through the desert—vast areas of empty space interrupted by the occasional shepherd grazing his flock on isolated patches of grass or a collection of mud huts whose inhabitants stood and watched us go by. I tried to stay vigilant with my gun pointed out of the truck and my finger just above the trigger, but something kept me from fully attending to my soldier's duties that day. It was as though fear had left me and something else, a new sensation, had momentarily taken its place. I felt enchanted by the countryside we were traveling through, with its rustic homes surrounded by small date palm trees and the still waters of the Euphrates; it was hard not to let my guard down. I needed to say good-bye to Iraq.

We arrived at al Assad and turned our weapons in to the battalion's supply sergeant, an act that marked a transition between the combat environment of ar Ramadi and the more relaxed al Assad, where soldiers had the luxury of walking around without wearing their combat gear. Before the introduction of the two-week R&R program, al Assad was used as a place for National Guardsmen to take three-day breaks. Now it functioned as a kind of combat desensitization post for soldiers leaving the battlefield.

That night we were visited by an army chaplain who gave us two briefings, one on readjusting to home and relatives, and another on suicide prevention. These briefings reminded me of the time our platoon went to see the combat stress team in ar Ramadi, which consisted of a psychiatrist and two assistants. The session started with them asking us to each talk about an experience we had had in Iraq that had an impact on our lives, and to then explain how we had dealt with such an experience. The stories all had to do with firefights and other combat-related events, and the ways to deal with such moments ranged from reading and writing or playing PlayStation. Once everyone was done "sharing," the team encouraged us to use one another's ways to deal with combat stress, and then they left.

Here, too, the briefings seemed more aimed at protecting the army's image than at helping the soldiers. A twenty-minute session centering on the admonition *Don't commit suicide* doesn't do much to ease the anguish of a soldier dealing with the horror, for instance, of having killed a child, just as a group session with a combat stress team isn't much help if your life is at risk twenty-four hours a day.

Ultimately, it was always the unit commander's decision

whether or not to let a soldier go home if he was stressed out due to combat. I think we all were stressed to a level that would be considered unhealthy by civilian standards, and, obviously, we couldn't all be sent home. But to have a psychiatrist tell a soldier struggling to cope with the stress of a recent firefight that he should play a video game was a mockery of one's intelligence.

The next morning we got on a Chinook helicopter that took us to Baghdad International Airport, which was heavily secured by U.S. soldiers but which also housed troops from Australia and England. Things had changed quite a bit from when we had first arrived in April. Back then the place had looked like no-man's land, with the area entirely deserted except for U.S. soldiers and military vehicles occupying the destroyed runway and airport terminals. Judging by the level of security I saw there now, I had no sense that the insurgency had eased up, but deep within the airport's grounds we were able to enjoy a meal at a fancy dining facility, run by a civilian catering company.

We were in Baghdad for just one day. The next morning we boarded an air force C-130 plane that took us to an army base in Kuwait. The base was in an area reserved exclusively for the U.S. military next to what looked like an international airport. During this stop the process of combat desensitization was upped another notch. We no longer had to wear our bulletproof vests or helmets and had only to show our military IDs to travel freely among the base's two post exchange stores, its Internet café, the fast-food outlets, and a travel agency, where we bought the plane tickets that would take us home from Baltimore-Washington International Airport — which was as far as the military paid for travel.

After one day in Kuwait we took a commercial aircraft to Frankfurt, Germany. It was the first commercial aircraft I'd taken since my original trip to the Middle East back in March. Boarding that plane gave me a certain sense of nor-

malcy and brought me closer to the nearly forgotten reality of
civilian life from which I'd traveled so far since leaving the
United States. It felt odd to be in an environment where there
were no machine guns sticking out of the windows, no bullets
flying, and no mortar or RPG attacks.

We stayed in Germany for two hours, just long enough to
refuel the plane and to be briefed again, this time on terrorism
and driving while intoxicated. The terrorism briefing consisted
of two instructions: the first was not to wear our uniforms at
home because terrorist cells operating in the States might try to
kill us — or hurt our families — for being in the army; the second
was not to give any information about our units in Iraq, even if
the person asking was a beautiful woman at a bar. The other
briefing was much simpler: "Don't drink and drive."

By the time we arrived in Baltimore we had been traveling for almost four days. Everyone was tired but there was no
mistaking the sense of relief and happiness at being back
home. To me it seemed like the fulfillment of an impossible
dream, the sudden return of a life that had just as suddenly
been taken from me. On touching down, the captain of the
plane welcomed us to the United States and everyone responded with loud cheers and applause.

As I transferred to a plane that would take me to Florida,
I found my mood alternating between joy and melancholy. I
knew I was happy because I was going to see my daughter and
family again, but it was less clear why I was also sad. Perhaps
it was because I knew I had to return to a war and occupation
I hated. Or it might have been the secret certainty that I would
not return, and that I was leaving the men of my unit behind
in a war where we did not belong, but also in a land where we
had created a brotherhood that can only flourish amid the
horror of war.

Once in Baltimore I changed my ticket, which had originally been for Miami, to an earlier departure to Fort Lau-

derdale. I wanted to maximize time with my family, of course, but I'd also heard the media knew about our arrival, the first homecoming of Florida's troops from the war, and I knew I didn't want to face reporters. I was afraid that I might not be able to stop myself from expressing my opposition to the occupation. I took a cab from Fort Lauderdale and surprised my mother when I arrived home.

Communication with my mother about the war had been extremely difficult. I hated the fact that I had been deployed to support an illegal war and an imperial occupation, completely ignoring international law. But as the missions had become more dangerous, the political and moral analyses of the war had become less important, finally giving way to a mortal fear of dying. Trying to keep my cool during combat missions was not easy, but it was nothing compared to the self-control required to keep calm while talking to my mother on the phone from Iraq. She firmly believed that we were fighting a war for the interests of a few U.S. corporations, for oil, and for empire. My participation in the invasion was a constant source of conflict for her because, on one hand, she believed the Iraqi people had a right to fight against an imperialist occupation, but on the other, she dreaded the idea that any harm should come to me. This mixture of anxiety, confusion, and shame was evident every time I spoke to her, and I felt terribly guilty for putting her through such intense suffering.

When I arrived at her apartment, she ran toward me and threw her arms around me, holding me tight and kissing my hair. I got the impression that she wanted to say something, but she was sobbing uncontrollably and couldn't speak. I couldn't say anything either; I wanted to appear strong and I knew that my voice was on the point of giving out. We stood there hugging, our eyes filled with tears. I didn't know whether this was the happiest day of my life, or the saddest.

The next morning I was able to see my daughter for the first time in nine months, a period which had seemed like a lifetime. I was filled with fear and uncertainty. She had only been two and a half years old when I left for the war, and I knew I had changed. At times I felt like a completely different person. Would she remember who I was? Could the new me still be a father to her?

Memories of al Assad came to mind, memories of when—between guard shifts, while lying on the concrete floor outside of the ruins that housed my platoon—I had tried to erase my guilt about what we were doing there by listening to classical music on my CD player. The truth was that I had abused prisoners despite knowing that it was wrong, because I was too afraid to take a stand against orders that undermined my morality. How could I ever teach my daughter right from wrong when I had done so much wrong myself? What moral authority did I have left to be a good father? As our time in Iraq continued and I became more and more preoccupied with the single task of surviving, these issues concerned me less and less. But now, at the door to Samantha's home, they all came flooding back to me.

As soon as the door opened, I picked up Samantha and held her in my arms. She explored my face for a few seconds with great seriousness.

"Daddy," she said, breaking into a broad smile.

I was awed at how much she had grown in nine months, and at how well she could now speak. As we hugged, all of my previous doubts receded and I knew that it was not too late to rediscover my old self and be a good father to my daughter once more.

Yet, soon enough my excitement was tempered by a deep sense of apprehension. Having put her through so much at such young age, was I going to abandon her again? Again I found myself fighting back tears as I took Samantha to the car where my mother was waiting.

"She recognized me," I said as I fastened Samantha's seat belt.

"Of course," replied my mother. "All she did while you were away was talk about you, right Samantha?"

Samantha did not answer; she just looked at me in silence. I knew my mother had done her best to keep my memory alive by showing Samantha pictures and videos of the two of us at the park across the street from our apartment, or playing in the ocean water when she was only a baby, or simply spending time together at home, eating, playing, or capturing the excitement of her precious little face on film as she conquered her very first steps when she was only ten months old. Now that we were together again, more common history could be made and recorded, but for how long?

Reclaiming my relationship with my daughter renewed my resolve to put pressure on the military to uphold its own rules and regulations and let me out of the service. I had some hope in this regard. After all, Ms. Tringially, the Florida National Guard civilian employee with whom I had spoken from Iraq, had said, "You have to be discharged from the military immediately." Surely she had not been talking about something she knew nothing about, not after a congressional inquiry had prompted an investigation into my case. She had also said that the regulation was clear, proving that the official army regulation preventing the involuntary extension of noncitizen soldiers beyond eight years did exist.

Finding the actual regulation was not so hard. I went to my unit's headquarters in Miami and explained the situation to an old acquaintance of mine, who now worked as a recruiter. He not only knew of the regulation, he had it with him, and even made copies of the section I needed to bring my case to the legal departments of the army.

After calling the various legal offices of the Third Infantry Division, I was referred to the transition department at
Fort Stewart, Georgia. But they claimed that they couldn't
help me because although I was on active duty status to serve
in the war, I was still a National Guard soldier. When I called
the Florida National Guard, they put me in contact with
Master Sergeant Wingard, a female career soldier who dealt
with personnel matters.

"Yes," she said to the extension of my contract beyond
eight years. "You should not have been extended. But we cannot help you; the entire Fifty-third Infantry Brigade (of the
Florida National Guard) falls under the command of the
Third Infantry Division. They are the ones who can discharge
you. If you were here, then I would be able to get you out."

"What do you mean 'If I were here'?" I asked.

"I mean, if you were in the United States," she responded.

"What if I were in the States, master sergeant?" I knew
by then she thought I was calling from Iraq.

"If you were home I would be able to get you a discharge," she replied, sounding absentminded. I imagined her
with the phone pressed between her head and shoulder while
handling paperwork with her hands and eyes.

"Well, I am in the United States," I said with a renewed
sense of hope. "I'm on leave from Iraq for two weeks."

"Oh, no, no, no, no," she said hurriedly. "That's not what
I meant. I meant, when your unit returns from Iraq, *then* I can
discharge you."

"But you just said that I should have never been extended."

"Yes, but you were." She sounded like she was talking
to a child who could easily be convinced. "Right now you're
on leave, and if you don't go back you could be charged
with AWOL, and you do know what that could mean, right,
sergeant?"

AWOL, or absent without leave, is a lesser form of desertion, which in time of war could be punished extremely harshly.

"I'm not talking about going AWOL," I responded defensively. "I'm talking about the fact that I shouldn't have been deployed at all, yet you're saying that I have to go back."

"You know, sergeant," she said in a higher tone of voice and stretching the word *know*, "it really strikes me as odd that you have been in the military longer than eight years and have not yet become a U.S. citizen."

"Well, master sergeant," I responded, "I had never thought about citizenship much, but I don't think that not being a U.S. citizen makes me a bad person."

"No, I'm not saying that," she said.

"You seem to be saying that the regulation can be violated, and that I can be extended illegally, but that within that illegal extension, I have to honor my two-week leave papers."

I was getting a bit bolder by then.

"All I'm saying," she said, sounding conciliatory, "is that you belong to the active duty component, and that you should work with your chain of command."

"What would be the point?" I asked in despondency.

"Well, sergeant," she said, ready to conclude the conversation, "they say the wheel that squeaks gets the most oil. Keep trying."

Encouraged by this unexpected response, I called the transition department of the Third Infantry Division. I spoke with Master Sergeant Summers, with whom I had spoken before.

"Well, yes," she said. "But you have to go back to your unit and have them discharge you before we can do anything."

"You mean I have to go back to Iraq so that I can be discharged from the military, and then come back to the United States?"

"Well, you're on leave, sergeant." A tiny hint of exasperation could already be detected in her voice. "You have to go back so you don't violate your leave orders."

"Yes," I tried to remain calm. "But why do I have to travel all the way back to Iraq to then get discharged here in the States?"

"Well, I can't give you your discharge papers; your unit commander has to do that and he's in Iraq."

The sudden confidence in her voice made it clear that she thought she had brought the matter to a close. My commander had to sign the paperwork, and in her mind, that meant I had to return to Iraq. In the past, I would have simply accepted this ruling, coming as it did from someone of a higher rank. Not this time.

"If I can get discharge papers signed by my battalion commander, then you can discharge me here, correct, master sergeant?"

"If you don't go back at the end of your leave you could be charged with going AWOL."

"Nobody is thinking about going AWOL." I was telling the truth at that time. "My question is this: Do I have to physically be in Iraq to be discharged by you? I mean, if I have my discharge papers *here*, signed and all."

She seemed to be thinking hard about her response, or perhaps she was thinking about the implications of her response. I decided to give her a hand.

"In other words, master sergeant, is there any regulation saying that I have to physically be in Iraq to be discharged from the army?"

After a short and thoughtful pause she answered. The lethargic voice seemed to carry the heaviness of an admission of defeat.

"No."

That was enough for me. I immediately sent an e-mail to

Captain Warfel, carefully explaining that I needed him to write a letter to Mirable asking him if he could approve and sign my discharge documents. I tried to sound respectful, and reminded him of his promise that, if the regulations said I should be discharged, he would let me out.

Warfel's reply was angry and far from encouraging, but it didn't surprise me. "Not only do I think your request is disrespectful," he wrote back, "I think of it more as cowardice. Rest assured I will write no such letter." Following my chain of command, I wrote next to Lieutenant Colonel Mirable. I explained the entire case in a lot more detail, and even cited the relevant regulations.

Mirable's response was far more astute and restrained than Warfel's. He said he would have his personnel officer look into the situation, promised a quick reply, and requested a "courtesy reminder" if I had not received an answer in three days.

By this time I had already been in the States more than a week. As my two-week leave approached its end, my mother's pleas that I not return became ever more persistent. She told me repeatedly that I should stay home regardless of what the army had to say about my legal right to be discharged. For her the war was illegitimate and because of that I simply had no obligation to return to it. She gave me a list of the names and addresses of people and organizations who could provide support to soldiers opposed to the war, although there were no known deserters at that time.

My initial unwillingness to openly defy the army was partly based on what I later realized was a naïve belief that following proper procedure, with a good legal claim, would get me out. I knew I had been illegally extended, and that after a congressional inquiry the Florida National Guard had determined that I was to be discharged immediately. Surely, I reasoned, the army would honor its own regulations, especially when a U.S. senator was aware of the situation.

And so three days later I sent my battalion commander the "friendly reminder" he had asked for. The reply stated that the battalion intelligence officers had already reviewed my case and found that I was supposed to stay with the unit until the end of the mission, and that only after the unit redeployed could I get out. Then, and only then, Mirable informed me, could I decide what I wanted to do with my life.

After thinking I was about to get out of the army and the war, a sense of impotence took possession of my inner self. How could it be? I had to go back to Iraq, brutalize the people, rape the land, and possibly die there, all against my conscience.

I wasn't sure what to do at that point. The regulations didn't really matter that much, nor whether the military could legally keep me or not; I couldn't care less about any of that. The fact was that I despised the war and myself in it, but I couldn't say that to the military. I had to go back to Iraq. I had to swallow my guilt, and my values, and my conscience, and I had to go back to the war and I had to find a way to survive there, not just in body but in soul. I had to find a way not to lose myself in the war, to return home still human so I could be a father to my daughter.

It was painful to think about her; either way she had much to lose. If I returned to the war, I could be killed in more than one way. It wasn't just the physical death; it was also the many deaths of the soul every time you kill a human being. Whether we squeeze the trigger, give the order, or simply stand idle in the face of senseless missions that result in the spilling of innocent blood, it doesn't make a difference. We die, little by little, each time someone gets killed, until there is no soul left, and the body becomes but a corpse, breathing and warm but void of humanity.

If I were to disobey the army, it could mean legal prosecution by the Uniform Code of Military Justice, trial by court-martial, and possibly the death penalty! And if not the harshest sentence, they still could put me in jail for a long time—five, maybe ten years. And how could I be a father in jail? How would jail change me? Would I be any good to anyone after five or ten years in prison? What if Samantha's mother decided to disappear and I never saw my little girl again? It could happen; and if it did, what power would I have before the law as a former "criminal" and a convicted army deserter?

No, I had to return. I could survive the war and then go home. We had already been deployed for over seven months and we probably only had a few months left before we would be redeployed to the States. I could go back and, once again, obey my orders, save my body, return home, and somehow rebuild myself.

But what about the Iraqis? We killed civilians. Had I killed them? What about the young man who threw the grenade? He was too far to reach us, he couldn't hurt us, but he threw a grenade; nonetheless, I had not killed him, had I?

Everyone fired at him. What about me? I couldn't remember shooting at him. He was in my sight and eleven bullets were missing right after the incident. But I don't remember shooting him. Firing eleven bullets takes an eternity; how could that eternity have been erased from my memory?

Oh, but there is a memory: He is moving very slowly within the sight of my rifle; his hand is about to throw a grenade, but right before he does, we open fire on him, and that's where the blank is. Then, the young man is dead in a pool of his own blood. Two men emerge from the crowd, hands up in the air; they take their dead, and then they are swallowed by it. We have just murdered their son. I see him over and over, and I see myself in a dark room, alone, counting the bullets I fired at that young man. Gone! Dead forever.

And the other images, are they real, or imagined? The faceless child standing by the headless corpse of his father — he is not real, is he? He is fatherless, maybe dead now, and forever faceless to me because I did not want to see it. It's easy to hurt them, and to kill them, and to kill the people they love, when they have no face.

And the seven civilians killed near that beautiful mosque — did they have faces? I remember one face, no three; I think I remember three faces. And what about the man in the car? No, I don't remember his face. I fired at him but he was probably dead by then. It was an automatic decision — I did not tell my body to point the rifle at him and squeeze the trigger; it just happened. He was meters away from me, and I shot him, knowing just that he was guilty. Of what? I don't know, of being shot, perhaps. How come I don't remember his face? He was so close. I just don't remember it. No images, none at all? Yes, there is an image, the image of a very brief moment. Flesh. Yes, flesh and blood. It wasn't a face; it was the flesh and blood of what once was his face. He was dead when I shot at him. He must have been dead, he had to be. He was dead.

And then there was the little girl, the precious little princess who roamed the streets of her kingdom, a kingdom we had occupied and destroyed. Her face was dirty, weather-beaten, and very, very beautiful. Her eyes were enchanting and her smile was uncorrupted by the death and destruction that floated around her. She reminded me of my daughter.

But I was blameless, and I didn't have to worry about losing my soul. I was a soldier. I had to go back to the men of my infantry unit and continue to do what my superiors told me to do. That's what soldiers do. I could not be blamed for this. My life could be mine after the war. For now, I belonged to the military.

I decided I had to call one of the organizations, the GI

Rights hotline in California, that helps soldiers with legal issues, from the list my mother had given me. I had two days of leave left.

"Can you ask for an extension of your leave?" the GI Rights counselor, Teresa, asked me in a worried tone. "We're going to need more time to find you an attorney who can take your case."

An extension? I had never thought about it. What would I tell them? That I needed time to find a civilian attorney to get me out of the army? It didn't seem very likely that that would work.

"How much time would we need to find one?" I asked.

"Well, do you have money to pay the attorney?" Her voice was sweet, and I wondered what she looked like.

"How much would it cost?" I asked, hesitantly.

"Well, we're looking at a writ of habeas corpus, which basically means that a civilian court reviews your case, and if it turns out that you're right, the civilian court asks the military to let you out. For an attorney to take your case, it could easily cost you between fifteen and twenty-five thousand dollars."

"No way!" I said, alarmed.

"Don't worry," she interrupted, trying to reassure me. "We can try to find you an attorney who would take your case pro bono. But that means that we're going to need some time."

"How much time?" I asked.

"Whatever you can get," she said. "Why don't I start looking for an attorney in your area while you try to get us more time, and then we talk again tomorrow?"

"OK," I said, fighting a strong sinking feeling.

When I got off the phone with Teresa, I called the Florida National Guard and was referred to the captain in charge of extensions. I left a message on her answering machine.

The next day Teresa rang back. Her news was not encouraging.

"I haven't been able to find anyone yet. Were you able to get an extension?"

"No," I said in despair. "I left a message on this captain's answering machine, but I haven't heard back from her."

"Have you thought about applying for conscientious objector status?" asked Teresa.

"Conscientious objector? Me?" I was surprised she had asked. "No," I said. "You know I am an infantryman who has been in combat already." I told her a little bit about my experience in Iraq.

"Yes, I know," she said, calmly and convinced. "It doesn't matter; you can still apply."

"But I'm not a conscientious objector."

"I think you are," she insisted. "I know you don't want to go back to Iraq, but let me ask you: would you want to participate in any war?"

I had never really thought about it. I knew conscientious objectors were supposed to be opposed to all wars, but I wasn't sure that was true for me. Anyway, it didn't matter because I had already fought in Iraq. Wasn't it too late for me to claim to be a conscientious objector?

"No, it's not," Teresa explained. "You could have had a change of heart because of your experience in Iraq. You seem to be doing everything in your power to stay out of the war, and from what you have told me, it seems to me like you have strong moral convictions against war and violence in general."

"No," I insisted. "I've fired at people, you know? I've been an infantryman in war. There's no way."

"Well, listen," she said. "Let me keep trying to find you a lawyer. Meanwhile I'll e-mail you the questions you have to answer for your conscientious objector application. Work on those while you wait for your unit to call you."

I agreed to look at the application, still not convinced. I printed the questions and placed them on the night table next to my bed, too nervous to read them. I lay in my room with the lights off, thinking about the war, about the men in my unit and the people of Iraq. I kept seeing images of the horrible experiences we'd been through while I waited for the phone to ring. I thought about my daughter, and then I fell asleep.

When the phone finally rang, the sound was loud and sudden. I didn't want to answer it, I was so terrified. As I opened my eyes I realized it was morning, which meant I had only one day left in the States.

"This is Captain Ash," said the female voice on the phone, sounding authoritative. "Is this Staff Sergeant Mejía?"

"Yes, ma'am," I said, sounding almost dead.

"I have spoken with your commander, Captain Tad Warfel," said Captain Ash. "He's your commander, isn't he?"

"Yes, captain, he is," I said, sounding more alive, but afraid that she would hear the loud beating of my heart.

"He alerted me that you might try to ask for an extension, and said that you were ordered to return to your place of duty, which is ar Ramadi, Iraq, as soon as your leave is over."

"Roger, ma'am," I said, and the entire world started to collapse on top of me.

"I reviewed your request," she said, continuing to push the dagger into my heart, slowly. "And I don't think you have a good case for requesting an extension. Do you understand that, staff sergeant?"

"Yes, ma'am."

"Today is your last day, isn't it, sergeant?"

"Yes, ma'am."

"When does your plane leave?"

"Tomorrow morning, ma'am."

"Well, I'm giving you a direct order to get on that plane tomorrow, sergeant."

"Yes, ma'am."

"You're a staff sergeant," she continued. "That means

you've been in the military quite some time, so you know the consequences of missing that plane."

"Yes, ma'am," I said.

"And you know that since you're not a citizen you could face deportation if you don't board that plane."

"Yes, ma'am! Like you said, I am a staff sergeant, and have been in awhile; I know the consequences, captain." There was an insolent sneer in my voice now, but she ignored it.

"Alright, sergeant," she calmly replied. "I'm just making sure you're clear on what could happen here."

"Thank you, ma'am!" I said, as sarcastically as I could. "And don't worry," I added. "I know the consequences."

That night when I spoke with Teresa, what was left of my world finally crumbled.

"They didn't give me the extension," I said to her. "I'm supposed to get on a plane tomorrow morning and head back to Iraq. What do I do now?"

She still had not found an attorney.

"Well, I can't tell you not to get on that plane," she said, a note of despair in her voice. "All I can say is that we will continue looking for a lawyer, and that we will try to get you out while you're in Iraq."

"But you don't understand, Teresa." I felt like I was dying as I said the words. "They don't care about the law in Iraq; all they care about is keeping their soldiers there, that's it. They're never gonna let me out if I go back."

"Well, maybe if we get you a lawyer they'll listen." I detected a combination of kindness and hopelessness in her voice. "But I can't advise you to stay."

I felt all alone in the world.

"Keep working on the CO claim." She sounded sincere, but I was in a state of total despair and abandonment. "And we won't stop working to get you back from Iraq."

I thanked her for her help, quite genuinely, and promised

that, whatever I did, I would keep her informed of my situation. But after that night, Teresa and I never spoke again.

I received the morning in bed, but without any sleep. I had to get up, find my itinerary, and prepare to leave. But there was no need to get up right away; it was still early morning and I had plenty of time. I was so tired, and my body felt so heavy. The hours passed and I stayed in bed. I didn't know exactly when I had to leave and I hadn't looked at the clock on the night table for a long time. But I knew I had to get up. I had to go back to Iraq. Before I knew it, night had fallen again. I had missed my plane. I decided I would go back the next day, and then I slept.

ELEVEN

A cool autumn rain was falling in New York City when I first visited the GI Rights advocacy group called Citizen Soldier, headquartered on Manhattan's Fifth Avenue. It was about a week after the official end of my two weeks of R&R leave and the beginning of my five months underground in the northeastern United States, where I had moved after realizing I was not going to return to Iraq.

Relocating to New York, one of the most liberal cities in the United States, was in part a search for "my kind," to be closer to people who had the same feelings about the war as I had. But it was also a move for reasons of safety. I hated leaving my home and family, particularly my daughter, for the clandestine life of a fugitive. But if I remained in Miami, where a poor public transportation system made it virtually impossible to avoid driving, I risked being pulled over by the city's police officers for a traffic violation, the most common way that AWOL soldiers are caught. In addition, there was the danger of being denounced by members of my local National Guard unit who were home on leave, or by the relatives of soldiers I knew who were serving in Iraq.

Trying to convince myself that going back to Iraq was the

right thing to do had proved completely unsuccessful. The reasons I had used in the past to justify my involvement in the war no longer carried any weight. It still hurt me deeply to think that the soldiers in my squad might be injured or killed without my being there; we had become very close to one another during the war, and it wasn't without much self-searching that I quit my job as their combat leader. But I had come to realize that individuals have to make their own decisions based on their conscience.

Many soldiers justify participating in wars they find objectionable with the argument that we're fighting for one another. Certainly that was an argument I wrestled with, but however much we said we were fighting for one another, the fact remained that we had no right to be in Iraq. Besides, as soldiers we had accepted that being in the military could one day put us in harm's way, but that wasn't the case for the Iraqi people. They had no choice about being swept up in the war and occupation that we imposed upon them. We were on their streets, patrolling their roads, invading their homes. It seemed to me that the real barbarity was the death and destruction we were bringing to those people.

But none of these reflections provided easy answers, and the truth is that there never was a moment of complete clarity at which I made a firm decision to resist the war; I simply didn't get on the plane when I was supposed to. I thought I would get on the next flight and then missed that one too, and then the following one, and then again, until one day I woke up simply knowing that I would not go back.

Deep inside I knew I had stayed behind for a reason, that there was a purpose for my coming home and for not returning. I knew that even if I didn't go back to Iraq, the war, for me, would be far from over; perhaps it was just beginning. It wouldn't be the same war, the one I had fought in the roads and alleyways of ar Ramadi, nor would it require me to carry

a rifle. I was done with that. This would be, first and fore-
most, a war waged within myself, one where my fears and
doubts would come face to face with my conscience, a war to
reclaim my humanity and my spiritual freedom. It would also
be a war against the system I had come from, a battle against
the military machine, the imperial dragon that devours its
own soldiers and Iraqi civilians alike for the sake of profits. I
knew that somehow I had to turn my words into weapons,
that speaking out was now my only way to fight.

Almost as soon as I arrived in Miami from Iraq, I started
to give interviews about the grim reality facing U.S. troops in
Iraq. A couple of days after I got back, Specialist Perez's
mother, Miladys Guerrero, had opened her home to a group
of soldiers' relatives for a religious service to pray for their
safety. (Early on in the invasion, when the war and the president still had strong public support, she had stood with my
mother and stepfather in downtown Miami holding "Bring
Our Soldiers Home" signs while wearing army fatigues.
Since then, she and my folks had been avoided like the plague
by the highly conservative and much larger Family Support
Group, made up of families of the other soldiers in my unit,
which perceived them as radicals.) After the service, a Fox
News reporter asked me, the only soldier present at the
event, for an interview. Shyly, and without expressing any
moral or political condemnation of the war, I made some comments that were critical of the military. I told the reporter
how guard units were not receiving the proper logistical support to perform combat duties. I explained how, contrary to
media reports, troop morale was extremely low, and how just
about everyone in my unit lacked a sense of mission and was
desperate to return. The story never aired.

But now that I was underground, things would be different. I would speak (concealing my identity) not only about
low troop morale in Iraq for lack of equipment and deploy-

ment extensions, but also about how our commanders were acting without the slightest regard for the lives of Iraqi civilians or soldiers in order to get awards, and of how we had abused prisoners. I would talk about my feelings concerning the war, and about why I wasn't returning. I would hold nothing back.

The first interview I gave was to a CNN reporter who had interviewed my mother in the past, when she and my stepfather, Julio, had first begun publicly protesting the war. Considerable care was taken to protect my identity. The cameraman kept my face in the shadows and I used the pseudonym Carlos, telling the interviewer simply that I was an Iraq vet, twenty-eight-years of age, unmarried with one child, an infantryman who had gone underground because of opposition to the war. A couple of weeks later the story appeared on national TV and radio in what I believe was the first broadcast interview with an Iraq war resister.

Through media contacts from before I went underground, I had gotten the contact information for a man named Steve Robinson, a retired Special Forces veteran who led an organization called the National Gulf War Resource Center, which provides support to veterans of the 1991 Gulf War. Steve in turn put me in touch with Tod Ensign, the director of the soldiers' rights organization called Citizen Soldier.

Thus a couple of weeks after the end of my leave I found myself on Manhattan's Fifth Avenue outside the address that Tod had given me over the phone. Looking at the building from the street, I thought at first I had arrived at the fancy headquarters of a well-funded organization. Once inside, however, I found that the Citizen Soldier offices were quite modest. Furthermore, far from the uptight, heartless image I'd always had of attorneys, Tod turned out to be a down-to-earth kind of guy, with a big smile and a physical resemblance to Christopher Walken—a similarity only enhanced by his heavy

New York City accent. As a young attorney in the sixties and seventies, Tod had been involved in the Vietnam GI resistance movement, and had helped underground soldiers living abroad with safe passage back to the United States, a legal defense, and the means to get their stories out to the media.

As soon as I spoke with Tod the door to a new world opened up before my eyes. I went from feeling powerless and alone to realizing that there was a whole network of people and groups, from women's rights organizations and antiwar veterans to military families and religious groups, who all felt as I did about the war.

Tod and I discussed how I was going to handle my absence from the military. We agreed that I should do everything I could to avoid getting arrested and then give myself up voluntarily while insisting in court on my right to be legally discharged from the service. This strategy of surrendering myself would defeat the charge of desertion, which is roughly defined as unauthorized absence from the military with the intent to remain permanently away.

Tod and I met many times during the following months to discuss what my eventual return to the military would look like. When the presidential primaries were in full swing with a number of antiwar candidates taking up the issue of Iraq in debates with their more conservative rivals, Tod suggested that the best strategy would be for me to surrender myself at a political event and make a major public statement while doing so, to pressure these candidates and hold them to their word. He thought that since I would be the first combat veteran to publicly denounce the war and refuse to go back to it, there would be wide media interest in my case, and that under the scrutiny of the public eye, the military would have to go easy on me.

But at that time I wasn't ready to hand myself over just yet. I had come to accept the possibility that I could be a con-

scientious objector and had started working on the application Teresa had given me. I also felt I needed to have a serious
face-to-face conversation with my legal counsel about what to
expect from a possible court-martial. This was the person who
would actually be handling my defense, as opposed to Tod,
who was in charge of the political and public relations side of
the case. For that, Tod explained, I would need to go to Boston
to meet his colleague, an attorney named Louis Font.

When I was ready to go, Tod took me to a newsstand to
get the bus ticket to Boston. To my astonishment the ticket
was only twenty dollars for a round trip.

"Why so cheap?" I asked.

"The Chinatown bus companies are always at war with
each other, so you're guaranteed to always get the cheapest
fares here," he explained.

This was only the first of many useful tips I would get
from Tod during my underground period in New York. Before long I knew all the cheap places to get great Middle
Eastern food, plus several safe places for clandestine media
interviews, mostly headquarters of nonprofit organizations
that, though they could not be overtly political, secretly ab-
horred the war and were happy to aid a soldier who was willing to speak out.

"And don't worry about New York City cops," added
Tod, smiling confidently. "They've got too much on their
hands to even care about policing AWOL soldiers."

He directed me to the subway train that would take me
home, and, as he nearly always did in the future whenever we
parted, gave me a full metro card for the train.

"There's about twenty bucks on it," he said, waving from
a distance as I descended into the subway station. "I only
used it a couple of times."

Attorney Louis Font was based just outside of Boston, in
Brookline, Massachusetts. I had spoken with him a couple of

times on the phone, but we had never met in person, and, for security reasons, he had not wanted to discuss the details of my case unless we were face to face. At that time, the government and media were really complicit in reporting that troop morale was high in Iraq, and I was the only combat veteran that Louis and Tod knew who was willing to openly discredit their line. That made me a wanted man and prompted Louis to suggest that I avoid Internet and telephone communication as much as possible.

My mother, my grandmother, my aunt Norma, and a friend who helped me move from Miami to the northeast all accompanied me on my first visit to Boston to meet Louis, who received us as family from the moment we set foot in his office. One of our main concerns was that Louis would not share our moral and political feelings against the war. But after we'd all introduced ourselves, Louis left the room and came back with a scrapbook filled with photos and newspaper clippings about his antiwar stance during the conflict in Vietnam.

Born in New York City of Puerto Rican parents and raised in the Midwest, young Louis Font had been somewhat of an army success story in its efforts to recruit Latinos into the U.S. military. He had graduated as one of the top students at the U.S. Military Academy at West Point, the most prestigious officers' school in the United States Army. The army then decided to send Second Lieutenant Font to Harvard's Kennedy School of Government, which is where the young officer first began to listen more carefully to his doubts about the Vietnam War, a conflict in which he was expected to eventually serve. It was then that Louis openly refused to deploy to a war he considered immoral, becoming the first officer in the history of West Point to publicly resist.

Tod Ensign, already an attorney, helped organize a legal and political defense for Lieutenant Font, who accused U.S. Army generals of war crimes against the people of Vietnam.

"I understand what you're going through, Camilo," said Louis with a kind smile.

It soon became clear that he certainly did understand, perhaps better than I did at the time. Back then Louis faced a sentence of up to twenty-five years in jail, and his trial lasted a whole year. But the public pressure that Louis's defense applied proved too intense for a military already battling severe internal conflicts of insubordination and mutiny. At the end, the machine gave in and Louis was released honorably from the army. I had traveled to Boston hoping to find an attorney who understood me; I had found inspiration and a role model.

It was cold in Boston when we left Louis's office on that that early fall afternoon. We roamed the streets for hours searching for a hotel, but all the rooms were booked by travelers making the annual trip to Boston for the foliage festival. When all seemed lost, Louis returned a call we had placed on his voice mail. The underground network of Peace and Justice, it seemed, had cast its net over Massachusetts as well as it had over New York. We were given the name and phone number of a person who could give us a hand for the night, even on such extremely short notice. We were not required to provide a name or an ID, but to simply say we had been referred by Louis Font. Before we knew it we were spending the night at a magnificent New England mansion on the outskirts of Boston.

There was no one waiting for us when we arrived, but the doors were unlocked and there were instructions for us on where to find the keys to our rooms. The note also included a courteous "Have a Pleasant Evening." I spent several nights at that same place in the following months, which welcomed not only weary travelers seeking quiet rest for the evening, but also different Peace and Justice activists, religious solidarity groups, and international students living on humble budgets.

Throughout the months that followed, my mother kept calling the army's deserter hotline to see if I had been listed, but my name never turned up. The police did not even visit my mother's house. Aside from a few nasty e-mail notes from Captain Warfel telling the Family Support Group that I was being sought for desertion, not much else happened.

But the military's apparent lack of activity in pursuing me did not mean I let my guard down; far from it. I understood the army's silence as simple caution. I was well aware of the violations the military had committed in my deployment and extension, and I thought they were simply trying to come up with a way to deal with me quietly and without damaging their public image.

The need for vigilance was all the greater because I continued to talk, under cover, to both national and international media outlets. Louis warned me that it was likely that someone in the military was monitoring all interviews given by soldiers about the war, particularly those of dissenting opinion — underground conscientious objectors who refused to return to the army. At that point, that pretty much meant me.

"Every time you give an interview, Camilo," Louis said to me once, "someone in the army, or maybe all the way up at the Pentagon level, says: 'Here is Camilo again.'"

"You really think so, Louis?"

"Of course. Think about it, Camilo; you're the only combat veteran who's been to Iraq, who's refused to go back, and who's speaking out against what he saw in the war. It is because you have been there that they don't want you to speak," he paused. "Make no mistake, Camilo, they know about you at the highest levels of government."

Bearing in mind these warnings, I stopped using my cell phone and my Internet account, and I also got rid of my ATM card. I made my phone calls from pay phones, trying to use a different one every time. If something sensitive needed to be discussed with Louis, I took a trip to Boston so that we could talk face to face. He advised me to avoid communication with anyone from my unit or the military in general, unless either he or Tod, or both, were present. I didn't let up on the press interviews, however. These were mostly set up by Tod, who arranged for them to be conducted at restaurants and cafés that were both safe and pricey.

"You'll be alright there," he would say as we rode the subway to some fancy Italian bistro. "They flew all the way here just to interview you; they've got money, so make sure they pick up the tab."

And indeed, reporters always did pick up the tab. But what caught my interest the most was not the food or who paid for it, but the approach the journalists would take in their questions. Most U.S. reporters, for instance, whether they agreed with the war or not, concentrated primarily on the pain of U.S. families and on the repercussions that my refusal to fight could have on the military.

"Don't you think," they would typically ask, "that if the army lets you go as a conscientious objector because of your opposition to the war in Iraq, it would open the door for everyone in the military to do the same?"

The unspoken attitude among these reporters seemed to me to be that soldiers, right or wrong, were supposed to keep their mouths shut and obey orders. Back then I took this simplistic analysis as a measure of the mediocrity of the U.S. media. I would nod my head pensively while the stern-faced reporter finished the question, even though I knew exactly where he or she was going with it; I could probably have written the answers to the questions asked and saved a lot of time. "Then no one would fight the war," would be the predictable answer to the predictable question.

I would say, however—as if answering the question for the first time—"But you don't have to worry about soldiers not wanting to fight, as long as there is a good reason for being at war. The problem is that we don't have a good reason for being in Iraq. I did not sign a contract to fight for oil in the Middle East, and I don't think anyone in the military did."

Then they would ask, "What would you say to the mothers of soldiers killed in Iraq then? That their loved ones died for oil? That they were mercenaries?"

I felt it wasn't for me to answer that question, since I was not the one who had sent their loved ones off to war, and since I wasn't the one making a lot of money in contracts to rebuild what *we* had destroyed (not that I had seen a whole lot of rebuilding of Iraq either). But I would always say: "I made my decision based on my understanding that this is a criminal, illegitimate war for empire." I would tell the reporter: "Had I died in the war, in my heart, I would have died a mercenary; I made a very personal decision not to. I would say to the mothers to voice their pain and to unite against the war to prevent more blood from being spilled unnecessarily."

My responses were honest, but the fact that I knew them by heart made me begin to feel like a bit of a fraud. I also felt bad about my answers because there was so much more to be said, in particular about the cost of the war to the Iraqi people. But I knew that most U.S. reporters were not looking for thorough answers to their questions—only sound bites. Still, I felt I had to work with what I had and try in every way I could to get some sort of critical perspective in front of a generally oblivious public.

Things were different with European reporters, who were more interested in the experiences that had made me into a conscientious objector. Most of their questions dealt with the everyday interactions between U.S. soldiers and regular Iraqis; they wanted to know about the raids, the curfews, the roadblock killings, and the abuse of prisoners. They also wanted to know if there were any soldiers from my unit, in ar Ramadi, who also opposed the war. I told them I didn't know much about soldiers agreeing or disagreeing with me, politically, morally, or spiritually. I only knew that although there wasn't a lot of open questioning of the war, there was intense disaffection with both the government and the mission.

I felt I could expand a bit more with European reporters than with their American counterparts, and I generally received a lot more sympathy from across the ocean than from within the United States; I was even offered help if I ever wanted to go to Europe, an offer made to me more than a few times.

"You could go to Europe, Carlos," said Patricia, a European reporter from a socialist newspaper, calling me by my most usual pseudonym. "Here you're going to go to jail."

"Maybe," I countered. "But this is my home."

"Yes, but you haven't done anything wrong," she insisted with a mixture of sadness and kindness. "Why stay here when you could go to Europe? People hate the war over there, you know?"

"I should stay precisely *because* I haven't done anything wrong," I said. "Besides, a lot of people here hate the war too."

She looked at me like I didn't know what was coming my way.

"Yes, but you will pay for your decision, Carlos," she continued, as if she could foretell the future. "You will pay."

Patricia and I met a few more times and became good friends. She never neglected to tell me that she thought I shouldn't surrender to the military when it was they who had committed the crime and not me. She argued that I already had a lot of healing to do from having been to war, and that if on top of that I ended up in jail, the psychological and emotional damage I would suffer might be beyond repair. I always told her that I had already decided to bring my case to the public arena and, if needed, to a court-martial. I tried to sound self-assured when I said this but in truth I was terrified of going public and surrendering to the army. A large part of me wanted to just go away quietly and pretend the war had never happened.

As my days in hiding became weeks and weeks became months, I began to feel more pressure to make my public surrender. The moral and intellectual clarity of mind I had found left me no options other than speaking out publicly against the war and refusing further participation in it. By now I had fully embraced the idea of conscientious objection and had spent countless hours filling out my CO claim. This process, together with the many underground interviews I gave, forced me to go back and relive my experiences in Iraq, and to reflect on their meaning. All this analysis and questioning of war, and of myself within the war, eventually served me as a vehicle toward absolute clarity of the wrongfulness not only of the war against Iraq, but of war in general. This growing conviction did not erase my deep-seated fear, sometimes bordering on horror, of going public and surrendering. Patricia's words kept echoing throughout my head: *You will pay, Carlos, you will pay.*

The widely broadcast capture of Saddam Hussein did not help ease my fears. The news media ceaselessly exploited the capture as if it justified the invasion and occupation. Never mind that no weapons of mass destruction had been found, nor a link between Saddam and al Qaeda—people were caught in a kind of trance by the media's spin and for a while it seemed as though everyone was cheering the war and the military. Once, on a CNN news program, Paula Zahn seemed to want to slap General Wesley Clark when he said he still did not think the war was justified.

"Even after the capture of Saddam Hussein?" she asked, astonished that anyone should think differently.

"No," said the general.

Clark's position did not seem, at least to me at that time, to be representative of wider public opinion. It was as though people were incapable of questioning the obvious. The government's and corporate media's spin of Saddam's capture had delivered its magic spell of deception. I wondered how a dissenting soldier would fare in the face of this widespread delusional conformity. With a public so complacent and so out of touch with reality, I would quite simply be fried, first by the war-hypnotized nation, then by the war machine and its judicial system that punished dissent.

I walked the streets of the massive, anonymous cities in the northeastern United States, spending entire afternoons in parks and museums, working on my never-ending CO claim, closing my eyes only to watch my resolve drown in the fear of my eventual public surrender, living in panic of the military and the government, afraid of the future, unable to really live. I felt like a coward for being unable to act on what was clearly my moral duty.

Every time I thought of going back to the military and going public, the deafening pounding of my heart paralyzed me. Tod kept telling me that perhaps we shouldn't wait too long, and every month he suggested that we participate in a rally or some other event, the idea being that we should make my surrender as open and public as possible to shine a spotlight on the military's handling of my case. Louis, understanding how frightened I was, didn't insist on my return being a media event. But he too wanted me to at least set a date for my surrender.

"Camilo, I know how hard it is," he said once. "I have brought clients back to the military completely drunk, because that's the only way they could do it—they were *that* afraid."

That wasn't really an option for me, as I knew I had to

have a clear mind if I was to say what I needed to say when I gave myself up. Again and again I was told how important it was for a soldier to speak out against the war from his personal experience of having been there. At that point, not one service member apart from me had come back from the war saying anything even remotely critical about the reality on the ground in Iraq. It was a heavy responsibility to bear.

"You're so courageous," people would say. "You are going to lead the way in a new movement of dissent within the military. Many more will follow you."

I would nod my head in acknowledgment, registering the words but often thinking about the punishment that would surely follow, and worrying about my own resolve. *Am I really courageous? I haven't done anything yet*, I would say to myself. And then other words would come to mind: *There has to be a first one, a voice that breaks the silence. There needs to be a first one.* And what I needed to do would become clear again.

A key event occurred after one of my visits to see Louis in Massachusetts. I was accompanied by Nancy Lessin and Charley Richardson, who had co-founded a grassroots antiwar organization called Military Families Speak Out, which my mother had joined back when I was still in Iraq. After a long conversation with Louis about my return to the military, Nancy and Charley took me to a place some forty minutes outside Boston that would play a major role in my eventual surrender to the army: the Peace Abbey, in Sherborn, Massachusetts.

We were greeted at the Abbey by its founder and director, Lewis Randa. Like many other middle-class kids, Lewis had joined the National Guard in order to avoid going to Vietnam. But during basic training he came to think that it was a dishonest way to avoid combat and instead applied for conscientious objector status, refusing to wear his military uniform and eventually going on a hunger strike as part of his protest. The military responded by attempting to dispatch him to active duty in Vietnam. Only the intervention of Senator Edward Kennedy secured his CO status and prevented him from being sent to war. From that point on, Lewis dedicated his life to the cause of peace, and, in 1972, he founded the Life Experience School, a program that empowers children and young adults to become peacemakers. Fourteen years later, Lewis expanded his work and opened the Peace Abbey, a refuge for people of all faiths and walks of life who want to learn about or practice nonviolence.

The Abbey is a place that must be experienced in order to be understood; no words can capture the spirit of the place that later became like a second home to me. A life-sized bronze monument of Gandhi welcomes visitors, and the grounds include an animal sanctuary that houses a cow, three pigs, a donkey, and two goats. The sanctuary is always open for people to spend time with the animals. Just outside the stable, at the base of a small hill, there is a tombstone inscribed with the words *Unknown Civilians Killed in War.* The memorial was unveiled by former heavyweight boxing champion of the world, war resister, and conscientious objector Muhammad Ali in 1994.

A couple of three-story New England homes flank the stable and overlook an old cemetery just outside the estate. One of the homes is a retreat with four rooms for visitors in search of peace and quiet, a multifaith chapel, a vegetarian kitchen, and a small library with a collection of books about peace and about the atrocities of war. The walls of the peace refuge are lined with news clippings about people who have paid a dear price for their peace activism and with relics of saints and people killed in their struggles for social justice.

The first time I entered the house I was struck by the soothing, spiritual music that filled the place with a sense of peace and harmony. I was then surprised by the sound of a mystical yet familiar refrain: the Islamic call to prayer. This was the first time I had heard the call since I had returned from Iraq, and it served as a reminder of the interconnections between people around the world, the unity of humankind that had brought me to the Abbey.

In a corner of the main house, inside the multifaith chapel, there is a shrine dedicated to the late Monsignor Oscar Arnulfo Romero, the Salvadoran archbishop who was assassinated in 1980 because of his commitment to peace and justice—making him the first bishop slain at the altar since Thomas Becket in the twelfth century. Photos of the moments after the arch-bishop's slaying were displayed next to a piece of bloodstained cloth from the altar at which he delivered his last mass. Monsignor's glasses were on display right next to the bloodstained cloths, enhancing both his powerful spiritual presence and the price he paid for speaking truth to power.

On the walls of a hallway of the other house were pictures of children. A legless child, severely mutilated by land mines, stared at me from one of the pictures. Another photo on the wall showed a newborn baby come into this world only to live a few moments of hell before dying. He had been born with extreme deformities caused by depleted uranium, a radioactive material used by the U.S. military to build munitions and armored plates for vehicles. Upon impact, depleted uranium–based projectiles and armored plates pulverize and get into the air and water, contaminating everything in their path and condemning people, including soldiers, civilians, and even unborn children, to a life of severe pain, deformity, and death by disease.

I didn't speak while looking at these pictures, but as I stared at the horrific images I was aware of a change occurring inside of me. I began to feel ashamed of my fear of going to jail and of being called a traitor. I realized that I had been a coward from the very beginning when I should have refused to be sent to war but did nothing. In Iraq, I had seen and participated in the brutal and abusive treatment of prisoners and civilians but had lacked the courage to disobey orders. Now, faced with a moral duty to publicly refuse and resist the war, I was paralyzed once again, too weak to break the chains of my own fear. But looking at the faces of those children, from times and lands unknown to me, I felt a new resolve and realized that I did have the strength to give myself up and to speak out when doing so. What's more, I knew the Abbey was the place where I wanted it all to happen. I would go public with my denouncement of the war and my refusal to return to it in this place that had been dedicated to peace from its very beginning.

When I subsequently told Tod of my plan, he expressed some reservations. He worried that the Abbey was too far from Boston and other major cities for reporters to make the journey there. But Louis insisted that it was important to choose a place where I would feel comfortable and my family agreed with him. Tod finally acceded and we began to plan for my public surrender to the military.

Up to that point most of my relatives, including my father, had been kept in the dark about my situation. Such secrecy was necessary for my safety, but also to protect those close to me from the possibility of harassment and prosecution by the army. But now that we had decided to go ahead with the surrender, we began contacting all available relatives and friends, as well as the different groups and organizations that opposed the war and wanted to stand by us.

We chose a date, March 15, 2004, almost exactly five months after the official end of my leave from the war, which, given the schedules of the people we wanted to invite, would allow as many people as possible to attend a press conference we planned to hold at the Abbey. After the conference I would be escorted to the place where I would surrender to military authorities. The media response to the news of my surrender was

very encouraging; it included an interview with Dan Rather for
60 Minutes, arranged for us with the help of Lewis Randa's
friend, the late Hugh Thomson. He had been the subject of one
of their stories, a short news documentary on the thirtieth anniversary of the My Lai massacre, which focused on Hugh's
heroic action in landing his helicopter to prevent more civilians
from being gunned down in the infamous Vietnam atrocity.

On the eve of my surrender, my family and I gathered
with reporters and friends for dinner and a few final interviews at the Life Experience School, which was located just a
few miles from the Abbey. Both of my parents were there, as
were my brother Carlos; my stepfather Julio; my maternal
grandmother Antonia; my aunt Norma; my uncle Alex; Louis
Font and his wife, Gale Glazer; a couple of reporters from
Chile; and some close friends of the family. After dinner we
all went back to the Peace Abbey, where a progressive band
from the area was giving a concert. My father and brother
joined in with some songs from Nicaragua. It was there that,
after five months of work and fifty-five pages, I was finally
able to finish my conscientious objector claim.

"You have to give it up, Camilo," Louis told me firmly.
"That's the only way we can submit it to the army."

The next morning Catholic bishop Thomas Gumbleton,
the auxiliary bishop of the Archdiocese of Detroit, arrived at
the Abbey. He gave the mass and then, together with a number of other witnesses, signed my conscientious objector application. Other people who were there to show their support
included Nancy Lessin and Charley Richardson from Military Families Speak Out, Fernando Suarez del Solar, whose
son Jesus was one of the very first U.S. marines killed in
Iraq; Dave Cline, the national president of Veterans for
Peace; and somewhere between sixty and eighty others who
opposed the war and stood in solidarity with us.

We didn't know what to expect in terms of media atten-

dance at the press conference that followed the religious service. I was concerned that Tod's point about the distance
journalists needed to travel might mean a poor turnout. But
the crowd of reporters, both international and national, that
greeted us on the front lawn of the Abbey surpassed our highest expectations. Lewis had arranged the event so that we answered questions standing next to the stone for Unknown
Civilians Killed in War, where a flame burned to honor the
dead. After a student of the Life Experience School sang the
Star-Spangled Banner, Bishop Gumbleton spoke briefly about
the long tradition of conscientious objection within the Catholic
Church, citing historical figures such as Saint Francis of Assisi and Saint Ignatius of Loyola.

I had decided not to write a speech, so after the bishop
spoke I gave a brief statement from the heart, saying simply
that I rejected all war, that I had been an instrument of violence in the past but was now choosing to be an instrument of
peace. I declared myself a conscientious objector, and said
that the war in Iraq was oil-motivated, that I was not a mercenary, and that I believed no soldier had signed up to travel
halfway across the world to fight for oil.

"So if you want to support the troops," I continued, "you
cannot support the war."

I concluded my remarks by referring to the decision of
voters in Spain just the day before, to elect a new prime minister who was committed to withdrawing all of Spain's troops
from Iraq.

"Yesterday the Spanish people voted 'no' to war. I hope
the American people can do the same in November. Thank
you very much."

"But, Camilo," yelled a newspaper reporter. "When you
signed for the military, you knew you could end up in a war.
What made you change your mind about it?"

"Well, I've been there and I can tell you it's not the people in power, the ones who declare wars, who pay the price; it's the soldiers, the civilians, and the innocent unarmed people."

"Yes, but you must have known that soldiers and people die in war," said a tall man in a blue suit who looked more like a Secret Service agent than anything else. "What was it that you saw that changed your mind?"

"Well, we were ambushed and people were killed. But I also think that, regardless of whether you happen to be sheltered in a palace or out in the streets getting ambushed like I was, simply going to war for oil is immoral."

"Camilo," said a woman from a prominent Spanish TV network, "what difference do you see between what is reported here about the troops in Iraq and what you experienced there?"

"Yes," I answered, glad that she had asked that question. "One huge disappointment is that the news media report that troop morale is high in Iraq, and that we're all happy to be there. This is not the case. We were all lied to about weapons of mass destruction and connections between Iraq and terrorism to justify the war. In reality we're giving terrorism a reason to exist with this war. But even for those who supported the war, the truth is, we all feel trapped there because the Iraqi people don't want us there and there is no sense of mission. There is no electricity, no water, nothing is being reconstructed; the feeling is that we're only there to watch our own backs."

A few weeks before my surrender, I had given an interview to a *Chicago Tribune* reporter. After meeting with me, he went to speak with people from my unit, which had by then returned from Iraq. When he talked to some of the soldiers about what I had said concerning the way our commanders had used us as bait to draw insurgents out and instigate firefights, a number of them confirmed my claim. Not surprisingly, my captain, who was also interviewed, took a different line. It was his comments, published that morning that the reporter picked up on:

"Camilo, your commander says you lost your nerve," he said, looking at the little notebook he held in his hand. "What do you say about that?"

"I say that I didn't lose my nerve." I looked right at the reporter as I spoke. "I actually did my job as a soldier."

"But what do you say to the soldiers in your unit," asked another official-looking man, "who may say you turned your back on them?"

"What I say to them is that I made a very personal decision to take a stand against the war, based on my own moral principles. And that even if they disagree with me now, maybe one day they will realize how we were lied to about this war. And I also say that today I speak for many soldiers who oppose this war but don't have the strength to come forward. I'm not turning my back on my comrades; I'm doing this for them."

"What do you think the military is going to do to you now?" asked an elegantly dressed woman journalist who was kneeling on the grass in front of me.

"I really have no idea," I said, and indeed that was the case. "But whatever happens, if I end up going to jail for many years, at least I'll have a clear conscience and I'll have peace because I know that God has already forgiven me."

From then on the questions became much more legal, so I asked Louis and Tod to provide the answers. After some other people present made brief statements on my behalf, Louis addressed the reporters, telling them that he was ready to defend me should the army decide to try me by court-martial but emphasizing that we expected them to deal with me administratively and give me conscientious objector status.

"During the Vietnam War," Louis said, "when President Bush himself was absent from his National Guard unit for

many more months than my client has been, the military dealt
with him administratively. We expect them to give Staff
Sergeant Mejía the exact same treatment."

After the press conference, friends, family, and I, together with as many reporters who could fit in, climbed
aboard a bus that Lewis had rented to take me to a military
base for my official surrender. The local police showed up just
moments before our departure, and when one of the activists
saw them approaching through the cemetery, a human wall
quickly formed around me to prevent them from taking me
away. It was only after one of the policemen explained that
they were there because a high number of vehicles were illegally parked outside the property that my friends relaxed.

When Lewis told the officer that we were about to leave
for Hanscom Air Force Base, some twenty minutes away
from Sherborn, the police offered to accompany us. And so
we set off with a police escort at the head of a long caravan of
supporters.

As we traveled along the suburban roads, my father and
brother played more Nicaraguan folk music, while some of
the reporters, including a production crew sent by documentary filmmaker Michael Moore, asked a few final questions.
When we got to the base, we were greeted by still more journalists and activists who had already set up their cameras and
sound equipment. Nearby, on the side of the road facing the
military installation, a rainbow peace flag and a Veterans for
Peace banner fluttered in the wind. I kissed and hugged my
friends and relatives, and then Louis and I were approached
by a couple of military policemen. It was clear that they had
absolutely no idea what was going on.

"Hello, sir," said Louis to the officer in charge. "My name
is Louis Font; I am an attorney representing Staff Sergeant
Mejía, who is here today to officially surrender to military
control."

After I gave the officer my military ID, he asked me to walk with them to the base. Before reaching the gate I turned back one last time to wave good-bye. All of my relatives and friends, my attorneys, just about all the peace activists, and even a few reporters from major news networks waved back. An air of profound sadness seemed to descend on the group. "We love you, Camilo!" a woman yelled, and the crowd responded with a mournful cheer.

Crying, my father turned to my mother. "What have we done, Maritza?" he asked with a torn voice. "Why have we given them our son?"

They stayed there for a while, watching closely as I was met by a squad of policemen wearing camouflage uniforms, radios, and guns. Finally, I was swallowed by a patrol car that took me away, into the unknown quarters of Hanscom Air Force Base.

TWELVE

It was clear that the officers at Hanscom were not aware of what had been going on outside their base that day. They didn't ask anything about the politics of my case, or even mention anything about my being absent without leave. They just wanted to verify that I was a member of the Florida National Guard unit from Miami and that was it. The airmen who were in charge of guarding me seemed almost afraid of me, and they treated me the way they would a powerful general or some other high-level figure. After a while they were curious to know if, besides being a National Guard staff sergeant, I also happened to be some sort of celebrity.

"Why were all those people out there with you, sergeant?" asked the young airman assigned to guard me.

"I don't know, man," I said, still shaken by the day's events. "I guess they were all there because they agree with me."

"Agree with you?" he asked with a slight frown. "And what about those TV cameras?"

"You'll find out soon enough," I answered, not wanting to get into any detail.

After verifying that I was a National Guard soldier, and considering that I had returned to military control on my own

volition, the leadership at Hanscom base decided I was not a
flight risk. Within a few hours of my surrender I had received
a one-way ticket home from a travel agency within the base
and was waiting for Louis to pick me up and take me to
Boston's Logan International Airport. My mother and aunt
were waiting there to fly home with me.

When Louis, Gale, and their daughter Emily dropped me
off at the airport, my mother and aunt were not the only ones
waiting for me. News about the first Iraq combat veteran to
publicly denounce the war was obviously spreading, and a
few reporters had gotten wind of the news that the air force
had decided to cut me loose and send me home on a plane;
they even knew what airline I was flying. A group of ten or so
was waiting just inside the terminal.

"No, I haven't been charged yet. I don't know what
they're going to do. No, they haven't mistreated me. I'm feeling well, thank you. I'm going to report to my unit in Florida,
probably tomorrow morning."

The group of reporters holding cameras and microphones
moved with us as we negotiated our way toward airport security. It felt strange to be getting so much attention, but that's
the way things had been since we walked out of mass at the
Peace Abbey that morning. Besides, Louis and Tod had told
me the presence of reporters reduced the likelihood of any
mistreatment by the military.

Things weren't very different when we arrived at Miami
International Airport later that night. Several local TV and
newspaper reporters were waiting for us just outside terminal
security when we arrived. I told them I planned to go home
and report to my unit early the next morning. My mother had
called ahead and arranged for Miladys, the mother of Specialist Oliver Perez and the woman who had hosted the first
prayer service I attended upon my return to Florida, to pick
us up. She took us to her house, where we watched the local

TV news. My surrender was a lead story and the coverage included interviews with some members of my unit, most of whom were not supportive of my stand. I couldn't help noticing that not one of the soldiers in my squad, nor even my platoon, was among those interviewed, though they all lived in the Miami area. Evidently, the news media from my hometown was not interested in what the people who had actually fought alongside me had to say.

Going home after leaving Oliver's place provided no rest from the media madness. The telephone was ringing off the hook. At first my mother fielded the calls, patiently explaining that we were exhausted and needed some sleep. But they didn't stop, and in the end, we had to take the phone off the hook. We awoke a few hours later to a full voice mail box and a news van waiting outside our building.

At the National Guard armory in North Miami, yet another posse of reporters awaited us, as did a Miami police detective who escorted me inside to meet with a major from the guard's legal department. When we were in the armory, the detective stopped for a moment and, after making sure there was no one within hearing distance, turned to me.

"Sergeant Mejía, I want you to know that besides being a police officer, I am a soldier. I am a sergeant first class in the reserves." He looked around for a moment. "I think you're right in everything you say, but you should know that there are serious consequences to your actions."

"I know, sergeant," I replied. "I know there are consequences."

"You could end up in jail, man. You're messing with the army."

"I know, sergeant."

"Alright, as long as you know," he concluded, sounding sincere. Then he went into one of the rooms to look for the major.

Inside the armory, which is nothing more than a huge basketball court, I saw that Oliver and Miladys were already there. They wanted to provide all the support they could as I surrendered to my unit. My mother and aunt, who had been talking outside to the journalists, joined us a few minutes later. Then we spotted my old platoon sergeant, Sergeant First Class Palango, walking around the court. He was wearing civilian clothes and talking into a cell phone in such a loud voice that it seemed he wanted us to hear everything he was saying:

"Yes, I'm here at the armory," he said, looking at his cell phone and then sneaking a peek at us, making sure he had our attention. "Yes, he's here." He walked a bit closer to us. "What!? I don't wanna talk to him, he's a deserter. Hey, what's going on, Specialist Perez," he said to Oliver, who was standing right next to me.

"Not much, sergeant," replied Oliver to Palango, who was now about three meters in front of us.

"Well, good to see you," said Palango, still holding the cell phone to his ear, even though it appeared his conversation had been over for a while. I wondered if he had even been talking to someone, or if he had just made it all up.

"Good to see you too, sergeant," responded Perez, but Palango had already taken off, the dead phone still at his ear.

Another man wearing civilian clothes approached us. He introduced himself as the husband of one the female sergeants who worked at the unit. He spoke to me in Spanish with a Caribbean accent.

"I saw you on the news yesterday," he said with a serious expression. "And I knew you would be here today. I brought this for you, so that it may protect you every step of the way." As he spoke he pulled a rosary from his pocket and pressed it into my hand. "God bless you, my boy," he said and disappeared across the room.

When I finally met with the major from the legal department in an office just off the court, he told me I was being
given a direct order to take a government van to the army
base at Fort Stewart, Georgia, where I should await word on
what the military intended to do with me. A team of soldiers
from my battalion had been assigned to escort me to the base.
We were to leave within a few hours.

Immediately I called Louis on my cell phone. When I told
him about the order I had just received, he was not happy. I
turned to the major.

"My attorney has asked me to tell you that we consider
this a punitive action by the military," I said. "The fact that I
have already surrendered twice on my own volition, first at
Hanscom base in Massachusetts, then here this morning, is
evidence of my intention to resolve my situation with the
army, and that there is no need to guard me."

"Oh, no, no, no," the major replied, evidently trying to reassure me. "We simply want to provide all necessary assistance to make sure you can get to Fort Stewart. We're doing
this to help you."

I relayed this to Louis, who was waiting on the phone.

"They don't want to help you, Camilo," he said. "They
want you under their control so as to keep you quiet. Can you
get to Fort Stewart on your own? Can Maritza and Norma
drive you there?" he asked, referring to my mother and aunt.

I told him they could.

"Well, then tell them that," he sounded impatient. "Thank
them for their offer, but tell them you would rather go there
on your own, and that you don't need to be guarded."

I relayed this back to the major. When he continued to insist on my going in the government van with an escort, Louis
asked to speak with him directly. They talked for a couple of
minutes and when the major handed the phone back to me,
Louis sounded a bit calmer:

"Camilo, I told the major that you will of course obey any direct orders given to you, but that if they force you to get on a government van to go to Fort Stewart under military escort we will consider that a punitive action by the military and will make an official complaint. He is going to check with his superiors. Call me back when they make a decision and don't do anything without letting me know."

About an hour later another major, a strong, mean-looking man, came into the office and handed a note to me.

"Staff Sergeant Mejía," he said, "since you have declined our help, I am issuing a direct order to you to report to Fort Stewart, Georgia, at no later than 1500 hours on 17 March 2004. Do you understand, sergeant?"

The note contained a written version of the order. After consulting once more with Louis, I signed and returned it. I was relieved I didn't have to leave that same day, because I had made arrangements to spend a few hours with Samantha. On my way outside to speak once again with the press, the legal department major stopped me.

"If you don't mind, Sergeant Mejía," he said. "I'm going to walk outside with you."

"I'm going to speak with the press," I replied to him, noticing that his buffed, mean-looking friend was close behind us. "Are you going to try to stop me?"

"Oh, no," he shook his head. "You can speak to them; I just want to answer any questions they may have for the military."

My mother, aunt, Miladys, and Oliver stood behind me as I addressed the media. The major was right next to me the whole time, while his mean buddy observed from a distance with his arms tightly crossed over his chest. I could almost feel his eyes burning into the back of my neck. But the military presence did not deter me from speaking my mind.

"The justification for this war is money," I said to the press. "And no soldier should go to Iraq and give his life for oil."

Some of the reporters had smiles on their faces, others nodded their heads in agreement; a few looked like they wanted to kill me. At one point someone asked if I was ready for what could happen to me and if I was ready to go to jail.

"I'm prepared to go to prison because I'll have a clear conscience," I replied. "Whatever sacrifice I have to make, I have to go there."

When the press asked about what measures the army would take, the major responded that a warrant for my arrest would be issued if I did not report to Fort Stewart at 3 P.M. the next day, but that there were no charges against me at that point. When asked how the army was treating me, I said they were treating me with respect and dignity. They then turned to Oliver, who said he supported me but that he probably would go back if the army called upon him to fight again. When they asked what he thought about me he said, "I think he's a brave leader and should not be prosecuted."

"Do you consider him a coward?" asked another reporter.

"No," said Oliver. "I fought next to him in many battles. He is not a coward."

I was only able to spend a little time with Samantha before I left for Fort Stewart that night. The drive there took close to nine hours, which meant we had to leave right after dropping Samantha off, spending the night on the road. Saying good-bye to her was painful. A grim uncertainty had hung over every occasion that I had seen her since I first learned of my deployment to the war, and this time wasn't any different. Though I felt relieved that I had finally started the process of resolving my situation with the military, I was also anxious. I didn't know if I would be deported or jailed for many years. The idea that I might not see my daughter again for a long time weighed heavily on me.

My mother and aunt did all of the driving while I tried to get some sleep in the backseat. Driving north from Miami,

which is at the southern tip of the Florida peninsula and populated mostly by Latinos, has the unique distinction of bringing travelers closer to the South as they travel north. With all
the media attention I had received since my surrender to the
military, I was reluctant to get out of the car when we stopped
for gas and food. At this time support for the war and the
president were running strong throughout Florida.

When we eventually arrived at the town right outside
Fort Stewart at around seven in the morning, I spoke briefly
to the small group of reporters waiting outside the hotel
where my aunt had made reservations; my mother had informed them of where to go for a short conference. The group
included a ubiquitous Associated Press correspondent, a couple of local paper reporters, and, to my surprise, an army
news crew with a video camera.

After sleeping for a few hours, we left the hotel for the
base. As we arrived, two men wearing civilian clothes got out
of an unmarked car. The guards at the gate evidently knew
who they were. One of them, well-built and wearing pitch
black sunglasses, walked over and introduced himself. He told
me he was with the CID, the military's Criminal Investigation
Department, and asked me to accompany him and his partner.

"Excuse me," asked my aunt Norma, who was standing
nearby next to my mother. "Can we come along? We can
drive him to wherever he needs to go."

"Don't worry, ma'am," the CID man reassured her. "We're
just going to take him to the unit he's being assigned to."

"Well, we can take him there," insisted my aunt.

The guy thought about it for a moment before assenting.
After reporting to my new unit and speaking briefly with my
newly assigned first sergeant, I gave my mom and aunt a hug
and assured them that I would be OK. Only then did they reluctantly leave for a nearby hotel, where they stayed for a
week.

I had begun the next stage of my journey through the U.S. Army, one that gave me new insights into that large and powerful institution. Leaders at Fort Stewart told reporters that they could speak to me only outside the base in order to avoid problems with other soldiers; they neglected to let them know that I had been given a direct order not to leave the post under any circumstances. With this decision, the army effectively suspended my interviews and public commentary against the war.

In addition to isolating me from the media and the world outside, they tried to keep me apart from the rest of the soldiers of the unit I had been assigned to, the medical holding battalion, known as Med-hold. The Med-hold was where they kept soldiers who either had returned from Iraq with some sort of medical condition or did not deploy to the war because of a medical problem. And then there were a few of us who were there because of legal reasons.

Most of the soldiers at the Med-hold felt like they were getting royally screwed by the military system. Particularly upset were those who had been injured in the war and had been waiting months for basic medical treatment. The barracks where they were stationed were unpainted cinderblock buildings, some of which didn't even have showers or toilets. They were also a good distance from the hospital, a particular problem for those whose war injuries made it difficult for them to walk.

It was clear that the army wanted to keep me apart from this smoldering discontent for fear that a war resister like myself might inflame it further. I was in the middle of dumping my belongings on a bed in the Med-hold barracks when the first sergeant rushed in and told me to pack everything up again.

"I'm sorry, Sergeant Mejía," he said urgently. "They made a mistake; we're actually going to put you in another building we have for noncommissioned officers."

I realized straight away that this was not a question of

putting me with other NCOs, because there were sergeants staying in the building we were in. The problem was that the interior of this building was open, with soldiers sleeping next to one another in a big room; they didn't want me to have that kind of close access to fifty other minds, particularly when most of them were already angry and critical of the army.

The other building, which was just across the street, was made up of two-person rooms, perhaps ten in all. In addition to having a lot more privacy, these quarters also had a common area with a refrigerator and a microwave oven, as well as showers and toilets. Two people had been kicked out of the building so that I could be given a room of my own, and I could sense the bad feeling toward me that this had created among my neighbors.

This awkward situation didn't last long because, within two or three weeks, the base received a number of brand new trailer homes. Everyone from the Med-hold battalion was moved into these, except me. Apparently it wasn't enough for the army to keep me in a room by myself; now they needed to keep me all alone in an entire building.

My work situation wasn't any different. At first they didn't know where to put me, and one of the first options that occurred to someone in my chain of command was to assign me to help to run the firing ranges, which would keep me a long way from the busier areas of the base. The problem with that assignment was that Louis had submitted my application for CO status directly to the post commander the day after my surrender at Hanscom base, and the regulations state that soldiers who have applied for CO discharge are not supposed to be given duties involving any type of combat training. This provision isn't always observed, but this time, given all the media attention surrounding my case, the army did not seem to want to take any chances and the range job was scratched.

Soon after that, I was assigned to the department in

charge of training at Fort Stewart. At first my work consisted
of moving furniture around, but the other two noncommissioned officers working with me had injuries and couldn't lift
anything heavy; I wasn't expected to do all the heavy work by
myself, so the people in charge left me pretty much alone. I
sat around and watched the TV news every morning. At
lunchtime, I would go to the nearest dining facility for a generally unappetizing meal, and would then return to the office
to lock up the door and call it a day.

This situation lasted until the secretary of the colonel in
charge of the department discovered that I had some basic
computer skills. She was particularly interested in my knowledge of PowerPoint, a knowledge that, however meager, was
still useful. Soon enough I was answering directly to either
her or the colonel.

At first I thought that maybe the colonel knew nothing of
my situation, or who I was, until one day when he came in the
office and asked me if I knew anything about a protest going
on outside the base in my support. I told him I didn't. When I
later reported to Louis about my brief conversation with the
colonel, he became irritated.

"You shouldn't have said that, Camilo." Louis's tone of
voice always dropped a level when he said my name. "Now he
can tell the general or whoever he reports to that you know
nothing about it."

"Why is that bad?" I couldn't see what the problem was.

"Because it means someone from the base can go outside
and tell the protesters that they can't be doing that on your
behalf when you know nothing about it."

I was beginning to see the picture.

"Everything you say to these people, Camilo, you can be
sure they will try to use to their advantage."

"So what should I say then?" I asked. "I really didn't
know there were people outside protesting."

"Well, you simply say, 'With all due respect, colonel, I have been advised by my attorney not to answer any questions before discussing them with him, but please feel free to give him a call,' and then you give him my number."

But I really found it hard to refer my superiors to an attorney every time I was asked a question or given an order. It felt like I was creating a wall between myself and the army which, after almost nine years of obedience, seemed almost impossible for me to do. This created particular difficulty when it came to my application for conscientious objection.

In my CO application I described in some detail the incidents concerning prisoner abuse at the al Assad base. At first this didn't provoke much action, or even interest, but after the international scandal broke concerning abuse at the Abu Ghraib prison in Baghdad, it seemed as though my chain of command invested a lot of energy and effort into getting me to fill out a different application, with a later date on its cover.

"Your attorney made a mistake in the original application," Captain Mohr, an affable yet stern infantry officer who served as my company commander, told me, adding, almost as an apology, "I'm just going by the regulations here."

"Roger, sir," I answered for perhaps the tenth time. "I spoke with my attorney about it, and he assured me that there is no mistake. He does not want me to refile the application. He actually wants you to give him a call."

"I am not going to give your attorney a call, Sergeant Mejía." I could tell the captain had a hard time harassing me, and for the most part he always tried to stay calm. "I am your company commander and I am telling you that this application needs to be refiled."

"Believe me, Camilo," Louis said later, "your company commander does not make any decisions. It is not he who decides how the military handles you; he just takes orders from way up."

It didn't matter how many times I told my first sergeant and company commander that I wouldn't do it; they continued to try to get me to file a new application, almost always claiming there had been some mistake in it, though every now and then they came up with new arguments.

"You see, Staff Sergeant Mejía," said Captain Mohr one time, "your attorney submitted the application directly to the CG."

CG stood for commanding general, which is the highest authority at a military base. In the case of Fort Stewart, this was Major General William Webster, to whom Louis had faxed my CO application on March 16, 2004.

"And the application is supposed to go up through your chain of command and work its way up. Your chain of command starts with me."

In the several decades that Louis had been working with military law, he had submitted many an application for conscientious objection and he knew the procedures inside out. He had been navigating the Uniform Code of Military Justice longer than Captain Mohr had been in the military, longer perhaps than Captain Mohr had been alive. There were no mistakes.

One likely reason the leadership at Fort Stewart was so bent on my refiling the application was the military's claim that Abu Ghraib was the product of a few apples gone bad, and only in the lower ranks. My CO claim contradicted this, describing how the highly secretive spooks were the ones running the operation, suggesting that authorization for the abuse came from high-level government officials. The procedures for how to carry out the abuse were passed on from one unit to another in crash courses, suggesting the abuse was systemic, not isolated. It also showed that the abuse of prisoners had started as soon as U.S. troops arrived in Iraq, even before the president announced the "end of major combat operations."

Before abuse at Abu Ghraib became big news, the military could easily dismiss soldiers' claims of prisoner mistreatment as unsubstantiated lies, or launch a ghost investigation with the results already written. But with massive amounts of evidence detailing cruel and unusual treatment at the Baghdad prison, the military suddenly had to at least pretend to take the claims seriously. Ignoring a conscientious objector application that described prisoner abuse, dated weeks before the Abu Ghraib scandal made the news, was not a good way for the army to protect its image, especially when the application was submitted by someone at the center of considerable media attention.

When the leadership at Fort Stewart finally recognized that I wasn't going to refile my CO claim, they started trying to rush the entire process. One day, without prior notice, a captain I had never seen before told me that he was my hearing officer and that my CO hearing was to be the next day. I had less than twenty-four hours to pull together my case, a task that required calling my witnesses, gathering all the evidence I wanted to present, and making sure my attorney made it to Georgia from Massachusetts.

"No, absolutely not," Louis said over the phone. "Not tomorrow, not the next day, and not until your court-martial is over. We have too much on our hands to deal with your CO hearing. You can tell the captain to give me a call if he has a problem with that."

This resulted in the further deterioration of my relationship with my immediate superiors. For them the matter was simple: I was just another soldier and I had to do what I was told. Only those higher up in the military hierarchy understood the larger political implications of my situation. But they did not deal directly with me; they just issued orders from their high positions of authority down to the company levels, where captains and first sergeants ran the show.

None of this was easy, but there were some good days

during the pretrial period. Strangely, one of the best moments was when I first learned that I would face a court-martial. The wait was over and I knew I would be going to trial. Even more important, I knew that because of the type of court-martial specified on the charge sheet, I could only receive a maximum of twelve months in prison. Up to this point, we really had no idea how the army was going to handle my case. There was the possibility that they would choose not to prosecute and just get rid of me quietly, administratively, and without punishment. But I had also faced the possibility of a long jail sentence.

On the day I was charged, Captain Mohr called me into his office. When I entered the room, I saw the main prosecutor, Captain Balbo, a short, somewhat overweight man, looking at me with dark, wounded eyes. Balbo seemed to be angry with me.

Mohr made me stand at attention and then proceeded to charge me under article 85 of the Uniform Code of Military Justice: desertion.

"Specification," he said, reading from the charge sheet that he held with both hands. "In that Staff Sergeant Camilo E. Mejía, did, on or about 16 October 2003, with intent to avoid hazardous duty, namely: service in Iraq, quit his unit, to wit: C CO 1st Battalion 124th Infantry, located at ar Ramadi and did remain so absent in desertion until on or about 15 March 2004."

Even more uplifting than knowing my maximum sentence could not exceed a year in prison was the support I received from other soldiers at the base who were aware of my refusal to go back to the war. Many of them had had similar or worse experiences in the battle-torn streets and alleyways of Iraq, and they knew I wasn't making things up. For the most part they just nodded their heads in approval upon recognizing me, but on more than one occasion, a reaffirming comment was whispered in my direction:

"You keep your head up high, sergeant. You did the right thing."

After my *60 Minutes* interview came out on CBS, more people began recognizing me, and several of them came over to shake my hand. On one occasion, the daughter of a high-ranking officer said she agreed with me 100 percent, and that more people were on my side than against me. Even some of the soldiers from my own unit, who were at Fort Stewart receiving treatment for injuries received in combat, were supportive, and most of them seemed glad to see me.

However, there were a few people who evidently had issues with what I had done. One was a soldier from my unit with whom I'd had a friendly relationship in Iraq but who now refused to speak to me or even acknowledge my presence. The other was Sergeant First Class Demarest, who was at Fort Stewart receiving medical treatment for injuries sustained in Iraq after I left. Before seeing Demarest for the first time since Iraq, I had heard that he was in pretty bad shape and had a hard time walking.

"Hey," I said to him one hot afternoon after formation. "I heard you were all messed up." I only realized after speaking that I could have expressed myself more sensitively.

"Oh, no," he said, frowning and refusing to shake my extended hand. "I think you're the one who's all messed up."

"Well, I'm not sure what you've heard, sergeant," I replied, retrieving my hand.

"It's not what I've heard." The tone of his voice was quite severe as he interrupted me. "You left your men, and you just don't do that. You're an NCO."

"I had my reasons for not returning." I was trying to sound conciliatory. Demarest was someone I respected, and his rejection hurt me deeply. "Maybe we should talk sometime."

"I don't think I've got anything to say to you, Mejía."

Before I could reply, he was walking off, shaking his head.

Demarest had always had an unusual gait, but by the way he was limping now I could tell his injury had been serious. Later that week I saw him again; this time we were standing next to each other in formation, to which I had arrived late.

"They called your name earlier," he said right after I took my place next him but always keeping his eyes to the front of the formation.

"Thank you, sergeant," I said, glad to find out we were on speaking terms.

After formation we both had to go to the company's office and we talked with each other while we waited. If I remember correctly, he told me an improvised explosive device had sprayed shrapnel through his lower body, and he had been evacuated to a medical facility near ar Ramadi. When he hopped on the first truck going back to the Eagle's Nest the medical unit almost charged him with being AWOL until they learned he had actually just returned to his unit.

"I just couldn't leave the men," he said.

"But you were in bad shape; you couldn't really do your job."

"I could do something." Demarest had replaced Barr as the first platoon's leader shortly after Barr was injured during Operation Shutdown. "Maybe I couldn't walk very well, but I could still be the platoon leader."

Demarest had never been an outspoken critic of our leadership, but I knew he and I had agreed on several issues regarding the unsoundness of our missions. I knew how perceptive and knowledgeable he was in terms of military strategy, and I knew he was a thinker, but up to that day I hadn't known how he felt about our deplorable command.

"If only you would have said something," he said after a long pause. "If you would have said something I wouldn't have such a problem with you."

"What do you mean by that, sergeant?" I wondered

whether he meant I should have said something critical about the government, or about our superiors in Iraq.

"About the things that were happening within our unit," he said.

"You mean the leadership, what our commanders were doing?" I asked. "You returned after being injured."

"I returned because of the men, not the leaders. I couldn't care less about the leaders."

"Well, I did talk about our leadership, publicly. I talked about how they used us for medals, about all the unnecessary killings, I was very critical."

"When?!" he asked, finally looking at me with a severe frown. "I never heard anything."

"I gave many interviews when I returned, but they were clandestine because I wasn't ready to surrender yet. I was putting together a legal defense." I felt the need to explain myself to him. "When I came back into the army," I continued, "I was still very critical, and I talked about everything."

He turned away from me. A frown on his face and a hard stare in his eye made me think something intense was going on inside of his head. We both remained quiet for a while. I didn't know to what extent he condemned my actions, but I sensed that perhaps a change in his attitude was beginning to take place. It was hard to figure out what he might be thinking. I had always figured Demarest as the type of soldier who was capable of analysis but who also took obedience to the military very seriously. That obedience, along with his unconditional devotion to the soldiers of his unit, seemed to place his sense of military duty, regardless of the mission, above any personal feelings or opinions.

"I'm glad you're listening to me," I said. The interruption of silence, or perhaps my words, seemed to have an emotional effect on him. "I'm glad you're talking to me."

Demarest pressed his lips together, for a moment acquiring the semblance of a father who's both too angry and too proud to talk to a son who has deeply disappointed him. I realized once again how my refusal to return to the war had hurt people within my unit; particularly hurt, I thought, were those who had been close to me.

"I had to talk to you," he said, turning to me with a sad smile. "No matter what you did, you're still one of my soldiers."

In spite of occasional uplifting moments such as that conversation with Demarest, the truth was I was more or less alone at the base, at least when it came to my criticism of the war and defiance of the government and military. The people at Fort Stewart, including me, did not appreciate the implications of the seemingly mundane issues surrounding my case. For instance, Captain Mohr had no idea why it was so imperative that I file a new CO claim; he just acted as a captain, followed orders, and did what he perceived to be his duty, which at times turned into flat out harassment. On my part, I found it hard to do everything Louis expected of me because I didn't share his knowledge and understanding of the military and government. He saw the intentions behind questions and conversations that I thought were casual and coincidental. He understood how difficult it was for me to be on my guard all the time, but he put a lot of pressure on me to be firm and remain strong.

"I know it's hard, Camilo," he would say. "I know they take you into rooms full of people who outrank you and expect you to say, do, or sign something. But you have to refuse, Camilo. You have to say no."

In the end, with just a few exceptions, I was able to follow Louis's directions and advice. But having to take a firm stand with my chain of command became a significant source of stress. Every time I received a phone call, I dreaded that it would be some new test of my resolve, something that I was no longer sure I had the moral strength to deal with. It got to the point where I developed an irrational fear of the ring tone of my cell phone. Even to this day, my heart skips a beat whenever I hear a phone with the same dreadful ring tone.

The command continued to try to get me to sign a new CO claim until just two weeks before the trial. They denied Louis's requests that I be allowed to travel to Miami for the purpose of conducting the defense investigation, insisting that I had to stay within the post to take care of my conscientious objector claim. They argued that letting me go would be detrimental to the good order and discipline of the unit. When Louis visited me at the base to prepare for trial, we had to conduct our meetings in army buildings because I wasn't allowed to go to a hotel, even the one just a couple of hundred meters away from the base's main gate. Several times Louis and I had to meet in parking lots, or in the food court.

Yet the maneuverings and tricks of the military in the two months between my surrender and my trial would pale in comparison to the blatant violation of its own regulations that occurred at the trial itself. I had figured the military penal code was highly biased, but the injustice I would witness in the three days of my court-martial proved to be beyond anything I had ever imagined.

THE TRIAL

The night before my trial opened, two to three dozen people protested outside the gates of Fort Stewart with "Bring Them Home" and "Free Camilo" signs. In the preceding weeks, my mother and aunt had made connections with peace groups around the country whose members had helped them rent a house near the base for people attending the court-martial.

The protest at the gate did not go unnoticed by the leadership at Fort Stewart, which responded by ordering me to inventory all my personal belongings and gathering my medical records in preparation for going to prison. They would later claim that this was all just normal procedure for anyone facing a court-martial, an affirmation of their guilty-until-proven-guilty approach to justice. They also tightened security at the fort, limiting access through the main gate to people who had a Department of Defense decal on their vehicles. Nonmilitary people attending the trial were directed to Gate Three, which was quite a distance away from the main entrance and unknown even to many soldiers on base. The signs to the gate were removed, perhaps in an attempt to get people lost and keep them out of the proceedings. On top of all this, passes allowing civilians into the base for the trial were limited.

On the morning of May 19, 2004, the first day of the trial, I was driven to the courthouse in the custody of two military escorts from the Med-hold unit. They were to accompany me at all times throughout the proceedings. The guards were as surprised as I was to see the level of security at the fort that day. The entire block around the courthouse had been sealed off with concrete barricades, traffic cones, and yellow "restricted area" tape. Military and civilian police officers patrolled the area and there was at least one police dog sniffing around the building.

I had been to the courthouse several times before, once for my own arraignment, and two or three other times to attend the courts-martial of other soldiers, something I did on Louis's advice to get familiar with military court proceedings. Though on the outside it looked like an ordinary old wooden building, the inside of the courthouse resembled a civilian court, with benches for the public arranged in front of two large tables for the defense and prosecution. In front of these were, to the left, the judge and, to the right, the jury. The witness chair was placed between the judge and the defense, directly facing the jury, which in a military tribunal is known as the panel.

If the arrangement of the courtroom was unremarkable, the number of military personnel attending the trial was not. From lowest-ranking privates to full-bird colonels, one half of the courtroom was entirely occupied by uniformed soldiers. I knew the trial had not been advertised at the base, and from attending prior trials, I knew that the post's courthouse was no social hangout among GIs, especially during duty hours. My impression was that this was just another deliberate measure to keep civilians out of the "army's business."

The other side of the courtroom was packed with family, friends, activists, reporters, and filmmakers. With the exception of the army photographers, all cameras had to be checked at the door, along with laptop computers, tape recorders, and cell phones. Recordings of the proceedings could only be made with paper and pen. Interviews relating to the trial were to be conducted at a designated media center, a mile away from the courthouse.

When I entered the courtroom I glanced at the prosecution, Captain Balbo, the portly man who had attended my arraignment, and Captain Lisa Bloom. As I continued to look around the room, I saw my mother, stepfather, aunt, uncle, and grandmother sitting behind the wooden railing that separated the defense table from the public. Behind them were representatives from Military Families Speak Out, Code-Pink, Veterans for Peace, and a number of other local antiwar groups. I took a seat with my defense team, including Captain Billy B. Ruhling, the military defense counsel, and waited for the proceedings to begin.

The court-martial lasted three days and had three main phases. My lawyers began the first phase of the trial by contending that the military had no jurisdiction to try me because I was a noncitizen soldier who had completed his eight initial years of service and had never applied for U.S. citizenship. This, they argued, made me nonextendable under army regulations. In addition, Gale had come across an international treaty between the United States and Costa Rica (of which I am a citizen), which states that Costa Ricans residing in the United States are exempt from all compulsory military service whatsoever. Based on the treaty and army regulation, together with a legal precedent in which the National Guard Bureau rejected a guard unit's request to extend another noncitizen soldier in almost exactly the same circumstances, the defense presented a motion to dismiss the trial.

The prosecution contended that the treaty, dating back to the year 1851, applied only to people who had been inducted or conscripted into the military, not those who had signed up voluntarily and enjoyed the "fruits and benefits" of the uniform. The term "compulsory service," Captain Balbo claimed, in a tone of barely suppressed anger, did not cover soldiers in my position because, if it did, it would apply not just to all Costa Ricans, but also to resident aliens from China, Ireland, Italy, Spain, and ten other countries.[1]

Next on the agenda was a request by the prosecution that the judge preclude the defense from putting the war and the U.S. government on trial, on the grounds that decisions concerning the armed forces should be left to the executive and legislative branches of government.

"In the instant case, Your Honor," argued Captain Balbo, "the accused and his defense team have signaled their desire . . . to put the United States government on trial for its actions and décisions: the motivation behind Operation Iraqi Freedom; the president's ability to deploy soldiers to that part of the world; the legalities and morality of that conflict."

This was one of the few moments during the three days of court-martial when I completely agreed with Captain Balbo. We were trying to do all that, and in a way we did.

Another petition by the government was that my fifty-five-page conscientious objector application, along with my personal beliefs, be found irrelevant and kept out of the trial.

"Evidence can be kept out, even if relevant," claimed Balbo, "if it would tend to confuse, unnecessarily burden, and delay the trial."[2]

It was evident that for the prosecution the entire trial was simply about whether or not I got on a plane to Iraq at the end of my leave. Everything else was irrelevant. The defense, on the other hand, wanted to argue that my decision not to return was justified on the basis of what I had encountered on the ground in Iraq and that evidence pertaining to that was both relevant and vital. To this end, we asked to bring in as a witness Professor Francis A. Boyle, a leading expert in international law, who was responsible for drafting the Biological Weapons Anti-Terrorism Act and served on the board of directors of Amnesty International. Professor Boyle spoke to the court via telephone.

Before Professor Boyle was allowed to say anything, the judge asked Louis if he could explain what his testimony was going to cover. Louis explained that the professor would offer evidence that the charge of desertion could not apply to someone who was authorized to leave their unit and that, under international law, I was authorized because I had been ordered, along with the rest of my platoon, to carry out an illegal act—namely, the abuse of prisoners at the al Assad air base.

After dealing with a couple of objections by Captain Balbo, the military judge agreed to allow the professor to be sworn. His voice sounded clearly across the courtroom from a speaker:

"Taking Sergeant Mejía at his word, it seems to me that he had formulated an opinion that he did not want to participate in war crimes. The abuses that are described here that took place at al Assad base clearly constituted war crimes under the Geneva Conventions of 1949 as well as the U.S. War Crimes Act of 1996. . . . My reading is that you had a wide-scale system of abuse at this facility constituting war crimes. And under the Laws of War, Sergeant Mejía had the right, if not the obligation, to abstain from any participation in the commission of war crimes, let alone doing it himself or turning people, prisoners, over, where they would be subject to abuse."[3]

In the course of Professor Boyle's testimony, Captain Balbo interrupted with various objections, some of which were sustained by the judge. The professor was not allowed to mention official reports of prisoner abuse at Abu Ghraib from the Red Cross or from General Antonio Taguba be-

cause, it was claimed, those matters were not before the
court. But without the discussion of those claims it was impossible to conclude that the abuse of prisoners committed by
my unit at al Assad was not an isolated incident but part of
something widespread and systematic. The judge forbade such
arguments not only because they established that the U.S. military was engaged in the commission of war crimes in Iraq,
devastating the charge of desertion, but also because when
these crimes are widespread and systemic, they become crimes
against humanity.

After Professor Boyle was dismissed by the court, Louis
requested that former U.S. attorney general Ramsey Clark
be allowed to challenge the prosecution's decision to prevent
the defense from raising broader matters concerning the U.S.
government and the role of its military in Iraq. After a number of objections, the judge agreed to call Clark.

Mr. Clark began his statement by referring to the court-
martial of Jeremy Sivits, one of the Abu Ghraib guards,
which was just beginning at that time:

"I hear from the prosecution today that, somehow or another, the military is not subject to laws. . . . I think that's the
worst message the United States could send to the world, and
I don't believe it for a minute.

"The cases in Iraq are important because they're tragi-
cally the prosecution of young Americans for, allegedly at
least, outrageous abuses of the person and dignity and rights
of Iraqi prisoners. . . .

"The first thing that most of us think of when we think of
Nuremberg and the charter, . . . which is binding in the United
States, is that obedience to the order of a superior is no defense
in the commission of a crime. I believe we would all have to desire that to be true, because criminal conduct will be irrepress-
ible if obedience to an order is a justification [of crime]."

Mr. Clark then turned his attention to my case:

"Here you have this young soldier . . . being told to continue the sleep deprivation of prisoners who have already been subjected to that sort of treatment. And it's hypothetical, in the sense that there is no evidence directly before the court at this time, but, on the basis of . . . his conscientious objector statement, we can see that his squad was ordered, directly, to violate the Field Manual 27-10 . . . which prohibits torture . . . , inhumane treatment, or willfully causing great suffering or serious injury to body or health.

"Now, here we have this incredible situation where the United States is seeking to convict soldiers in [Iraq] for alleged violations of the rights of prisoners and, at the same time, prosecuting a young soldier halfway across the world because he did what he was authorized to do under international law, what he had a duty to do under international law; . . . [he] refused to return to a duty that would involve him . . . in war crimes.

"The word 'quit' is defined in Article 85 as a person who leaves or fails to return without authority. His authority is the Nuremberg Charter. It's The Hague and Geneva Conventions. . . .

"To simply try to rule out [his CO application] would eliminate important evidence that the court would have to hear to make full determination of the applicable law in the case.

"The thing you have to hope for most is that the message be that [the] United States military intends, fully, to comply with the requirements of International Law. . . ."

The trial went into a recess immediately after Mr. Clark's argument. When it reconvened, Louis complained to the judge about the exaggerated level of security on the base that day, claiming it served to taint and prejudice the trial and the members of the panel, who all worked at the base and would recognize that this was not normal. It occurred to me that the extra guards were also being used to send a message to the soldiers of Fort Stewart's Third Infantry Division, who were gearing up to return to Iraq: it would be a bad idea to follow in my footsteps.

Louis then entered into a discussion with the court concerning which witnesses we would be allowed to subpoena. We certainly had an impressive list of people we wanted to call, including the spooks who had been in charge of the detainee camp in al Assad, as well as high government officials such as Defense Secretary Donald Rumsfeld; Lieutenant General Ricardo Sanchez, commanding general of U.S. forces in Iraq; and Major General Geoffrey Miller, deputy commanding general for detention operations. The rationale for calling these witnesses to the stand was to explore the policy behind the interrogation of detainees in Iraq. We hoped to show how a policy and an atmosphere of abuse had filtered down from the highest levels of the U.S. government to regular soldiers such as myself.

It soon became clear that the prosecution had control over almost every aspect of the trial. After saying he would look into the exaggerated level of security, the judge quickly ruled testimony by most of our witnesses as irrelevant. The highest military officer who would be compelled to testify was my old battalion commander, Colonel Mirable, who was also on the prosecution's list.

Other crucial defense witnesses who were not allowed to be called included Master Sergeant Wingard, who had told Louis my deployment to Iraq had been due to a computer glitch on the Florida Guard's database, and Kathy Tringially, who had informed me that a congressional inquiry on my case had concluded that I should be discharged immediately from the service. A colonel with the National Guard Bureau who had rejected a petition by a guard unit to stop loss, or extend, a noncitizen soldier in a position almost identical to mine was also ruled out.

At the end of the first day of the court-martial the judge responded to our pretrial motions. He informed us that none of the allegations of prisoner abuse described in my CO claim could be brought before the members of the panel. No proof of the illegality of the war within the context of either military or international law could be explained to the jury, no allegations of war crimes or of crimes against humanity could reach the ears of those deciding the "merits" of the case. In effect, my entire CO application was to be banned from the trial.

It was almost six o'clock in the afternoon when we left the courtroom. Nearly all of our pretrial motions had been denied, and our essential witnesses had been precluded from testifying. We headed directly to the media center, where a number of local and national reporters were waiting for us. After answering a few questions, I went to see some of the friends and activists who had come to lend their support and then headed to the food court to get something to eat. Almost immediately, I ran into Oliver Perez and two other guys from my squad in Iraq: Estime and Funez. They were there to testify at the trial.

For the most part Estime and Funez seemed glad to see me, although I did sense some emotional distance between us. Perhaps they weren't sure if I was the same person they had known in Iraq, or maybe they thought my becoming a conscientious objector had in some way turned me against them: the myth of the pacifist spitting in the face of the returning soldier. There was also clear resentment that I did not return to them.

"I just think you did what you did for the right reasons, sergeant," said Estime. "But you went about it the wrong way."

I wanted to explain everything to them, to tell them that leaving them in Iraq was the hardest thing I had ever done in

my life, but they were witnesses in the trial who had not yet
testified, so I had to be careful about what I said.

"Mejía," said Funez, almost to himself, his lips pressed
tight together, "how did you get yourself into this, man?" He
seemed to feel sorry for me.

I smiled back, trying to reassure him. I knew I had no regrets, and that if I was going to jail, it wouldn't be with a bitter heart.

"Well, you guys," I said, "I have to get ready for tomorrow. God knows what will happen, but when this all over I
hope we can all get together again, the whole squad."

"Alright, sergeant," said Estime. "Take care of yourself."

"I'm glad to see you guys." I said. I really was. "It's good
to see that you're OK."

Funez shook my hand and stared at me for a moment.

"Take care, man," he said.

Oliver waved good-bye. I smiled and waved back, got
into my car, and drove to my room; it had been a long day.

The second day of the court-martial started at eight-thirty the
next morning. The first order of business was to interview
members of the jury. All the members of the panel had regular monthly meetings with the commanding general at the
base, General Webster—the general who had ultimate and
absolute authority over the trial. Louis's questions, therefore,
focused on possible bias and prejudice. He asked the members if they thought I was guilty of desertion simply for being
accused of it, or, put another way, whether I could still be
proved innocent after being charged with the crime.

Louis also asked the members if they felt under any command pressure to vote on a certain verdict, or if anyone had
told them it was their duty to convict. The questions would
have seemed silly to me just a day or two before, but after the
judge had given the prosecution everything they requested

and denied all our motions, I understood what Louis's concerns were. In the end, two of the highest-ranking jurors, both colonels, were dismissed. One had a reputation of being soft on convicting, while the other had a reputation of being hard. But it occurred to me during this process that everyone in the court worked for the same boss. In the case of *The United States v. Staff Sergeant Camilo E. Mejía-Castillo*, just about everyone there, including me and one of the defense attorneys, plus the judge, the jury, most of the witnesses, the accuser, and the prosecution, worked for the U.S. government. Perhaps that's why the Uniform Code of Military Justice has a conviction rate of 98 percent.

The business before the court on this second day was also to argue and assess the merits of the case for the jury to decide whether to find me guilty or innocent. The government's evidence consisted primarily of paperwork showing the date I was supposed to leave the States to go back to Iraq. The judge had basically limited the case to the question of whether or not I got on a plane. All other considerations, legal, political and moral, were deemed irrelevant.

Captain Balbo, opening the case for the prosecution, addressed the panel:

"This case is about a deserter. It's about a squad leader who abandoned his soldiers at the very time they needed him the most. It's about an NCO, a staff sergeant, who turned his back on everything the noncommissioned officer corps stands for."

The prosecution was adopting a twin-pronged strategy of showing me in as negative a light as possible while emphasizing how dangerous the situation in ar Ramadi was, in order to justify the criminal element of the charge.

Given the restrictions imposed by the judge, Louis was limited to simply contradicting the prosecution's image of me and showing that I really was a "good soldier" who might have made an honest mistake:

"It is my honor and privilege to represent Staff Sergeant Mejía. . . . I respectfully submit to you that the picture that you will receive [of him] overall will be far different than what Captain Balbo has just said to you now. . . . I expect that the evidence will be that Staff Sergeant Mejía . . . was a good squad leader; that he took care of his men; [and] that he was concerned about their welfare."

The first witness called for the prosecution was Captain Warfel. Using my old commander's testimony, Captain Balbo attempted to show that the situation in ar Ramadi was extremely volatile and that they badly needed me to return.

"What types of casualties did your company sustain?" asked Captain Balbo.

"The majority of the casualties," responded Captain Warfel, "were from improvised explosive devices, IEDs. Also, several RPG injuries, mortar round injuries, indirect fire injuries."

"And approximately how many people deployed with you, in your company?"

"When I left Fort Stewart," continued my former CO, "I had about 131 soldiers in my company."

"And when you redeployed," went on Balbo, looking really stern, "how many came back as a group?"

"Redeployed ninety-five soldiers."

"What happened to the others? Were most of the medical evacuations the result of enemy contact?"

"I believe every one of them was," responded Warfel.

"Were there any particular awards given?" continued the prosecution.

"Yes, I had twenty-four Purple Hearts awarded in my company," responded Warfel, in a low yet proud voice, referring to awards given to soldiers for injuries sustained from enemy fire.

It was very frustrating to see him there sounding concerned, when just about everyone in our company knew that his personal ambition had contributed significantly to the casualty figures. My old commander also failed to mention that many of those who were seriously injured were not sent to get proper treatment; instead they were kept in Iraq so that our company would not fall below combat strength. The captain, whose military service had mostly been in the National Guard and who had no combat experience prior to Iraq, appeared to have more medals than most of the active duty members of the panel, including career officers with the rank of colonel.

Louis honed in on this in his cross-examination of the captain.

"By the way, were you injured in Iraq?" he asked Warfel, to everyone's surprise.

"Yes, I was," responded the captain.

From talking to other members of my unit, I knew that much fun had been made of the captain's alleged injury.

"And did you receive a Purple Heart?" Louis continued.

"I've been put in for a Purple Heart, yes."

I noticed that the members of the panel seemed to be following this line of questioning with particular interest.

"And who put that in?" Louis continued.

"Went through my battalion," was the response.

"I'm asking who is it that put you in for a Purple Heart, sir?"

"Who specifically filled out the paperwork?" asked Warfel nervously, knowing exactly what the question was.

"Objection, Your Honor," protested Captain Balbo. "Relevance?"

"The objection's overruled," responded Colonel Smith, the judge in the case.

"I believe it was my company's XO," responded Warfel, referring to our company's executive officer, Lieutenant Green.

"And my company medic, and battalion surgeon. It takes accumulation of paperwork to do that."

"And those are people under your command, is that correct?" Louis asked, "[the ones] who put in that paperwork?"

"One of the three that would be involved, are, uh . . ." The captain was having trouble putting a sentence together. "Under my command."

"What were your wounds, sir?"

"I had grenade shrapnel wounds to my right forearm," replied the captain, probably fearing that Louis would ask him to show his injuries to the court.

"And how is your right forearm today?" asked Louis.

"Fine," said Warfel.

"And there is no shrapnel that got into your wound, is there?"

"Objection, Your Honor," said Balbo, in defense of his star witness. "This is outside the scope of the direct."

The judge sustained the objection.

"How was your arm within hours after this wound? . . ."

"Objection! Your Honor." Captain Balbo sounded furious, and the colonel finally relented. It was unusual for the judge to give Louis room to do anything and every time he did, Balbo gave the impression of being profoundly betrayed.

The next witness to take the stand was Specialist Oliver Perez, who was called by the defense team to testify to my character as both a leader and a person. The defense strategy was not to deny that the situation on the ground in Iraq was hazardous but rather to show that even under such adverse conditions I led my squad to the best of my ability.

"What was Staff Sergeant Mejía like as a squad leader in Iraq?" Captain Ruhling, our military defense attorney, opened the cross examination.

"He was a great leader," responded Oliver. "He always

took care of his men, and if he considered there were flaws in the planning [of our missions], he brought them to the attention of those higher up, which not everyone did. . . . He looked out for his men."

He was then asked whether he trusted me.

"From what I saw, from what I experienced, he was very truthful. I trusted him with pretty much all my life. "

"What types of missions did he lead you on?" Captain Ruhling asked.

"Ambushes, all types, patrols, cordon search; just regular sweeps of the city; setting up defensive positions outside at night . . . just regular stuff."

"During those types of missions, did you encounter much resistance?"

"Yes," said Oliver. "We did."

"And how did he react in those situations?"

"He reacted bravely," Oliver replied without hesitation. "He always kept control of his squad and he never showed any fear. He always had his men in control as a good squad leader does. . . . I never really saw any incompetence or anything of that nature."

"Did he ever question planning that the command was using?" continued the defense captain.

"At times he did."

"Did he have the moral courage to raise those concerns?"

"Yes, he did."

"What are some types of character traits that you expect a noncommissioned officer to have?" asked Ruhling.

"He should have the confidence to lead his men. That's the first thing men notice about their leaders. . . . He should care for his men all the way; have the mission in mind all the time, but at the same time, keep his men in mind."

"So," went on Captain Ruhling, "with those traits in mind

as your ideal noncommissioned officer, on a scale of one to ten, with one being just an absolute cluster and ten being the ideal NCO, where would you place Sergeant Mejía, based on your experience with him?"

"No doubt," said Oliver, firmly. "I'd honestly put him at a ten; a nine or ten."

Captain Balbo then took the witness.

"Specialist Perez," he began.

"Yes, sir."

"You were surprised when the accused didn't return to Iraq, weren't you?"

"I was, sir," responded Oliver.

". . . The responsible thing for him to do would have been to come back and support you. Isn't that right?"

"That's correct, sir."

"Do you think what he did is a good example of an NCO?"

"As an NCO," reflected Oliver, "I don't believe it was a good example, no."

". . . Now, Specialist Perez," continued the prosecutor, "you mentioned how the accused had a calming effect on his men, isn't that right?"

"That's correct."

"And you said that he had the confidence to lead his men, isn't that right?"

"That's correct."

"It must have been a real shame that you didn't have that calming effect for five months, isn't that right?"

"It was a blow," said Oliver, more to himself than to the court.

"And knowing that," Balbo went on, "you still want to rank him as a ten?"

"That's correct."

"Nothing further, Your Honor."

Captain Balbo again appeared angry, as he did for much

of the trial. I had never seen anyone as emotionally invested in hurting someone's image as Balbo was in hurting mine.

"Why is it that you still consider him a ten, despite that disappointment?" asked Captain Ruhling on redirect.

"As an NCO, he still can lead his men; even today, in battle . . . if he were to go back, he could still lead his men. . . . I would put the trust of my life in his hands, because he will lead his men to battle. And as long as he does that . . . I worked with him on the intense situations, battles, conflicts, things of that sort, I still have the trust in him, so I'm going to rate him as high as I did."

I had a hard time fighting back the tears after Oliver's testimony. Though I came to realize that it was the right decision, indeed the only decision I could have taken, it had been very painful for me to leave my squad behind. It was primarily because of them that I had almost returned to Iraq.

Oliver was right in that he could still trust me with his life, but I knew that I would never again put myself in a position where I might have to lead an infantry squad into battle. Morally I could never again embrace going to war.

Private First Class Estime was the next witness called to testify:

"[He] talked to us. Came with open arms; talked to us as like," he paused to think for a moment, "more as a father. . . . He looked out for us; made sure we had everything we needed. . . . He put us before himself, that's what he did."

"Do you trust him today?" asked Captain Ruhling. "As he sits here?"

Estime replied that he did, but as his testimony progressed it was clear that he was considerably more critical of my behavior than Oliver. When asked about whether he respected my decision-making judgment, he didn't hesitate to distinguish between his opinion of my leadership before and after I left Iraq.

"Well," he said, "leading up to when he left, his decision [making] was great to me. . . . If he made a decision, I followed it."

Balbo tried to make the most of Estime's more critical stance by contrasting his own behavior with mine.

"You missed seeing your sister after she was in a car accident, didn't you?" asked Balbo.

"Correct, sir," responded Estime.

"And the accused went home before you did, didn't he?"

"Yes, sir."

"In fact," Balbo paused momentarily, "you always stayed and performed your job, didn't you?"

"I had to, sir."

"You had to because it was your duty."

"That was my duty," responded Estime.

Estime was someone I'd had a special relationship with in Iraq. I didn't feel resentful of Estime's testimony, but I do wish I could have explained to him why it had been impossible for me to take any other course than to reject the war.

The final testimony was reserved for me, though, given the restrictions imposed by the judge, there really wasn't much left for me to say in my defense. At that point, the judge had already forbidden us from mentioning anything to do with war crimes or crimes against humanity. I could not be asked questions dealing with the abuse of prisoners in al Assad, nor could I go into the details of my conscientious objection claim. The only thing I could say was that I had applied for CO status and that I thought conscientious objectors shouldn't be ordered to do missions that would violate their beliefs.

Our defense, then, was limited to explaining to the panel members how, even though the court had ruled that I didn't have authority to remain absent from my unit, I sincerely believed at the time that I did have such authority. This argument is known as *mistake of fact*.

For its part, all the prosecution had to show was that I had not been permitted by anyone in my leadership to remain away from Iraq, that my leave papers required me to return, and that I was physically able to get on the plane. Beyond these considerations, no questions of substance were asked by Captain Balbo at any time.

Closing arguments were delivered the next morning. Balbo, who spoke first, took the opportunity to paint me as a self-serving liar and coward who tried to cheat the system to avoid danger. He urged the panel members to do what the entire court-martial had been assembled to accomplish:

"The government asks you to find the accused guilty of the charge of desertion."

Louis's closing argument was more comprehensive and articulate than Balbo's but he was crippled by having to start his defense with the admission that I had made a mistake, albeit an honest one, in not returning to Iraq. He tried his best, within the restrictions placed on him by the court, to raise some of the details in my CO application, including my having witnessed civilian killings and having been baptized in Iraq. He reiterated the testimony of my fellow soldiers, all in an attempt to counter Balbo's allegation that I was a fundamentally dishonest person.

Captain Balbo then had the opportunity to rebut Louis's statement, but did little more than repeat his previous claims that ". . . The accused was not a good soldier" and that I had failed in the most basic responsibility of the mission, which was that of "Showing up!"

After closing arguments, the judge gave instructions to members of the jury concerning the procedure they were to follow in conducting their deliberations. They were dismissed to deliberate and returned some two hours later.

"Accused and counsel, please rise," said the judge. "Colonel Nicolle," continued the judge, this time to the president of the jury, "you may announce the findings of the court."

The pepper-white-haired colonel read the verdict from the panel section without standing up:

"Sergeant Mejía-Castillo, this court-martial finds you, on the specification of the charge: Guilty. On the charge: Guilty."

Shortly after the finding was read, the court was closed for lunch. Given the restrictions placed on the defense, it should have come as no surprise that I was to be found guilty. Yet right to the end I clung to the hope that justice would be served, and as we left the court I felt bitterly disappointed that the verdict had gone against us.

The final stage of the trial, the sentencing phase, began after lunch. The government sought the maximum penalty: a year in prison, demotion to the lowest rank, and a bad conduct discharge. The defense requested no punishment at all and for me simply to be discharged and sent home.

The first two witnesses called to the stand were for the prosecution. I wasn't surprised to see my old platoon sergeant, Sergeant First Class Vernon Williams, called first for the prosecution. Though we had never been enemies, I had more than once questioned his authority in Iraq, and that had created friction between us. However, I was not at all prepared for the way Williams distorted things from the stand. When asked about my performance, he told the court that I had been a good soldier up to the moment of Operation Shutdown, but that after then my behavior had significantly deteriorated. He suggested that this was specifically linked to my learning of the injury suffered by Recio.

"Did the accused have a reaction to that injury?" asked Balbo.

"Yes," answered Williams. "When I got back [from a mission at the palace], Sergeant Demarest said to me, 'Mejía re-

fuses to go out, says he's not going on patrols with us anymore.' . . . And I said, 'Let me talk to him.' He came into our
room. If I recall correctly, it was me, Sergeant Demarest, and
Mejía inside the room. We basically discussed why he didn't
want to go out.

"And what did he say to you?" continued the prosecutor.

"He said it was too dangerous. He said it was too dangerous and it was crazy that they have us doing the same thing
over and over. . . . I explained to him," continued Williams,
"that when we do things we don't do things repetitiously.
We're not going to do the same thing over and over again."

Williams omitted the fact that we had gone out on exactly
the same patrol and that that was precisely what we had done
for four nights running, a decision that had contributed
greatly to our company's four casualties and the decapitation
of one civilian. We had been doing things repetitiously to instigate battles so that our officers could get awards; *that* had
been the concern, and that's what I had explained to him.

"'This is not a time for you to crumble. Behind the cur-
tains, yeah, that's fine; everybody's hurt; everybody's mournful, that's fine,'" Williams, the man who'd advised me to tell
my superiors I was afraid of battle rather than file a formal
complaint against my battalion commander, claimed he had
said to me. "'But in front of your men,'" he continued, "'you
can't give a demeanor where you're too afraid to perform
your job.'"

Williams finished his testimony by telling the court that
he had pushed for me to be given leave to take care of my immigration issues in the full expectation that I would return,
and that he had been disappointed that I had not done so.

I remembered things differently: he had encouraged me
to stay in the States, at one point even saying, "What are they
going to do to you? Your green card is expiring; there is nothing the military can do to you."

Louis's cross-examination focused on my refusal to go out on the fifth night of Operation Shutdown.

"Did you ask him, 'What do you mean by too danger-ous?'" inquired Louis.

"Negative, I didn't."

"Did he say to you, four nights in a row, the very same thing?" Louis continued.

"Correct," interrupted the sergeant first class. "But he didn't say in specific why it was too dangerous. I didn't ask. And the reason I didn't ask is because I didn't care. I'm the platoon leader. I choose the missions and we do the mis-sions. . . . If I need input, I'll ask for input or guidance, but at the same time, I'm not going to have my squad leader tell me what he won't do and tell me what I will do. That's unaccept-able, sir."

Williams's true colors finally surfaced at this point. He could not allow any questioning of his authority, and the real source of tension between us was the fact that, on occasion, I had done just that.

I did not know what to expect when I heard that the next witness to take the stand for the prosecution was Funez. He was the person who seemed to have made the most effort to understand my doubts and fears when we were in Iraq, but I was never sure of how much he really understood me.

Captain Balbo opened the questioning:

"Would you please describe how the accused functioned as a squad leader?"

Funez paused before answering, choosing his words carefully.

"He took care of all of us, you could say. He's a pretty charismatic person. He knew his job. He's an E-6.[4] He's been around for a while, so he knew what to do."

"Would you say he was technically and tactically profi-cient?" continued Balbo.

"In a way, yeah."

"Could you be a little more precise?"

"I mean, no one's perfect," Funez continued. "I would say some things he did well, and some things he didn't."

"On a scale from one to ten," said Balbo, sounding more like a defense counsel, "one being very poor and ten being excellent."

"Maybe an eight," Funez replied. "I would say eight."

"What would you say his best skill was?" asked Captain Balbo.

Again Funez paused, thinking about his answer.

"Well, Sergeant Mejía made sure that everyone was taken care of in whatever little ways he could. . . ."

"As a member of his squad, how did you feel when you realized he wasn't coming back?" Balbo continued.

"I was really disappointed. I was angry," he responded with a really stern voice. "But mostly disappointed . . . because I felt that he was better than that; he was smarter than to make that move."

Captain Balbo then returned to the NCO creed, which described how a good leader should act. He had questioned me about the creed, and I had told him that I didn't remember it well. From then on he used my not knowing the creed by heart as irrefutable evidence of my poor leadership.

"Now that you're an E-5," continued Balbo, calling Funez by his new rank, "I assume you're familiar with the NCO creed, right?"

Captain Balbo couldn't understand that infantry soldiers didn't carry a copy of the creed into battle, or that not knowing the creed by heart was not enough to convict me.

"Not by heart," said Sergeant Funez, "but I get the gist of it for right now."

"And knowing why we're here today," continued the captain, ignoring what Funez had said, "and that the accused has been convicted of desertion, do you think he embodied all the values found in the NCO creed?"

"Like I said before," said Funez with a bit of a hard tone, "I don't know the NCO creed by heart and I would assume that maybe, to put it a certain way, maybe being loyal to us . . ." he trailed off and then paused for a second. "I mean, at least I felt through the time we spent together, I befriended him in my own way, and I really respect him and he was like a brother." He paused again. "We all became brothers. We had a love-hate [relationship], like everywhere; just conflicting personalities. But I don't think you just leave the . . ."

"As a subordinate of his," interrupted Balbo, ". . . you said you felt like a brother; would you have rather him have returned?"

Funez seemed to be experiencing a real conflict during his testimony, but Balbo never thought of giving him a moment to put his emotions into words; he just hammered upon his anger and disappointment to hurt my image.

"Yes," answered Funez. "Because I think that there is a right way and there is a wrong way. I'm just that type of person. There's always a right and a wrong."

"And how would you describe his actions?"

"I believe it was the wrong way to go about it. Some right steps, but in the big picture it was just the wrong move."

During redirection, Captain Ruhling attempted to bring out the complexities in Funez's attitude toward me and what I had done.

"It's hard testifying like this, isn't it, Sergeant Funez?" he began.

"I don't like being in a courtroom, sir," replied Funez, avoiding the real question.

"But you really like Sergeant Mejía?" Ruhling inquired.

"Yes, I do."

"In fact, you think he's a good person, don't you?"

"Yes," he admitted. "He's a great person."

"Someone you can still look up to, despite your misgivings?" Ruhling asked, though his words were more of a statement than a question. "Someone that, even though, as you said it, made a wrong choice, you still respect?"

"Of course."

"And you paid pretty close attention to the way he handled himself on missions and after missions, didn't you?"

"Yes," responded Funez.

"And after missions, he was very contemplative, wasn't he?"

"Yes, sir."

"Very conscientious about thinking through whether this was the right mission to do or not and were these people the right people or not?"

Without making it explicit, Ruhling appeared to be referring to my feelings after civilians were wrongly arrested, or when prisoners were abused, or innocents killed. Funez seemed to understand what he was getting at:

"After a firefight or a raid, Sergeant Mejía would reflect on what had happened, just like all of us did. But he would take it to another level. . . . I would think about things for five minutes, and then it would be out of my mind. Sergeant Mejía would just keep analyzing the situation, I think overanalyzing it. And of course, there's some days you have bad days; some days you have really bad days."

I thought Funez put that in exactly the right way: some days we had bad days; some days we had really bad days. There were never good days.

"In particular," continued Captain Ruhling, gently, "he focused a lot on the human side of the mission, right?"

"Yes," said Funez, "very much so."

"And those were pretty significant thoughts for him?"

"Most definitely," answered Funez.

"Do you think he's the type of person who would not come back just on a whim?"

"Oh, no."

"Is it more consistent to say that he's the type of person who would have tried to do some research on the steps necessary to try and do it the right way before he would make a decision?"

I felt a little uncomfortable about the way Captain Ruhling put that question because I knew my decision had been based on conscience, and that investigating the legal issues involved hadn't really come into it. But I recognized that it was hard for him to take any other route in a courtroom where any consideration of morality had repeatedly been ruled out of order.

"Yes," responded Funez. "I believe he would have."

"Thank you, nothing further."

Funez was the last witness brought to the stand for the prosecution. Now it was the defense's turn. We first called on my former counselors from the University of Miami, José Rodriguez and Dr. Victoria Noriega. I was both moved by and grateful for their testimonies, which painted a very positive portrait of me as a student and human being. They were followed by Fernando Suarez del Solar, whose son, a marine, had been killed in Iraq under friendly fire by a cluster bomb. Francis Boyle, the law professor from the University of Illinois who had previously testified by phone, now made an appearance in person to explain how the Laws of War, as described in Field Manual 27-10, related to the prisoner abuse contained in my CO claim, the use of which had been permitted for the sentencing phase.

The last witness we called, before I myself closed for the defense, was Lieutenant Barr, the leader of first platoon during Operation Shutdown; although he didn't explicitly make the point, his testimony seemed to indicate that our leadership had exposed us to danger for their own personal advancement.

"Essentially," said Lieutenant Barr about Operation Shutdown, "we were setting ourselves up for failure by going to the same place at the same time."

"And the next day," Louis continued, "did you take up these concerns with Captain Warfel?"

Lieutenant Barr confirmed that he had done so, repeatedly, but that Captain Warfel had appeared to take no notice of what the lieutenant said. After the mission went on in exactly the same way for three nights straight, on the fourth night, the lieutenant approached again.

"Prior to the fourth time going out," explained Barr, "the conversations between Captain Warfel and I became increasingly heated. . . . my position was that I didn't understand why we weren't using the tactical knowledge we had and incorporating some . . . common sense into this." continued the lieutenant. "The chances of us getting attacked . . . with each time going out there, were increasingly likely."

"Now," continued Louis, "were you the only person in your platoon who felt this way? . . ."

"No, sir," Barr replied emphatically.

He then went on to tell the court how his insistence that Captain Warfel modify the mission had worsened the relationship between the two men, to the point where the captain began to undermine his lieutenant openly in command meetings. After the exchange on the fourth night again proved fruitless, Barr said that he had resigned himself to getting the mission done in whatever way he could. He then proceeded to describe the attack that night in graphic detail, stopping periodically to compose himself when his recollection of what happened appeared to overwhelm him.

He told the court how, in spite of his best efforts, his platoon was badly hit and how his medic, Specialist Mayorga, had lost half of his hand to enemy fire but had still managed to oversee the treatment of Recio, who almost died. He described how his wounded platoon sergeant, Mateo, climbed up on a destroyed vehicle to man the machine gun. It became clear, over the course of his testimony, that giving up on his previous insistence that the mission was fatally flawed had become a demon that still haunted the lieutenant.

"When you look back on it, Lieutenant Barr," Louis probed gently, "do you have concerns about how forcibly you presented the case for changing the mission?"

Lieutenant Barr, evidently upset, confirmed that this was the case.

"I've been in for quite a few years, and though I don't claim to know everything, it just didn't make any sense. Captain Warfel and I were at odds quite a few times. He had a tough job to do, as we all did, and I brought my concerns up as best as I could. . . . Worst of all was that maybe it didn't need to happen. I felt pretty lousy, because I . . . personally, I felt as if I caved in . . . that I should have done things differently."

In his cross-examination, Balbo concentrated on the way Lieutenant Barr himself had continued to do his duty even when, after the attack, he had been reassigned to a still more dangerous mission, leading convoys from ar Ramadi to al Assad. No mention was made of Warfel's decision to fire the lieutenant from his job as first platoon leader. Instead, Balbo asked if, given the guilty verdict of desertion, Lieutenant Barr would want to have me working for him.

"No, sir," Barr replied.

Finally it was my turn to take the stand. Louis had explained to me that this final opportunity to address to the court was known as an unsworn statement, and that I could not be cross-examined about it.

"This is your opportunity to address the members and the judge, Camilo," Louis had told me during lunch with him and

Gale on the second day, after the guilty verdict had been
delivered.

"You can talk to them about your volunteer work in Miami, about your helping homeless people. You can also tell
them about being in three honor societies at the university."

Louis was doing his best not to seem too concerned about
the possible outcome of the sentencing, but he couldn't hide
an intense emotional investment in what might happen next.

"You should also talk to them about your relationship
with Samantha," he went on, "about all the things you do together. Tell them how hard it would be for her to not have her
father around."

I thought about all this for a moment and realized I really
didn't feel comfortable raising such issues. I hadn't done anything wrong—quite the contrary in fact—and begging for the
leniency of the court just didn't seem right. On the other
hand, I felt an obligation to my defense team to do my best to
avoid going to jail. When I told Louis about my discomfort I
saw that he understood immediately. He exchanged looks
with his wife and then it was she who spoke.

"They've already found you guilty, and they've probably
already decided to give you the maximum sentence. So why
ask for clemency? Tell them what's in your heart, Camilo, and
don't hold anything back."

I was grateful to Gale for these directions. When I took
the stand for the last time, I reviewed the testimony of the
various witnesses we had heard, emphasizing again that my
objection to the way Operation Shutdown was organized was
not that it was dangerous, but that it was unnecessarily so. I
reiterated that it was unacceptable that the lives of soldiers
and civilians should have been put at risk in pursuit of honor
and medals for those in command. I then turned to address
the panel directly:

"I have a great respect for this court, and I have a great

respect for you. . . . I stand convicted. I am guilty. . . . You have the power to put me behind bars for a year and to discharge me with a bad conduct discharge. But with all the respect that you and this court deserve, I have to tell you from the bottom of my heart that I sit here a free man, and that I will sit behind bars a free man. . . . I followed my conscience and made those decisions from the bottom of my heart. My actions and my beliefs in war and after war have set me free, and, with all due respect, I have no regrets. Not one.

"It will be sad if I end up going to jail. I have a daughter. It will be painful not seeing her. Many people love me, my attorneys included. They will pay the price also. I'm not going to say that it won't bother me, but I will go there with honor, knowing I did the right thing.

"Yes, you have the power to convict me, to sentence me, to discharge me with a bad conduct discharge. . . . I have been a bad soldier according to you, and you have that much power, but [remember] I am part of the military. . . . I am one of you, and this is my family too.

"We're all on trial. Not just me, sitting here, but everybody here in uniform, everybody in this country. . . . War crimes? Abuse of prisoners? The U.S. Army? No. A few privates, perhaps, one sergeant; they did that. They did that because they didn't have the courage to do what I did, because they were lost in a situation where it's hard to tell the difference between right and wrong. Perhaps they were afraid not to do what they were told by people who are higher ranking. Perhaps they decided that it was easier to do what everybody else was doing. So now it's easier to judge these people and put them on trial and blame it on them. . . . I'm not saying they're not responsible. They have some responsibility, just like I have some responsibility for the things I did in Iraq. Of course I do. But if we really want to look at ourselves as a military, and we really want to keep our pride and honor as a military, then we have to start from the top. . . .

"It's your decision, not only as members of this panel . . ."

"OK," said the judge, looking at me. "You need to stop rebuking the members of the panel. If you need to get in focus again, you can do so, but you need to stop directing comments directly to members."

"I respectfully object, Your Honor," said Louis, getting up.

"Well," the judge replied, "counsel can't do that, so the accused can't do it either." He turned to me. "Go ahead."

"I understand, Your Honor," I replied. "We're all on trial because it takes outstanding leadership and it takes moral courage to do what you believe to be right, even at personal cost. And not being an attorney, I didn't know the extent of that cost, but I knew that I would bring my case to the courtroom, and I knew the consequences. I knew that many offenses and possibly many years in prison were on the table. But I believed so strongly in what I did and, respectfully, I suggest to you that I have committed no crime in coming here because sometimes it's not easy to provide leadership and, as twisted as it might sound, I believe right now, sitting in this chair, that I am providing that leadership. Now I feel free. I have nothing further, Your Honor."

As I stepped down from the witness stand, several people in the audience stood up and began applauding. I could see that my aunt and uncle were both in tears. When I looked at my mother I saw that she was not crying. I knew she was pain-stricken, but she was determined to remain stoic and strong. Louis and Gale stood up to take me back.

"Alright," said the judge addressing the audience sternly. "Sit down."

No one paid him any attention and he was forced to repeat himself.

"Sit down," he shouted above the din. "Sit down and be quiet."

Eventually the courtroom fell quiet and the judge asked to hear closing arguments. The prosecution took the stand first, with Balbo continuing his campaign to denigrate my character. But now he had to at least allow the possibility that I had been a good leader.

"Even if you believe that Staff Sergeant Mejía was a great squad leader," he said, as bad tempered as ever ". . . that's all the more reason he needed to stay. If he felt he was some pillar of virtue in an otherwise difficult place, if he had a better sense of right and wrong, if he felt that his soldiers were in danger, if he felt they lacked leadership, he needed to stay, not run away. . . . He didn't take responsibility when he made his statement." He stared at the panel with an indignant frown on his face. "He feels he did nothing wrong. He has no regrets. He stands before you defiant and, worst of all, knowing that he abandoned his men. Not once did he have the decency to say he was sorry. Accordingly, the government asks this panel to recommend the maximum sentence."

Louis began his argument in his usual elegant and gentle way, without anger and without raising his voice, relying on the wisdom and the precision of his words.

"Members of the panel, it's an honor to represent Staff Sergeant Mejía in a case that goes to the core and the fundamental values of the United States Army. What I have in front of me is a book called *The Armed Forces Officer*, published by the Department of Defense."

Louis held the book up to show the court.

"It never hurts to go back to the founding principles of our army, and there is one particular passage here that is very relevant to what is going on right now in this courtroom and around the world, should the U.S. Army continue ordering people to do things like Staff Sergeant Mejía was ordered to do."

After Balbo's objection to the passage was overruled by the judge, Louis read from the book:

"Within our school of military thought, higher authority does not consider itself infallible, either in combat or out. In any situation where a majority of military-trained Americans becomes undutiful, that is sufficient reason for higher authority to resurvey its own judgments, disciplines, and lines of action."

Louis closed the book after reading the passage.

"What an amazing concept for a military," he observed. "So higher authority in the U.S. military does not consider itself infallible. Here we have a thinking army, people who are required to think, not just to do, and Staff Sergeant Mejía has shown us that he's a thinking person."

Louis then went back to Operation Shutdown, and told the panel that what had happened on the fifth night of the mission was that a number of thinking persons, including me, had caused the leadership to resurvey its judgments and lines of actions in combat. He told them that in my unsworn statement, in a much larger sense, I had requested them to resurvey their own line of action.

"Maybe he's a loner at this time," continued Louis, referring to me. "But I respectfully submit to you that there may be more like him—perhaps hundreds, or thousands, or ten thousands in the future, if higher authority does not resurvey it own judgments and disciplines and lines of action.

"I respectfully submit to you that the appropriate option here, in this historic trial, is no punishment at all, and to let Staff Sergeant Mejía continue his life, to have his conscientious objector hearing, and move on. That is what I request on behalf of my client, and I respectfully suggest to you that that is what would be the very best that could happen in this

case not just for my client, but for the United States Army as
a whole."

With that, the end of his closing argument, Louis took his
seat. The judge then briefed the panel on the proper procedure to arrive at a sentence and they left to make their delib-
eration. Despite the considerable amount of evidence and
testimony before them, they returned to the court within only
twenty minutes. The judge called the court-martial back to
order and addressed the president of the panel.

"Have you determined a sentence in this case?"

"We have, Your Honor," Lieutenant Colonel Nicolle
responded.

The bailiff passed a sheet of paper containing the sentence to the judge, who examined it briefly, without showing
any reaction whatsoever. The judge asked the bailiff to return
the sentence sheet to the president of the panel and, looking
toward our table, said:

"Accused and counsel, please rise."

We all did.

"Colonel Nicolle," said the judge, "you may announce the
sentence of the court."

"Sergeant Mejía-Castillo," said the colonel, "this court-
martial sentences you to be reduced to the grade of E-1, to
forfeit $795 pay per month for twelve months, to be confined
for twelve months, and to be discharged from the service with
a bad conduct discharge."

When the time came for me to be escorted out of the
courtroom to be taken to jail, I asked for a moment to say
good-bye to my family. I embraced my stepfather, uncle,
aunt, and grandmother. I then turned to my beloved mother.
Seeing her reminded me of where my moral strength had
come from. She had raised me to always question and to
always do the right thing, regardless of the consequences.

There were no signs of defeat on her face; she told me she loved me, and she kissed me good-bye.

As I walked out of the courthouse I was not sad or bitter, nor was I afraid. Instead, I experienced a deep sense of empowerment on that beautiful day.

Looking back, I can see what a long trip it had been to arrive at an understanding of my life that today seems perfectly clear. I realize now that my refusal to participate in a morally indefensible war was one I should have made from the beginning. But it took the experience of going to war for me to see things in a broader perspective and realize that I was, deep down, a conscientious objector.

It can be claimed that a particular war is justified politically, or that it has the support of the international community and the blessing of international law. But these arguments can never convey the images, the sounds, the smells, or anything that remotely depicts the full horror of war. Escaping those arguments is the irreversible damage war always inflicts upon humanity, and upon everything worth loving on earth.

War, ultimately, is the destruction of life.

Even if before deploying to Iraq I had been convinced by the lies that we were going to find weapons of mass destruction, and that we were fighting against global terrorism, and even if all those lies had turned out to be true, there is no doubt in my heart that, today, I still would hate and oppose *all* war.

There were times in Iraq when I failed to see things the way I was supposed to as a soldier, when I knew that what we called targets were in fact homes, public squares, or markets, when I knew that what we called enemy combatants, terrorists, or Saddam loyalists were in fact people, sons, daughters, parents, human beings. On those occasions, when I destroyed human life in failing to refuse my orders, I also failed myself, my soldiers, the Iraqi people, and humanity.

I should have resisted my orders, and I should have fought for the dignity and preservation of life. I didn't because I was too afraid, because even without chains or shackles, I was still a prisoner, a prisoner of my own fear. I knew the right path to take; I knew what my actions should have been, but I didn't feel free to do what in my heart I knew to be the right thing.

I now know exactly what it was that so empowered me as I left my trial. Though I was handcuffed as I walked down the steps of the courthouse to the police vehicle, that was the moment that I gained my freedom. I understood then that freedom is not something physical, but a condition of the mind and of the heart. On that day I learned that there is no greater freedom than the freedom to follow one's conscience. That day I was free, in a way I had never been before.

NOTES

1. Record of Trial: Staff Sergeant Mejía-Castillo, Camilo E., Volume II of V, p. 67.
2. Ibid., pp. 97–98.
3. Ibid., p. 110.
4. E-6 is the pay grade corresponding to the rank of staff sergeant in the U.S. Army.

ACKNOWLEDGMENTS

A special thanks goes to Chris Hedges, for your solidarity, for taking the time to write the preface to *Road from ar Ramadi*, and for having the moral courage and integrity to tell the truth about war.

My friend Silvia Giagnoni spent many hours providing crucial editorial advice during the drafting of the preface. Thank you so much!

I would also like to recognize the hard work and dedication of the people at Haymarket Books who made this paperback edition possible. In particular I want to thank my dear friend and comrade Jared Rodriguez, who spent a whole afternoon trying his best to make me look handsome for the new cover; Julie Fain, Dao Tran, and Rachel Cohen, who handled all the production, overseeing all the changes and editorial work; Eric Ruder, one of the main advocates for Haymarket to publish the book and Josh On, who was responsible for the new cover design. And last but not least, Anthony Arnove who found the memoir a new home in this paperback edition, and who had the good heart to accommodate my last minute editorial requests.

ABOUT HAYMARKET BOOKS

Haymarket Books is a nonprofit, progressive book distributor and publisher, a project of the Center for Economic Research and Social Change. We believe that activists need to take ideas, history, and politics into the many struggles for social justice today. Learning the lessons of past victories, as well as defeats, can arm a new generation of fighters for a better world. As Karl Marx said, "The philosophers have merely interpreted the world; the point however is to change it."

We take inspiration and courage from our namesakes, the Haymarket Martyrs, who gave their lives fighting for a better world. Their 1886 struggle for the eight-hour day, which gave us May Day, the international workers' holiday, reminds workers around the world that ordinary people can organize and struggle for their own liberation. These struggles continue today across the globe—struggles against oppression, exploitation, hunger, and poverty.

It was August Spies, one of the Martyrs who was targeted for being an immigrant and an anarchist, who predicted the battles being fought to this day. "If you think that by hanging us you can stamp out the labor movement," Spies told the judge, "then hang us. Here you will tread upon a spark, but here, and there, and behind you, and in front of you, and everywhere, the flames will blaze up. It is a subterranean fire. You cannot put it out. The ground is on fire upon which you stand."

We could not succeed in our publishing efforts without the generous financial support of our readers. Many people contribute to our project through the Haymarket Sustainers program, where donors receive free books in return for their monetary support. If you would like to be a part of this program, please contact us at info@haymarketbooks.org.

Order these titles and more through our online store available at:
www.haymarketbooks.org or call 773-583-7884.

ALSO FROM HAYMARKET BOOKS

Beyond the Green Zone:
Dispatches from an Unembedded Journalist in Occupied Iraq
Dahr Jamail • Foreword by Amy Goodman • Independent jouralist Dahr Jamail presents never-before printed details of siege of Fallujah and examines the origins of the Iraqi resistance, bringing us inside the Iraq we never see. $20, hardcover. ISBN 978-1-931859-47-9.

Welcome to the Terrordome: The Pain, Politics, and Promise of Sports
Dave Zirin • This much-anticipated sequel to *What's My Name, Fool?* by acclaimed sportswriter Dave Zirin breaks new ground in sportswriting, looking at the controversies and trends now shaping sports in the United States—and abroad. Always insightful, never predictable. $16. ISBN 978-1-931859-41-7.

In Praise of Barbarians: Essays Against Empire
Mike Davis • No writer in the United States today brings together analysis and history as comprehensively and elegantly as Mike Davis. In these contemporary, interventionist essays, Davis goes beyond critique to offer real solutions and concrete possibilities for change. $15. ISBN 978-1-931859-42-4.

Sin Patrón: Stories from Argentia's Occupied Factories
The lavaca collective, with a foreword by Naomi Klein and Avi Lewis • The inside story of Argentina's remarkable movement to create factories run democratically by workers themselves. $16. ISBN 978-1-931859-43-1.

Between the Lines: Readings on Israel, the Palestinians,
and the U.S. "War on Terror"
Tikva Honig-Parnass and Toufic Haddad • This compilation of essays—edited by a Palestinian and an Israeli—constitutes a challenge to critially rethink the Israeli-Palestinian conflict. $17. ISBN 978-1-931859-44-8.

No One Is Illegal: Fighting Racism and State Violence
on the U.S./Mexico Border
Justin Akers Chacón and Mike Davis • Countering the chorus of anti-immigrant voices, Davis and Akers Chacón expose the racism of anti-immigration vigilantes and put a human face on the immigrants who risk their lives to cross the border to work in the United States. $16. ISBN 978-1-931859-35-3.

A Little Piece of Ground

Elizabeth Laird • Growing up in occupied Palestine through the eyes of a twelve-year-old boy. $9.95. ISBN 978-1-931859-38-7.

The Communist Manifesto:
A Road Map to History's Most Important Political Document

Karl Marx and Frederick Engels, edited by Phil Gasper • This beautifully organized and presented edition of *The Communist Manifesto* is fully annotated, with clear historical references and explication, additional related texts, and a glossary that will bring the text to life. $12. ISBN 978-1-931859-25-7.

Subterranean Fire: A History of Working-Class Radicalism in the U.S.

Sharon Smith • Workers in the United States have a rich tradition of fighting back and achieving gains previously thought unthinkable, but that history remains largely hidden. *In Subterranean Fire*, Sharon Smith brings that history to light and reveals its lessons for today. $16. ISBN 978-1-931859-23-3.

Soldiers in Revolt: GI Resistance During the Vietnam War

David Cortright with a new introduction by Howard Zinn • "An exhaustive account of rebellion in all the armed forces, not only in Vietnam but throughout the world."—*New York Review of Books*. $16. ISBN 978-1-931859-27-1.

Friendly Fire: The Remarkable Story of a Journalist Kidnapped in Iraq, Rescued by an Italian Secret Service Agent, and Shot by U.S. Forces

Giuliana Sgrena • The Italian journalist, whose personal story was featured on *60 Minutes*, describes the real story of her capture and shooting in 2004. Sgrena also gives invaluable insight into the reality of life in occupied Iraq, exposing U.S. war crimes there. $20, hard cover. ISBN 978-1-931859-39-4.

The Meaning of Marxism

Paul D'Amato • A lively and accessible introduction to the ideas of Karl Marx, with historical and contemporary examples. $12. ISBN 978-1-931859-29-5.

Revolution and Counterrevolution: Class Struggle in a Moscow Metal Factory

Kevin Murphy • Murphy's wealth of research and insight deliver an exciting contribution to the discussion about class and the Russian Revolution. $20. ISBN 978-1-931859-50-9.

The Women Incendiaries: The Inspiring Story of the Women of the Paris Commune Who Took up Arms in the Fight for Liberty and Equality

Edith Thomas • *The Women Incendiaries* tells the often over-looked story of the crucial role played by women during the Paris Commune of 1871, one of history's most important emxperiments in working-class democracy. $16. ISBN 978-1-931859-46-2.

The Dispossessed: Chronicles of the *Desterrados* of Colombia

Alfredo Molano • Here in their own words are the stories of the Desterrados, or "dispossessed"—the thousands of Colombians displaced by years of war and state-backed terrorism, funded in part through U.S. aid to the Colombian government. With a preface by Aviva Chomsky. $14. ISBN 978-1-931859-17-2.

Vive la Revolution: A Stand-up History of the French Revolution

Mark Steel • An actually interesting, unapologetically sympathetic and extremely funny history of the French Revolution. $14. ISBN 978-1-931859-37-0.

Poetry and Protest: A Dennis Brutus Reader

Aisha Karim and Lee Sustar, editors • A vital original collection of the interviews, poetry, and essays of the much-loved anti-apartheid leader. $16. ISBN 978-1-931859-22-6.

The Bending Cross: A Biography of Eugene Victor Debs

Ray Ginger, with a new introduction by Mike Davis • The classic biography of Eugene Debs, one of the most important thinkers and activists in the United States. $18. ISBN 978-1-931859-40-0.

What's My Name, Fool? Sports and Resistance in the United States

Dave Zirin • *What's My Name, Fool?* offers a no-holds-barred look at the business of sports today. In humorous and accessible language, Zirin shows how sports express the worst, as well as the most creative and exciting, features of American society. $15. ISBN 978-1-931859-20-5.

Literature and Revolution

Leon Trotsky, William Keach, editor • A new, annotated edition of Leon Trotsky's classic study of the relationship of politics and art. $16. ISBN 978-1931859-16-5.